DISCOVERING HISTORY
Tsarist Russia
1801-1917

John Hite

Causeway Press

Introduction

A Introduction to the series

This book is the first of a series written to assist those students and teachers who believe that studying History should be an active, skills-based process, and not just the assimilation of a vast amount of material. It is primarily aimed at 'A' and 'AS' level students but its approach should also make it suitable for 'open learning' courses, and for students in Further and Higher Education. It is designed to develop historical skills to a high level, as well as to assist the study of the historical content covered in each book. It has been influenced by the impact of GCSE, and the moves being made to make 'A' level more compatible with a skills-based approach.

Although in recent years a number of books have been written with the 'A' level student in mind, in many cases they have just been surveys of a topic, interspersed with the occasional document. Others have been produced in a rather intimidating format, with little appreciation of the value of pictorial evidence and analytical charts.

In this series great stress has been placed not just on lively presentation, but on how a variety of ways of conveying historical evidence and analysis can help to develop a greater range of skills.

Though each book does cover, at a general level, the chief content of the period, the depth of treatment varies considerably. In many areas, the key points will be covered in an analytical chart rather than in the text itself, freeing space to be used for primary evidence. Certain important themes, however, are treated in more depth than in all but specialist books. This will enable teachers and students to have easy access to the level of detail and analysis necessary for gaining the highest grades in examinations. With this in view, and to allow students to appreciate a range of historical interpretations, several exercises are based on extracts from specialist historians.

Causeway Press Limited

P.O. Box 13, Ormskirk, Lancs. L39 5HP

© John Hite
First published 1989, Reprinted 1992, 1995

British Library Cataloguing in Publication Data
Hite, John
Discovering History; Tsarist Russia 1801-1917.
1. Russia, 1796-1918
I. Title
947.07

ISBN 0-946183-53-8.

Typesetting by Image Photosetting, Aughton, Lancs.
Artwork by The Art Factory, St. Anne's-on-Sea.
Printed and bound by The Alden Press, Oxford.

Worksections

Each chapter has at least one worksection, mostly using primary evidence, designed to develop a range of skills. The exercises can be tackled using material from the book. They take a variety of formats, and can be used flexibly; many are suitable for oral work; others can be set as formal written tasks. In most chapters specific marks have been allocated to at least one exercise on evidence so that it may be set as a formal assignment. Students and teachers can obviously select the exercises they find most useful.

Structure of charts

A large number of maps and charts have been used. To ease cross reference, they are numbered firstly by chapter, then by order within the chapter, ie Chart 6.5 is the fifth chart in chapter 6.

B Introduction to Tsarist Russia

Nineteenth century Tsarist Russia is a fascinating period of history, not just in its own right, but for the light it sheds on current problems in the Soviet Union and in the world in general. As in the nineteenth century, the questions of reform (economic and political) and the nationalities question are currently major issues in Russia, and many countries face the problem of terrorism.

This book surveys the last century of Tsarist Russia before the regime collapsed during the First World War. It concentrates on the last seventy years when pressures for change were developing. In the early chapters, the period is treated chronologically by reign, reflecting the importance of the personality and policies of individual tsars as absolute rulers of Russia. In the later chapters, some broad themes, cutting across the reigns of tsars, are considered in depth.

Throughout the book stress is put on the development of historical skills. Particular skills are highlighted in some sections, as shown in the following table.

Skill	Section
Handling evidence: documentary documentary and pictorial	Alexander II 1905 Revolution, Opposition
Use & interpretation of statistics	Economic development
Historical controversy	Alexander II, Nicholas II
Causation	1905 and 1917 Revolutions
Role of the individual	Tsarist ministers Alexander II, Nicholas II
Continuity and change	Conclusion

Contents

Acknowledgements

The authors and publishers are grateful to all those who permitted the use of copyright material in this book. Due acknowledgement has been made to each source in the text.

Statistics

C. Trebilcock, Industrialisation of the Continental Powers, Longman pp. 75-77, 81-83.
M. Falkus, The Industrialisation of Russia, Macmillan pp. 75-77, 81-83.
G. Katkov (ed), Russia Enters the Twentieth Century, Methuen pp. 81-83.

For help and advice

Dr. P. Gatrell of Manchester University.

Every effort has been made to locate the copyright owners of material included. Any omission brought to the publisher's notice are regretted and will be credited in subsequent printing.

Dedication

To Phil

1 Tsarist Russia 1801 — 1917

A Broad nature of the period

Tsarist governments faced many problems as they attempted to modernise Russia's backward economic and social structure. In order to maintain her great power status modernisation was necessary despite its potential effect on the position of the tsar. The period was marked by reform, repression, and revolution. Tsarism collapsed in February 1917, to be replaced by a communist government in October.

The nature of historical analysis of Tsarist Russia has been greatly influenced by this eventual establishment of Communism. Some historians highlight the significant progress made by tsarism from the 1880s, and point to the tragedy of revolution. Others, often Marxists, identify the profound contradictions within tsarism as it tried to modernise whilst maintaining its absolute political structure. They consider revolution inevitable.

The period has traditionally been seen as one of alternation between reform and repression, associated with the reigns of various tsars. Taking this view the century began with the 'liberal' Alexander I, whose reign was followed by a bleak period of repression under Nicholas I, which then prepared the way for the 'Great Liberator' Alexander II. His assassination in 1881 led to another period of repression under Alexander III. His son Nicholas II tried to continue this policy, although he was forced to make concessions in the 1905 Revolution. This book will, however, attempt to show that such a neat pattern is in many ways misleading.

B Key questions

i) How successful were the reforms of Alexander II in solving the problems of Tsarist Russia? Did they create more problems than they solved?
ii) How important was opposition to the tsarist regime?
iii) What were the nature and effects of economic change?
iv) Why did tsarism survive the Revolution of 1905?
v) How responsible was Nicholas II for the eventual collapse of tsarism?
vi) Could Tsarist Russia have modernised without reforming the autocratic system?

C Tsarist Russia in the early nineteenth century

The character of Tsarist Russia in the early nineteenth century was largely determined by her geographical position and previous history. The original state of Muscovy had gradually established itself as a major power, in both Asia and Eastern Europe. Two authoritarian features developed. Autocracy developed to prevent the fragmentation of the Empire, and serfdom to control scarce labour. During the seventeenth century the powers of the tsar over the nobles had increased. In return for serving the tsar, the nobles had been granted full control over their peasant serfs.

In 1812 Russia had had to face the onslaught of Napoleonic France. Though she had apparently triumphed, the contrast between Russia and Western Europe, revealed by the war, set the scene for the key issue of the nineteenth century, that of modernisation.

The chief features of Tsarist Russia are identified on charts 1.3 and 1.4.

D The debate over Russia's relationship with the West

Since the reign of Peter the Great (1682-1725), who had tried to modernise Russia, there had been tension over her future course. In the 1840s a lively debate emerged over Russia's relationship with the West. Two broad trends developed. The Westernisers admired the political and economic advances made in Western Europe, and argued that Russia should imitate her neighbours, just as she had done under Peter the Great. Their critics, the Slavophils, admired Russia's own distinct culture based on the Orthodox Church and mir. They saw the West as corrosive of Russia's communal, religious traditions. Whereas the Westernisers argued for change, the Slavophils either looked to preserving the status quo, or, with the later Populists, argued that Russia could develop a form of socialism based on the peasant commune rejecting Western style industrialisation. These two outlooks were to permeate the major economic and political debates throughout the nineteenth and into the twentieth century.

Worksection 1

A. Russia in the early nineteenth century

A.1. Interpretation of maps and charts.

Look carefully at charts 1.2, 1.3 and 1.4

i) Use this information to describe why Russia was considered a backward country in the early nineteenth century. Refer, for example, to her political, economic, social and financial systems.

ii) Do you consider it is convincing, as Smith does (chart 1.3), to use geographical factors to explain the character, and by implication, the political structure of states? Explain your answer.

iii) Which other country has fairly similar geographical features? What differences and similarities in its history can you identify?

iv) How appropriate was the description of the tsar as 'Tsar of all the Russias'?

A.2. Nineteenth century Russia compared to modern societies.

Below is a list of 20 words which might be used in a description either of Tsarist Russian society and government in the early 19th century, or of modern day Britain. Study charts 1.3 and 1.4.

i) Divide the words into two lists, one containing words suitable to describe Tsarist Russia, the other modern Britain.
ii) Try to link the words in contrasting pairs.
iii) Compare and discuss your results with those of other students, assessing the validity of such generalisations.

autocratic	orthodox	corrupt
dynamic	decentralised	repressive
arbitrary	diverse	hierarchical
lethargic	democratic	honest
responsible	centralised	egalitarian
inefficient	irresponsible	justified
libertarian	efficient	

B. Westernisers and Slavophils

B.1. Study the two pictures of cities A and B, and coat of arms C.

A

B

i) Which city looks typically Russian? Why?
ii) Which looks less Russian? Why?
iii) One is St Petersburg, one Moscow. Referring to chart 1.3, explain the different characters of the two cities. What two trends in Russian history do these different cities represent?

C

iv) The Romanovs adopted the double headed eagle of the Byzantines. Some historians suggest this was particularly appropriate. Consider the points raised in question iii) and explain whether or not you agree.

B.2. The Westerniser-Slavophil debate.

Read page 4, then the following two extracts. As you read, try to identify the differences between the two outlooks expressed by the writers.

a) Literary critic V. Belinsky (1811-48):
'Everything great, noble, human, and spiritual came up, grew, burst into splendid bloom, and brought forth sumptuous fruit on European soil. The diversity of life . . . the refinement of customs, art, science, the subjugation of the unconscious forces of nature, the victory over matter, the triumph of the spirit, the respect for human personality, the sacredness of human right, in short, everything that makes one proud of being a man . . . all this is the result of the development of European life.'
(Quoted by Christian, D. (1986), *Power and Privilege* p.54)

b) Kireevski:
'Theology in the West assumed the character of rational abstractness; in the Orthodox world it retained an inner wholeness of spirit . . . In the West, there were universities for scholasticism and law; in ancient Russia, monasteries for prayer . . . There, a state organisation based on violent conquest; here, one based on the natural development of the people's way of life, permeated with the unity of a fundamental belief. There, a hostile division of classes; in ancient Russia, their harmonious association in all their natural variety . . . There, improvements were always accomplished by forcible change; here, by harmonious natural growth . . . There, the precariousness of each individual regulating himself; here, the firmness of family and social bonds . . . There, the foppery of luxury and the artificiality of life; here, the simplicity of basic needs and the courage of moral fortitude.'
(Quoted by Christian, D. (1986), *Power and Privilege* pp. 54-5)

i) Which writer is a Westerniser, and which a Slavophil? Give reasons for your choice.
ii) Look at the following paired phrases. Divide each pair into phrases which describe aspects of:
a) European society admired by Westernisers and criticised by Slavophils.
b) Russian society admired by Slavophils and criticised by Westernisers.

religious faith/rational criticism
uniformity/diversity

individuality/communal traditions
gradual growth/drastic changes
control of nature/harmony with nature
complexity/simplicity

iii) What do you think might be the attitude of each of the two groups to:-
a) the commune or mir (see chart 1.2 and page 18),
b) railways,
c) industrialisation.

Chart 1.1 Time and genealogy

A. Basic chronology 1801-1917

1801 Accession of Alexander I.
1805 Russia beaten by Napoleon at Austerlitz.
1807 Tilsit Treaty with Napoleon.
1812 Napoleon invaded Russia; retreated. Russian army followed French back into Europe.
1814 Russian Army reached Paris. Congress of Vienna met.
1815 Alexander I established Holy Alliance.
1820 Troppau Protocol redefined Holy Alliance.
1821 Greek Revolt against Turkey. Russia did not intervene.
1825 Death of Alexander I and Decembrist Revolt.
1825 Accession of Nicholas I
1831 Polish revolt crushed.
1833 Münchengrätz Treaty.
1848 Russia untroubled by revolution and in 1849 helped Austria crush Hungarian Revolt.
1850 Russia supported Austria at Olmutz.
1853 Beginning of Russo-Turkish, later Crimean War.
1855 Nicholas I died.
1855 Accession of Alexander II.
1856 Peace of Paris.

1861 Emancipation Edict led to wave of other reforms.
1874 Failure of 'To the People' movement.
1877 Russo-Turkish War.
1878 Russian diplomatic humiliation of Congress of Berlin.
1881 Alexander II assassinated.
1881 Accession of Alexander III. Emergency decrees.
1890's Rapid industrialisation. Witte Finance Minister.
1894 Death of Alexander III.
1894 Accession of Nicholas II.
1895 Nicholas dismissed reform hopes as 'senseless dreams'.
1904 Outbreak of Russo-Japanese War.
1905 Bloody Sunday and Revolution.
1906 First Duma met. Vyborg Manifesto. Stolypin agrarian reforms.
1907 Second Duma, and change to electoral law.
1908 Diplomatic defeat over Bosnia-Herzegovina.
1914 Outbreak of First World War.
1915 Nicholas went to war front.
1917 Feb. overthrow of tsarism.
Oct. Bolshevik seizure of power.

B. Family Tree of Romanov Tsars in 19th Century.

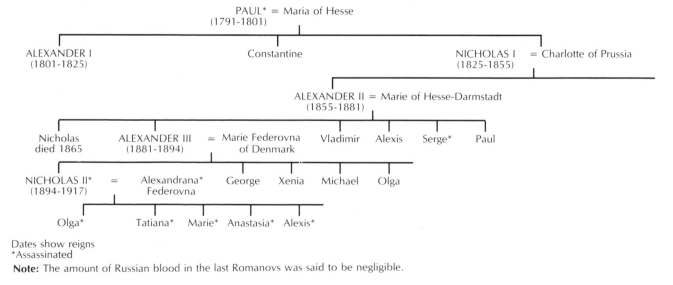

Dates show reigns
*Assassinated
Note: The amount of Russian blood in the last Romanovs was said to be negligible.

Chart 1.2 Glossary

A. Important terms

i) **Autocracy** - System of government where there were no legal restrictions on the power of the monarch, and all power was concentrated in the monarch. Like absolute monarchy.

ii) **Serfdom** - Social system in which nobles (gentry) owned their peasants (serfs), whom they could buy and sell, punish, and who had to work for their lord, or pay him money. System became firmly established in the late 17th century, when it was dying out in the rest of Europe. The question of serfdom became the major issue of the century until it was formally ended in 1861.

iii) **Mir or Commune** - Russian village organisation run by heads of households. Form of peasant self-government. Admired by many socialists as a form of primitive socialism. Seen by the government as a force for stability. Mir's powers weakened after 1905 revolution in order to encourage greater individualism.

iv) **Russification** - Policy of forcing Russian language, Orthodox religion and culture onto minority groups. Refusing to allow such groups to develop their own cultural and political structures.

v) **Slavophilism** - Trend which admired distinct Russian/Slav traditions, believing Russia to be culturally, morally and politically superior to the West. (See page 4.)

vi) **Panslavism** - Developed from Slavophilism. Believed in Russia assisting fellow Slavs, especially by liberating those under Turkish rule in Balkans; and linking them under Russian protection.

B. Other terms

1. Institutions

i) **Obshchina** - Another word for mir.

ii) **Zemstvo** (plural zemstva) - Form of elected local government set up after 1864. (See page 27).

iii) **Duma** - Elected parliament established in 1906. (See pages 49-51)
NB. Term also applied to elected town councils set up after 1870 (ie urban Zemstva). This use is rare.

iv) **Soviet** - Technically means council, so can be used to describe 1810 State Council. This use is rare. Normally refers to elected councils set up by workers in 1905, and which re-emerged in 1917. (See page 38).

v) **Zemsky Sobor** ('Assembly of the Land') -Assembly of nobles and other social groups called to consider important issues. Had last met in the 17th century. In 19th century some nobles wanted it re-established.

vi) **Holy Synod** - Body of bishops, headed by lay Chief Procurator, which ran the Orthodox Church as virtually a government department.

vii) **Third Section** - Secret police 1826-1880.

viii) **Okhrana** (Literally guard) - Secret police 1881-1917.

2. Administrative Units

i) **Guberniya** - Province. 50 in European Russia, each headed by a governor.

ii) **Uezd** - Subdivision of province. County.

iii) **Volost** - Subdivision of uezd. A canton, a group of several villages comprising from 300 to 2,000 male peasants and their families.

3. Russian measurements

i) Distance - **Verst** = 1.06 km.
Area - **Des(s)yatin** = 1.09 hectares = 2.7 acres.

ii) Weight - **Pud** =16.3 kg.

iii) Money - **Rouble** - Value fluctuated considerably in the 19th century. In 1897 its value fixed at 1 rouble = 2s 1d (ie about 10p).

iv) Dates - Till 1918 Russia operated under the old Julian Calendar, which meant in the 19th century Russian dates were 12 days, and in the 20th century, 13 days behind those used by the rest of Europe which used the Gregorian calendar. All dates in this book are old style.

4. Economic terms

i) **Obruk** - Money payment by serfs to lords.

ii) **Barschina** - Labour service performed by serfs for lords.

iii) **Khutor** - Individual farm, separated from mir. (See chart 7.8).

iv) **Otrub** - Individual farm, still in village. (See chart 7.8).

v) **Kulak** - Rich peasant (literally 'fist').

vi) **Kustar** - Craft manufacture; domestic industry.

vii) **Artel** - Co-operative association.

5. Political groups (for details, see chapter 8, especially chart 8.1)

i) **SRs** - Socialist Revolutionaries.

ii) **Populists** - Radical group looking to Russian people for support.

iii) **SDs** - Social Democrats (Marxists).

iv) **Mensheviks** - More moderate section of SDs.

vi) **Bolsheviks** - More radical section of SDs, led by Lenin.

vii) **Octobrists** - Moderate Liberal party 1905 onwards.

viii) **Kadets** (or Cadets) - Constitutional Democrats. More radical Liberal Party.

ix) **Progressists** (or Progressives) - Moderate Liberal Party formed in 1908 mainly by commercial and industrial circles.

x) **Black Hundreds** - Reactionary political organisation formed in 1905 by the Union of the Russian People. Engaged in violence in support of autocracy. Extreme nationalists, and anti-semitic. Slogan: 'Beat the Yids and the Intelligents: Save Russia.'

6. Miscellany

i) **Old Believers** - Dissident branch of church, disagreeing with changes made in the 17th century. Powerful in some communities.

ii) **Pogrom** - Anti-Jewish riots.

iii) **Ukase** - Royal decree.

Chart 1.3 Geographical aspects

GENERAL LANDSCAPE

'It was a hard land, whose overpowering landscape reduced men and their works to insignificance. Towns and villages, in Gogol's phrase, were like 'little dots', marks imperceptibly stuck upon the plains.' (Smith, (1971). Russia of the Tsars p.5).

POPULATION

Size
1812 41 million
1913 166 million

RUSSIA: Population in 1900 approx. 128 millions, (European Russia 87m, Ukraine 20m, Don Caucasus 5m, Lower Volga 4m, Siberia 5m, Asiatic Russia 7m).

GEOGRAPHICAL: (see map)

DISTRIBUTION: 1812 Urban population 4%

SOCIAL: Russia's Social Hierarchy

GENERAL

- European Russia vast lowland plain.
- No large mountains nor seas to protect most of her boarders.
- Poorly defended by nature so required vast military burden on people.

MOSCOW

- Capital of old Russia.
- Typified traditional Russia: tsars crowned there.

ST PETERSBURG

- Built by Peter the Great on the Baltic marshes as a 'window on Europe'.
- Centre of European influences.
- Official capital since 1712.

TEMPERATURE

▓	Below −40°C
▨	−40° − −20°C
▧	−20° − 0°C
░	0° − 20°C
□	Above 20°C

POPULATION 1900

● one dot equals one million persons

ECONOMY

- Overwhelmingly agricultural.
- Some industry, eg wool, linen, silk, leather, iron.
- Urals world's leading iron producer in early 19th century.
- Textiles at Moscow, St Petersburg.
- Largely serf based, inefficient.
- Primitive communications: first metalled road only 1830s; railways and steam boats 1850; 1800 600,000 employed as haulers on rivers.
- Long winters encouraged peasant handicrafts as vital supplement to farming; so local, small scale industry developed; hindrance to major expansion.

URALS

- Mark traditional boundary between European and Asiatic Russia.

Russia's Social Hierarchy

Non-productive classes (11.4%) Educated classes

Officials and *Ranznochintsy*

Productive classes (88.6%)
(Peasants and urban working classes and small traders)

Ruling elite (0.25-0.5%)
Military (5%)
Merchants (0.5%)
Nobility (1.1%)
Ranznochintsy (3.7%)
Clergy (1.1%)
Meshchane (3.7%)
Urban working classes and small traders
Cossacks and other peasants (1.5%)
State peasants (32.7%)
Landlords' serfs (50.7%)
Peasants (84.9%)
Rural working classes

▨ Predominantly urban

SOIL AND CLIMATE

KEY

▓	Black Earth Region. Rich as any in Europe. Glacial clays and decaying vegetation formed fertile soil. Thin in north, deeper in south.
░	Other chief agricultural areas
▨	Mountains
M	Rich mineral deposits
North	Plentiful rain
South	Periodic droughts hit agricultural lands
– – –	North of this line subsoil permanently frozen
x x x x	North of this line snow on the ground four months a year (see diagram of temperature)

Rivers:
useful for internal transport, but problem of freezing; limited use for international trade as most flowed into landlocked or ice-bound seas.

JULY

JANUARY

ECONOMY

- Poverty of masses and serfdom discouraged enterprise, but
- State under Peter the Great (1682-1725) had boosted industry by establishing factories, giving orders, tax exemptions.
- Factories founded for state needs, eg shipbuilding, iron, or luxury market.

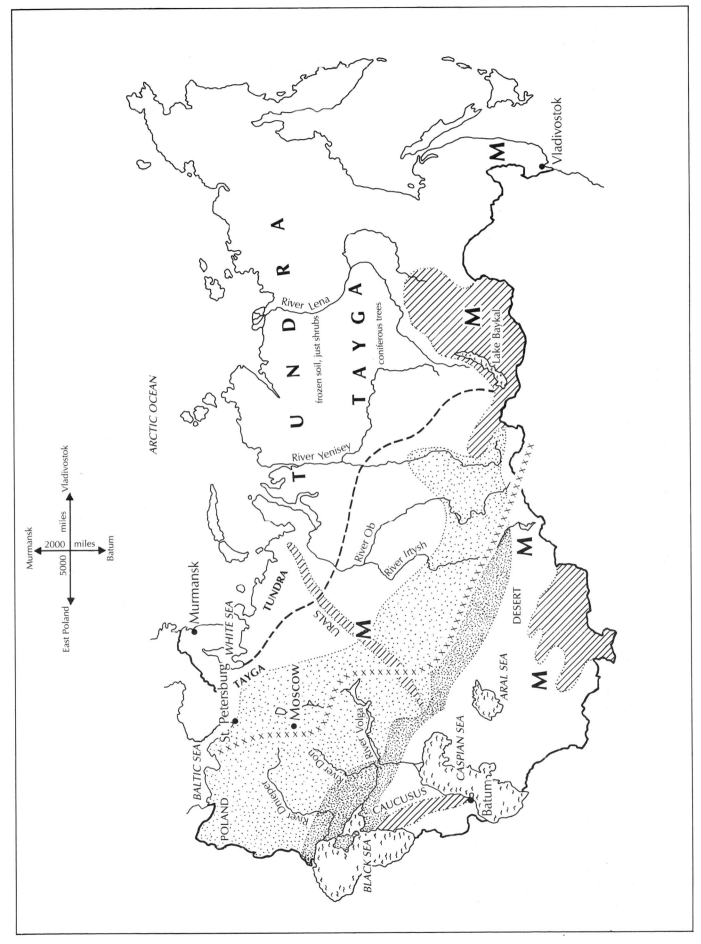

ARCTIC OCEAN

T U N D R A

frozen soil, just shrubs

River Lena

T A Y G A

coniferous trees

Lake Baykal

M

Vladivostok

River Yenisey

River Ob

River Irtysh

M

Murmansk

WHITE SEA

TUNDRA

TAYGA

URALS

DESERT

ARAL SEA

M

St. Petersburg

Moscow

River Volga

CASPIAN SEA

BALTIC SEA

POLAND

River Dnieper

River Don

Batum

CAUCUSUS

BLACK SEA

M

Murmansk ↕ Vladivostok

2000 miles

5000 miles

East Poland ↔ Batum

9

Chart 1.4 Political aspects

Budget of the Russian government in 1846

Expenditure
- Other (14%)
- Ministries of Justice and Education (4%)
- Ministry of Finance (13%)
- Imperial Court (7%)
- Army and fleet (45%)
- Loans (17%)

Income
- Other (22%)
- Customs (18%)
- Tax on salt (5%)
- Tax on Vodka (30%)
- Direct taxes (25%) (Mainly poll tax and *obrok* of state peasants)

KEY
- – – – Limits of authorised Jewish settlement
- 1858 Date of Conquest
- JEWS Minority groups
- ⊙ Centre for exiles
- ⇧ Areas of actual and hoped for expansion

AUTOCRACY (See also Chart 1.2)
- Absolute monarchy.
- Developed to keep vast, diverse state together, and to organise resources to defend extensive, weak borders.
- Power centralised in dual capitals, St Petersburg, Moscow.
- 1613 Romanov Dynasty founded.
- Article 1 of Fundamental Laws ' The Emperor of all the Russias is an autocratic and unlimited monarch. God commands that his supreme power be obeyed out of conscience as well as fear.'

ARMY
- Over 1 million in 1826.
- Conscripts served for 25 years; great dread for ordinary Russians.
- Fierce discipline; soldiers could face up to 12,000 lashings.
- Military colonies on borders.

SERFDOM (See also chart 1.2)
- About half peasants were serfs, the other half were state peasants, ie similar condition but owned by state; state peasants most common in north, and centre-north.
- Serf law; 'The owner may impose on his serfs every kind of labour, may take from them money dues and demand from them personal service, with this restriction, that they should not thereby be ruined...'

CHURCH
- 15th century offshoot from from Greek Orthodox.
- Moscow considered as 'Third Rome'; God's city.
- Belief in special religious destiny of 'Holy Russia' which represented the true faith.
- Close link between patriotism, church, government. Assumed all loyal subjects should belong to state church. Education Minister Uvarov's official slogan: 'Orthodoxy, Autocracy, Nationality.'
- Church seen as arm of the state: headed by Over Procurator of Holy Synod, lay figure appointed by the tsar.
- Church catechism: 'God commands us to love and obey

from the inmost recesses of the heart every authority, and particularly the Emperor.'

EDUCATION
- Very limited provision.
- In 1800 only one university (Moscow).

BUREAUCRACY
- Over half a million officials (chivovniks).
- Needed to carry out central government orders.
- Top levels gained nobility.
- Notorious for inefficiency, delays and corruption.
- Irresponsibility of bureaucracy was described by a noble in a report to Alexander II in 1850s:
'All power is centred in the hands of the chivovniks...a savage and greedy horde which has taken possession of Russia and enjoys without inhibition the rights of conquerors. It plunders all classes of people, robs the Imperial Treasury... Having bound the hands of Ministers by centralisation, paper formalism and countless signatures having freed itself in this manner from inspection and verification on the part of the central government, being everywhere the persecutor of freedom of expression....'

POLICE AND JUDICIARY
- Ordinary police supplemented by the Third Section, then Okhrana which penetrated all aspects of Russian society.
- Strict censorship.
- Judges had neither independence from the government, nor respect from the people.
- Lords and police could enforce arbitrary punishments.

GENTRY
- Vital prop for government.
- Only possible major source of officials as middle class so weak.
- Exempt from poll tax.

EXILE
- Siberia used since 1648 for criminals and political opponents, especially

1825 Decembrists, 1863 Poles, Socialists etc.
- Also indebted Jews, rebellious serfs.
- 1891 estimated 40,000 criminals; 50,000 political prisoners; 100,000 Poles.

POPULATION

1897 Census	Nationality by mother tongue
Great Russian	55.6m
Ukrainian	22.4m
Polish	7.9m
White Russian	5.8m
Jewish	5.0m
Kirgiz	4.0m
Tatars	3.4m

BLACK SEA
- Crucial strategic area for Russia, for access to Mediterranean.
- Exit (via Straits) controlled by Turkey; Russian desire to gain Constantinople.

COSSACKS
- 'Free warriors' originating from independent Tatar groups.
- Established several independent, self-governing communities.
- Given special privileges in return for military service.
- Reputation for rowdy, violent living; insubordinate.
- Had been rebellious, but by 19th century incorporated into tsarist army.
- Most loyal, ruthless supporters of the regime.

UKRAINIANS
- Largest national minority, though very similar to Russians.

JEWS
- Mainly confined to 15 provinces of Pale 1815-1917.
- Of 5 million, only 300,000 outside this area.
- Discriminated against, eg not allowed to own, work on land.
- Periodic pogroms (anti-Jewish riots) from 1881 onwards.

POLES
- 1815 Kingdom of Poland ruled by tsar.
- 1831, 1863 rebellions.

FINNS
- 1809 Grand Duchy ruled by tsars till 1917.

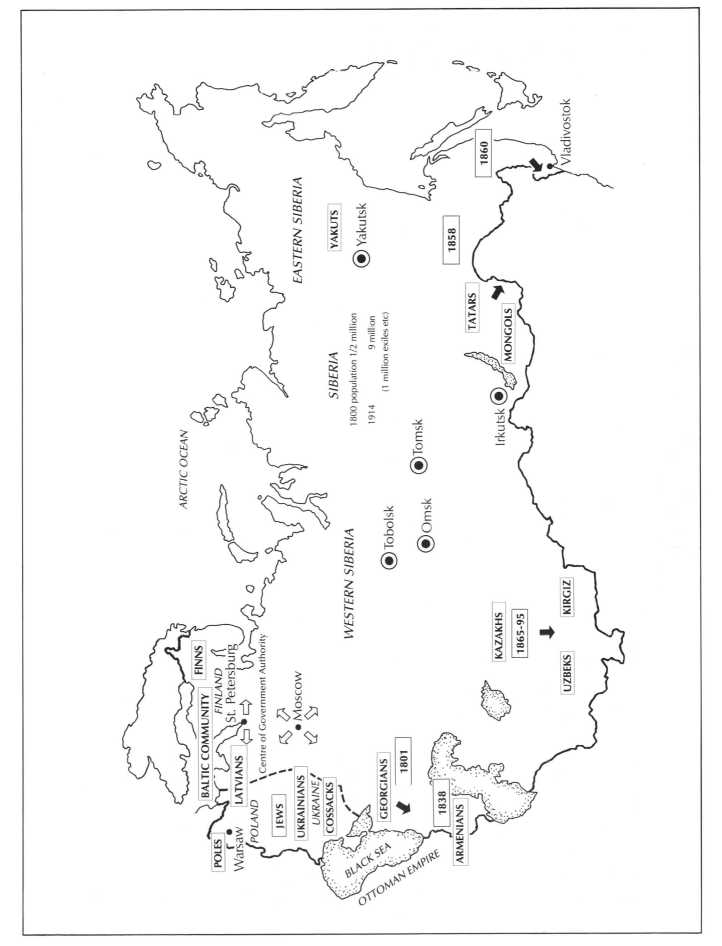

ARCTIC OCEAN

EASTERN SIBERIA

YAKUTS
⊙ Yakutsk

1858

1860

Vladivostok

WESTERN SIBERIA

SIBERIA

1800 population 1/2 million

1914   9 million
           (1 million exiles etc)

TATARS

MONGOLS

Irkutsk ⊙

⊙ Tobolsk

⊙ Tomsk

⊙ Omsk

KIRGIZ

KAZAKHS
1865-95

UZBEKS

FINNS

FINLAND
St. Petersburg

Centre of Government Authority

Moscow

BALTIC COMMUNITY

LATVIANS

JEWS

UKRAINIANS

UKRAINE

COSSACKS

GEORGIANS
1801

1838

ARMENIANS

POLES
Warsaw

POLAND

BLACK SEA

OTTOMAN EMPIRE

11

2 The Reigns of Alexander I and Nicholas I

A   The reign of Alexander I 1801-1825

(see chart 2.1)

In many ways the key issues that were to face tsars throughout the nineteenth century first arose during the reign of Alexander I. Russia became involved in the struggle against Napoleon who headed a nation modernised by the French Revolution. Russia's defeat of Napoleon in 1812 seemed to confirm her status as a great power. However, when the Russian army pursued Napoleon back to Paris, its noble officers came into contact with a modern state, and were shocked by the contrast with their own country. This contrast was to become greater, and more apparent as the century progressed.

The major issues of the reign are identified on chart 2.1. Some historians suggest that the greatest chance to break with Russia's authoritarian past and to develop along liberal constitutional lines, similar to the West, came during the reign of Alexander I. That this failed to occur has been attributed both to the sheer weight of authoritarian pressures in Russia, and to the personal inadequacies of Alexander himself.

Study of Alexander I has highlighted the inconsistencies of his character and policies. In his youth he criticised both serfdom and autocracy; when he became tsar he established commissions recommending their abolition, and supported constitutions in other countries. Yet at home his reforms, after initial relaxation of police control, were minor.

This apparent contradiction has been explained in various ways:

a) a reflection of his personal inadequacies, in particular an inability to formulate clear policies;

b) a reflection of the general situation and obstacles to change, such as illiteracy, the shortage of trained, honest administrators, and the difficulties of trying to reform against reactionary pressures at court and in the country at large;

c) the actions of a youthful liberal reformer who later became converted to reaction;

d) the tactical actions of a frightened conservative, who only made moves towards reforms as a form of 'insurance' to cover himself in the event of revolution (a view argued by the Soviet historian Okun. See article by Young, in Kochan, L. (1967), *Russian Themes*.)

A wise historian might suggest there are elements of truth in most of these explanations.

B   The reign of Nicholas I 1825-1855

(see chart 2.2)

There is less debate about the reign of Alexander's brother, though it was not merely the period of repression often portrayed. Certainly Nicholas was worried by the attempted Decembrist revolution that tried to prevent his accession, and he increased the repressive machinery. On the other hand, there was a series of minor administrative and social reforms. However, he left his son Alexander II a difficult inheritance, with Russia facing defeat in the Crimea, and with irresistible pressures for major reforms.

Worksection 2

A. Contemporary views on Russia

A.1. Interpreting historical evidence.

Read the following statements.

a) Extract from Prince Volkonksy's Memoirs:

'The campaigns of 1812-14 brought Europe nearer to us, made us familiar with its forms of state, its public institutions, the rights of its people. By contrast with our own state life, the laughably limited rights which our people possessed, the despotism of our regime first became truly present in our heart and understanding. (Quoted by Kochan, L./Abraham, R. (1983), *Making of Modern Russia* p.156.)

b) Returning Napoleonic war veteran Yakushki:

'Seeing the insipid life in St Petersburg and listening to the babbling of old men praising the past and deprecating every progressive step was unbearable. We were a hundred years from them.' (Quoted by Westwood, J. (1973), *Endurance and Endeavour* p.33)

c) The Decembrist Bestuzhev explains his involvement to Nicholas I:

'We shed our blood (against Napoleon) and now we are forced once more to sweat under feudal obligations. We freed the fatherland from the tyrant, and now we ourselves are tyrannised over by the ruling class . . . Did we free Europe in order to be put in chains ourselves? Did we grant France a constitution (Alexander's support for restoration of constitutional monarchy in France 1814) in order that we dare not talk about it, and did we buy at the price of our blood pre-eminence among nations in order that we might be humiliated at home?'
(Quoted by Crankshaw, E. (1978), *Shadow of the Winter Palace* p.56)

d) Count Speransky, Alexander's adviser, on the nature of Russia:

'The authority the sovereign wields over the landlords is in no way different from the power the landlord has over his peasants . . . I find in Russia only two estates: the slaves of the sovereign and the

slaves of the landlords. The former are called free in relation to the latter, but there are no free men in Russia except beggars and philosophers.'
(Quoted by Crankshaw, E. (1978), *Shadow of the Winter Palace* pp. 93-4)

    i) How does extract (a) help explain why the revolutionary Herzen said that 'Russian history began in 1812'?

    ii) What do the four extracts have in common?

    iii) How do extracts (a), (b) and (c) help explain why Nicholas was so determined to reduce contact with the rest of Europe?

    iv) How does Speransky's comment indicate one of the reasons why both Alexander I and Nicholas I felt unable to end serfdom? (Consider, how nobles might react to the loss of their power over their serfs.)

A.2. Study the English cartoon on Nicholas I and the Polish Revolt.

    i) What criticisms made of Nicholas in the speech are reinforced by the drawings?

    ii) Which do you consider the most effective form of criticism, the speech or the drawings? Why?

    iii) Is the relationship between Nicholas and the Poles portrayed as purely a brutal, repressive one? How accurate was this view of relations between tsar and people?

    iv) Of what value to the historian is this piece of evidence?

B. Assessment of Alexander I and Nicholas I

B.1. Study chart 2.1. on Alexander I.

    i) Draw up a list of points to substantiate the view of Alexander I as a 'liberal', and another to support the view of him as a 'reactionary'.

    ii) How appropriate do you consider these terms? Explain your answer.

B.2. Study chart 2.2 on Nicholas I.

    i) To what extent does the evidence there justify the view of Nicholas as a merely repressive monarch?

    ii) Why was his country not in 'good order' by 1855?

B.3. Study charts 2.1 and 2.2, and page 12. Then read the following extracts from historians describing the policies and reigns of Alexander I and Nicholas I.

    i) Decide which tsar or reign is being described, and explain your decision.

    ii) Choose four of the extracts, and explain to what extent you agree with them.

a) 'The most complex and most elusive figure among the emperors of Russia.' (Charques, R. (1959), *Short History of Russia* p.125)

b) He 'took a perverse pride in Russian backwardness and tried to preserve it without contamination by the West.' (Smith, D. (1971), *Russia of the Tsars*, p.17)

c) 'Within an enveloping political absolutism the system of bereaucratic tyranny, barrack-room discipline and police supervision which -------- imposed on Russian society bore only a delusive appearance of strength.' '(Charques, R. (1959), *Short History of Russia* p.141)

Nicholas I and the Polish Revolt
English cartoon

'Gentlemen! I know you wish to address me; but to spare you from delivering a pack of lies, I desire that you hold your tongues. How can I put faith in you, when you hold the same language to me as on the eve of the Revolution. My much lamented and august brother, Alexander, was treated with the blackest ingratitude after all the blessings which he heaped upon the Polish rebels. And you would treat me — your soft-hearted, generous, and consoling father — just the same, if you had the power. But I have taken the sting out of you, my dears! I have raised the citadel; and I declare, that on the slightest movement of you for the recovery of your Liberties, I will blow you all to hell; and there shan't be a single Pole left to tell the tale. Ungrateful slaves! are you totally incapable of appreciating the blessings and the tender mercies hourly bestowed on you by me — your most paternal guardian genius? Do I not allow you to eat, drink, sleep, walk and talk every day without punishment for such luxuries! Do not I allow you to wear your chains that they may not incommode you in walking? — Do not I allow you to be whack'd by the knout, instead of the English cat-o-nine-tails! Do not I (God be merciful to me for my mercies!) allow your discontented countrymen to be hanged only, in lieu of being roasted alive; or sent to Siberia, instead of the gallies! Are not the most rebellious of you merely cut into four quarters when they ought to be chopped into pieces? Look at all that, you ungrateful slaves, and remember me in your prayers sent to your Creator, for such God-sends as you continually enjoy under me, your affectionate, but much ill used father, and sovereign protector, — Nick-alas!'

d) 'His apparent inconsistency was perhaps due to a conflict of two consistencies, his fear of disorder and his wish for improvement . . . His ideas and thoughts led lives independently of what (he) happened to say at any particular time.' (Westwood, J. (1973), *Endurance and Endeavour* p.18)

e) 'The reign of ------- was not a development but a prolonged situation.' (Crankshaw, E. (1978), *Shadow of the Winter Palace* p.50)

f) 'His actual achievements as a political and social reformer were negligible.' (Young, article in *Russian Themes,* ed. Kochan, L. (1967) p.63)

g) He 'postponed and finally evaded the solution of his problems.' (Smith, D. (1971), *Russia of the Tsars* p.17)

h) 'A conscientious ruler who seriously desired the welfare of his subjects and his Empire.' (Lincoln, B. *History Today, Vol 21,* 1971, p.80)

i) 'The reign of ----- represented the highest development of autocratic monarchy in Russia, yet like all high points, it contained in itself the main elements that caused its subsequent decline.' (Morris, T. (1985), *European History 1848-1945* p.80)

C. Concluding essay

Use the ideas in the charts and exercises, and wider reading, to write one of the following essays.

a) Was Alexander I's reputation for baffling inconsistency at home and abroad justified?

b) 'A long period of repression and gloom.' Discuss this view of the reign of Nicholas I.

Advice. Both these essays could be tackled by first putting forward points that support the statement, and then considering counter points. Both titles cover two aspects, so in the Alexander essay be sure to discuss both domestic and foreign policy, and in the Nicholas essay discuss the extent of 'gloom' as well as the obvious repression. This latter essay raises an interesting point. Even if you are perhaps unfamiliar with an idea in an essay title, or initially fail to see why it has been used, you still have to address the specific question set, and not the one you might have preferred.

The Alexander I question addresses the central debate about the reign. It could be tackled by considering the extent to which the inconsistencies in action during his reign were due to the character of Alexander, and to what extent changes of policy were more a product of the context within which he operated. The question requires consideration of explanations for inconsistency (in order to address the term 'baffling') as well as identification of them. One needs to consider the issue of inconsistency within each sphere of policy (domestic, then foreign), but one could also discuss any inconsistency between domestic and foreign, eg over constitutional monarchy. One could also consider Okun's line, and argue against there being any inconsistency.

In the Nicholas essay with the reference to 'gloom', you could refer to the overall atmosphere in Nicholas's Russia, particularly after he became worried by the 1848 Revolutions, and the feeling of decay which failure in the Crimea served to encourage. A reference to the flowering of literature during Nicholas's reign might challenge the quotation, although some of this was critical of the regime. It would also be legitimate to point out how hard it is for the historian to gather firm evidence about the atmosphere in a country, particularly one where expressions of opinions were as tightly controlled as in Nicholas's Russia. You will be given credit for points like this for it shows your understanding of the problems of historical evidence and interpretation.

Chart 2.1 The reign of Alexander 1801-1825

A. Character
i) Upbringing.
  – Educated in the enlightened atmosphere of Catherine the Great's reign by liberal tutor La Harpe.
  – Character still unformed when he became tsar at 23. Perhaps affected by the sudden acquisition of unlimited power.
ii) Personality.
  – Romanov charm; attractive, but insubstantial character.
  – Had short-lived enthusiasms.
  – Never sure of himself, indecisive, but also intransigent temper.
  – Dissimulator. Perhaps he never grew up.
  – Impenetrable.

Chart 2.1 *continued*

B. Alexander as Tsar

- —Probably involved in aristocratic plot against his father, and felt guilt about his murder in 1801. May have helped cause his restless spirit.
- —Indecisive: hid from major decisions.
- —Easily influenced, eg early on by young liberals; then Speransky; Napoleon briefly 1807; Golitsyn 1812; mystical Madame de Krudener 1815; reactionary Arakcheyev 1810 onwards.
- —Soon lost his enthusiasm for reforming Secret Committee, and shelved reforms.
- —Not attracted to routine of government.
- —1812. Initially firm against Napoleon; then suffered depression, till recovered with role of 'Liberator of Europe', which flattered his vanity. 'For twelve years Europe has regarded me as a mediocrity. Let us see what they have to say now.'
- —After 1819 virtually left Arakcheyev to rule at home, and spent hours in spiritual contemplation.
- —Rushed around Europe, and his Empire.
- —Considered abdicating; and rumours he had done so in 1825 when he died of typhoid.

C. Domestic policy

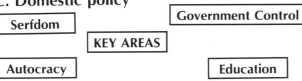

Serfdom   **Government Control**

KEY AREAS

Autocracy   **Education**

Serfdom

a) Attitude: As a youth, he criticised serfdom. 1814. He said, 'With God's help, serfdom will be abolished in my lifetime.'
b) Actions:
  i) 1801-3. Secret Committee of reformers to plan abolition; not enacted.
  ii) 1815. Arakcheyev asked to devise scheme for gradual emancipation; shelved.
  iii) Only concrete action was a few minor reforms, palliatives, ie:
  —1801 Lords could not advertise serfs for sale.
  —1803 Emancipation by mutual consent (47,000 of 17 million private serfs set free in 20 years).
  —1809 Lords could not punish serfs with penal servitude.
  —1819 Baltic serfs liberated without land.

Autocracy

a) Attitude: 1796. He said, 'Hated despotism everywhere and in every form.'
  —1798 He spoke of 'national assembly and free consitution.' Attracted by American constitution.
b) Actions:
  i) 1801-3. Unofficial Secret Committee to discuss political changes.
  ii) 1809. Speransky drew up a draft constitution for a system of elected bodies, headed by a Duma and State Council. Not enacted, apart

from appointing an advisory Council of State in 1810.
  1812. Speransky was dismissed.
  iii) 1818-19. Novosiltsov drew up draft constitution; accepted but not enacted.

Overall, some bureaucratic changes occurred, eg new ministries, Council of State, but there was no move from autocracy to more representative government.

Government control

- —1801. Initial relaxation, ie exiles recalled, secret police, censorship reduced; increased contact with West.
- —Some brutal punishments, eg nostril splitting and judicial torture abolished.
- —But from 1819 repression increased, especially as brutal Arakcheyev dominated government. Provoked 1825 Decembrist revolt.
- —Universities closely controlled; stress on religion; censorship tightened.
- —1815. 'Military colonies' developed to settle returning soldiers and their families. Cheap defence, but tight discipline.

Education

- —1804. Education Statute established hierarchy of schools from parish to universities, and a Ministry of Education. Initially study abroad was encouraged, and a liberal atmosphere prevailed.
- —5 new universities founded. Number of pupils trebled, but still most Russians uneducated.
- —After 1815, this liberal approach ended, Church influence increased. Purges of liberal and foreign elements. Reactionaries appointed to key posts.

D. Foreign policy

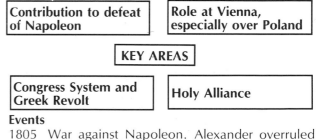

Contribution to defeat of Napoleon   **Role at Vienna, especially over Poland**

KEY AREAS

Congress System and Greek Revolt   **Holy Alliance**

Events

1805 War against Napoleon. Alexander overruled cautious General Kutuzov, and Russians engaged French in battle, but were defeated at Austerlitz.
1807 Friedland defeat, led to Treaty of Tilsit. Europe carved up, and Russia joined Continental System.
1808-9 Conquered Finland. Its constitution kept.
1810 onwards. Growing antagonism to France over Duchy of Warsaw, Turkey, trade etc.
1812 French invasion. Battle of Borodino was a bloody draw. Moscow abandoned and burnt. Napoleon forced to withdraw. Alexander ordered army to follow French back into Europe.

Chart 2.1 *continued*

1813 Alexander led anti-Napoleonic campaign; joined by Prussia and Austria.
1814 Major role at Congress of Vienna; gained most
1815 but not all of Poland. Granted her a constitution and Parliament. Favoured constitutional monarchy in France.
1815 Set up Holy Alliance, along principles of peace, justice and charity. Turned into reactionary alliance under influence of Metternich.

1818 Aix, 1820 Troppau, 1821 Laibach Congresses; Alexander favoured military action against revolts.
1821 Torn over Greek Revolt, but refused to help Greeks.

E. Overall assessment

A reign of contradictions, both as regards Alexander personally, and his policies. Liberal and reactionary elements. Has been seen as a missed opportunity for major reforms after 1812-1815 military success.

Chart 2.2 The reign of Nicholas I 1825-1855

A. Character

i) **Upbringing**
   – Illiberal education.
   – As third son of Tsar Paul, trained for military.
ii) **Personality**
   – Happiest dealing with military matters.
   – Obsessed by discipline, order, obedience.
   – Narrow intellect; unimaginative.
   – Temperamentally unsure of himself.
   – Suspicious; trusted no one.

B. Nicholas as Tsar

   – Firm believer in personal autocracy; a God-given duty.
   – Felt personally responsible for the material and spiritual welfare of his subjects; tried to prescribe exactly what his subjects should think. Once said: 'I am a sentry at outpost on guard, to see all and observe all. I must stay there until I am relieved.'
   – Exercised great personal control in all state affairs, both domestic and foreign; unable to distinguish between trivial and essential matters.
   – Conscientious; great energy, often began work before dawn but eventually drove himself to death.

   – Felt reform necessary in some areas, but must come from the tsar.
   – 1855. Caught chill and died, broken by Crimean disaster.

C. Domestic policy

Overall nature: bleak repression, but also some reforms. The 'Nicholas System', ie paternalist conservatism via vast bureaucratic apparatus.

Repression

   – Frightened, made suspicious by Decembrist Revolt.
   – 1826. Set up Third Section of Personal Chancery; secret police headed by Benckendorff, permeated Russian society, virtual state within a state, independent of normal process of law, preventive arrests. Also seen as having paternalist role by Nicholas, ie. Third Section, as guardian of public order and morality. A means to extend his concern for his subjects' welfare.
   – Nicholas expanded Personal Chancery as means to keep control over administration.
   – Tight censorship, foreign travel restricted.
   – Secondary education restricted; greater government control of universities, especially after the European revolts of 1830. Press and the Church launched counter-offensive to buttress the system.
   – 1831. Cholera epidemic led to revolt by military colonies; repressed by mass floggings. Over 100 died. Earned him nickname, 'Nicholas the Stick'.
   – 1848. European revolutions worried Nicholas, and repression intensified. Early paternal conservatism degenerated into sterile reaction.
   – Massive administrative system; bureaucratic tyranny, with barrack-room discipline, enforced by vast police system; over 2000 suspects shadowed.
   – Great flow of exiles (150,000) to Siberia.

Reforms — More positive aspects

Series of pragmatic reforms, generally by-passing traditional bureaucracy.

Chart 2.2 *continued*

a) Finances
  – Finance Minister Kankrin enacted major financial reforms; created stable currency.

b) Law
  – Second Section of Imperial Chancery under Speransky 1829-33 codified Russian law. Major achievement. Raised doubts as to legal basis of serfdom.

c) Serfdom
  – Nicholas aware of problem as 'powder cellar under the state', and between 1826-48 he set up 10 secret committees to study improvements.
  – Minor reforms, ie 1833 auctions of serfs ended; Fifth Section of Personal Chancery set up to help state peasants via improved agriculture, education, health.
  – But growing peasant unrest; over 700 risings.

d) Economic
  – Slow spread of railways; 700 km by 1854.
  – Growth of cotton, metallurgy, sugar-refining.
  – Factory workforce trebled to ½ million.

e) Literature
  – 'Golden Age' of Russian prose and poetry, eg Pushkin, Gogol.
  – Indirect means of political and social criticism, eg Belinski.

D. Foreign Policy

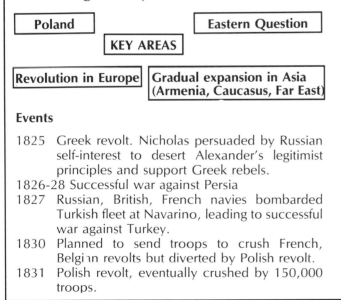

Events

1825 Greek revolt. Nicholas persuaded by Russian self-interest to desert Alexander's legitimist principles and support Greek rebels.

1826-28 Successful war against Persia

1827 Russian, British, French navies bombarded Turkish fleet at Navarino, leading to successful war against Turkey.

1830 Planned to send troops to crush French, Belgian revolts but diverted by Polish revolt.

1831 Polish revolt, eventually crushed by 150,000 troops.

1833 Münchengrätz agreement with Holy Alliance powers (Austria, Prussia).
  Treaty of Unkiar Skelessi. Russia gained rights over Straits.

1841 Straits Convention. Russian rights reduced, but still gained security by closing Straits to all warships when Turkey at peace.

1846 Minor Polish disturbances, chiefly in Austrian Galicia and Cracow.

1848 Terrified by European revolts; Nicholas nearly sent 400,000 troops West. Restrained Prussia in war with Denmark.

1849 170,000 troops sent to crush Hungarian revolt.

1850 Influenced Prussia to give way to Austria at Olmütz.

1853 War against Turkey, Russian successes, then she evacuated Danube provinces, but still British-French expeditionary force attacked Crimea.

1855 Russia clearly losing Crimean War.

Assessment

  –Nicholas content with his nickname, the 'Gendarme of Europe'.
  –Also preoccupied with Turkey, which he called 'sick man of Europe'. Early cautious policy successful, but Nicholas's obstinate conceit, combined with Franco-British aggressive stupidity, led to disastrous Crimean War.

E. Overall assessment

  –Policy summed up by Education Minister Uvarov, 'Orthodoxy, Autocracy, and the National Way of Life.'
  –Succeeded in maintaining system, but there was growing peasant unrest, and an increasingly critical intelligentsia.
  –After 1848 paternalist system collapsing into vast bureaucratic jungle.
  –Increasingly irrational repression not a secure basis for future.
  –Foreign policy failure, combined with collapsing system of government, paved way for reforms of Alexander II.
  –Said to his heir in 1855 'I hand over to you my command unfortunately not in as good order as I would have wished.'

3 The Reign of Alexander II

A Introduction

The disastrous legacy of Nicholas I meant that change was bound to come to Russia. Hence the reign of Alexander II was arguably one of the most important periods of Russian history. Many historians, such as Kennan, believe that if Alexander II had been prepared to grant moderate political concessions then Russia might have been set on the course of gradual development into a constitutional monarchy. But though Alexander did, at last, tackle the urgent problem of serfdom, like all other tsars (with the possible exception of Alexander I) he was determined to maintain autocracy. Furthermore, the nature of the ending of serfdom (emancipation), the major social reform of the reign, has also been seen as a missed opportunity to provide long term security for the tsarist regime.

B The emancipation of the serfs

The question of serfdom had for long been seen as central to the fate of Russia. Since the late 18th century there had been increasing criticism of the system. Peasant unrest was growing and in the 1770s there had been a vast serf uprising led by Pugachov. But the dangers of ending what was seen as a pillar of the whole tsarist system were also considerable. As Nicholas I said,

'There is no question that serfdom in its present state in our country is an evil, palpable and obvious to everyone. However, to attack it now would be, of course, an even more disastrous evil.' (Seton-Watson, H. (1967), *The Russian Empire* p.227).

The shock of defeat in the Crimean War finally convinced the new Tsar that the problem of serfdom had to be tackled. Alexander asked the nobles to consider ways of emancipating the serfs, but they failed to take up the challenge, so he laid down the broad outlines. He was concerned that peasants should see a real improvement in their lives, whilst estate owners' interests were also protected as much as possible. (Tsars Peter III and Paul I had been murdered by disaffected nobles.) In 1861 the complex Emancipation Decree (really 22 acts) was issued, giving personal freedom to 50 million serfs, and providing a state supported means for them to buy their lands. (See chart 3.1 for details.)

The actual effect of emancipation varied considerably, depending both on the existing system of land-holding and agriculture, the approach of landlords, and variations in the edict. Thus peasants in Polish territories were rewarded for their general passivity during the noble-led rebellion, whilst peasants in the more fertile Black Earth region, where land was highly valued, lost heavily. The overall impact on the peasantry was far less beneficial than the term 'emancipation' might suggest.

Worksection 3 part 1

A. The nature of serfdom

Examination of primary evidence.

A.1. Read the following description of serfdom in the 1840s (made by the German traveller Haxthausen), and answer the questions which follow.

'The following information was given to us concerning the division of land in the village communes. The principle is that the whole of the land (tillage, meadows, pasture, woods, streams, and so on) belongs to the population of a village community regarded as a whole, and in using these communal possessions every male inhabitant has a right to an equal share. This share is therefore constantly changing; for the birth of every boy creates a new claim, and the shares of those who die revert to the commune. The woods, pastures, hunting grounds, and fisheries remain undivided and free to all inhabitants; but the arable land and meadows are divided equally, according to their value, among the males . . .

The land is first divided, according to its quality, position, or general value into sections, each possessing on the whole equal advantages. The sections are then divided into as many portions, in long strips, as there are shares required, and these are taken by lot. This is the usual plan, but each region, and frequently each commune, has its local customs . . .

The facts here described constitute the basis of the Russian communal system, and one that undeniably possesses great advantages for the social condition of the country. The Russian communes possess an organic coherence and compact social strength that can be found nowhere else, and yield the incalculable advantage that no proletariat can be formed so long as they exist with their present structure. A man may lose or squander all he possesses, but his children do not inherit his poverty. They still retain their claim upon the land, by a right derived, not from him, but from their birth as members of the commune. On the other hand, it must be admitted that this fundamental basis of the communal system, the equal division of the land, is not favourable to the progress of agriculture, which...under this system could for a long time remain at a low level.'
(Quoted by Christian, D.(1986), *Power and Privilege* p.41)

i) How does the commune system illustrate Russia's backwardness? (Had a similar system ever existed in Britain, for example?)
ii) How might the commune system help explain Russia's large population rise in the 19th century?

iii) What evidence does Haxthausen give in the second paragraph for the problems the government had in drafting the emancipation legislation for the whole of the Empire?
iv) What indications does Haxthausen give why:
   a) most peasants favoured the commune system,
   b) tsarist governments also favoured it,
   c) economists criticised it,
   d) non-Marxist socialists were attracted by it?

B. The emancipation process

Three exercises on primary and secondary evidence.

B.1. Alexander II introduces Emancipation.
Read the following extract from a speech made by Alexander II to the State Council in January 1861, and answer the questions which follow.

'The matter of the liberation of the serfs, which has been submitted for the consideration of the State Council, I consider to be a vital question for Russia, upon which will depend the development of her strength and power. I am sure that all of you, gentlemen, are just as convinced as I am of the benefits and necessity of this measure. I have another conviction, which is that this matter cannot be postponed; therefore I demand that the State Council finish with it in the first half of February so that it can be announced before the start of the work in the fields . . .

For four years now it has dragged on and has been arousing various fears and anticipations among both the estate owners and the peasants. Any further delay could be disastrous to the state . . . Although the apprehensions of the nobility are to a certain extent understandable, for the closest and material interests of each are involved, notwithstanding all this, I have not forgotten and shall never forget that the approach to the matter was made on the initiative of the nobility itself, and I am happy to be a witness to this before posterity . . .

I hope, gentlemen, that on inspection of the drafts presented to the State Council, you will assure yourselves that all that can be done for the protection of the interests of the nobility has been done: if, on the other hand you find it necessary in any way to alter or to add to presented work, then I am ready to receive your comments; but I ask you only not to forget that the basis of the whole work must be the improvement of the life of the peasants, an improvement not in words alone but in actual fact . . .

My late father was continuously occupied with the thought of freeing the serfs. Sympathising completely with this thought, already in 1856 while in Moscow I called the attention of the leaders of the Moscow nobility to the necessity for them to occupy themselves with improving the life of the serfs, adding that serfdom could not continue for ever and that it would therefore be better if the transformation took place from above rather than from below.'
(From Vernadsky, G. ed. (1972), *Source Book for Russian History Vol 3* p.599)

i) Why, according to Alexander II, was the liberation of the serfs so important? (2 marks)
ii) Give three references in the speech to show the need for speed over emancipation. (3 marks)
iii) Why do you think Alexander refers to his father's concern to free the serfs? (2 marks)
iv) Alexander says that all members of the State Council are as convinced as he of the benefits of reform. Given the aristocratic membership of the State Council, does this in fact seem likely? Is there any evidence later on to suggest it was not really the case? (3 marks)
v) Alexander also states that the approach for emancipation was made by the nobility. Is there any evidence in the speech to suggest that this too was not really the case? (2 marks)
vi) Why do you think Alexander made these comments about the initiative and support coming from sections of the nobility? (2 marks)
vii) What evidence is there in the above speech to support each of the following views:
   a) 'Alexander II deserves to be called the Tsar Liberator, with a genuine concern for the welfare of his people.'
   b) 'Emancipation was a conservative reform designed to salvage as much as possible for the nobility.'
   c) 'Emancipation was a precarious balancing act.' (6 marks)
viii) With which of the above views do you most agree? Why? (2 marks)
ix) What qualities of Alexander II as ruler of Russia does this speech show? (5 marks).
x) How valuable is it as a piece of evidence? Give your reasons. (3 marks)
(Total 30 marks)

B.2. Read the following account by Acton of the emancipation process, and answer the questions below.

'The government's overriding concern to ensure domestic stability ruled out the possibility of landless Emancipation. It was axiomatic that peasant agriculture must not be jeopardised, that the peasantry must remain closely bound to the land, and that the spectre of a restless, landless proletariat must be avoided. The sharp rise in disturbances between 1857 and 1859 underlined the dangers of an excessively harsh settlement. Nevertheless, while the statute was taking shape the nobility were able to reduce the quantity and quality of land in peasant hands and to extract limited amendments to the legislative proposals. In acquiescing, the government was well aware that the final terms would provoke peasant hostility, and took suitable precautions. In the capital the police told employers to work their men to the point of exhaustion the day before the terms were to be made known in order to leave them too weary to protest. The statute was promulgated during Lent, in the hope that abstention would find the peasants in subdued mood. The military were fully alerted and when the village priest read out the details the police were in attendance to stifle the groans of disbelief with which

they were met. Throughout, the Tsar had made abundantly clear his wish to damage the position of the nobility as little as was compatible with social order, and with the parlous condition of the State Treasury. In doing so he avoided confrontation: the State continued to be guided by a primary concern for the interests of the landed nobility.'
(Acton, E. (1986), *Russia* p.75)

i) To what extent does Acton's analysis support the evidence from Alexander's speech on the following issues?
   a) The reasons for emancipation.
   b) Alexander's preparedness to respond to noble criticism of the Edict.
   c) Alexander's genuine concern to improve the position of the serfs.
   d) The need to balance the interests of serfs and nobility.
   (4 x 2 marks)
ii) Was the government confident it had successfully balanced competing interests? Explain your answer. (2 marks)
iii) What two reasons does Acton give why the government was unable to protect the interests of the nobility as much as they would have liked? (2 marks)
iv) Would you expect Acton to agree with the view of Alexander II as the 'Tsar Liberator'? (3 marks)
(Total 15 marks)

B 3. Read the concluding words of the Imperial Edict proclaiming emancipation in 1861, and answer the questions which follow.

'And now we confidently hope that the freed serfs, in the presence of the new future which is opened before them, will appreciate and recognize the considerable sacrifices which the nobility has made on their behalf . . .

Only by assiduous labour, a rational expenditure of their strength and resources, a strict economy, and above all, by an upright life, a life constantly inspired by the fear of the Lord, can they hope for prosperity and progress.

And now, my orthodox and faithful people, make the holy sign of the cross and join thy prayers to ours, invoking the blessing of the Most High upon the first of thy free labours, for this alone is a sure pledge of private well-being and the public weal.'
(Quoted by Smith, D. (1971), *Russia of the Tsars* p.57)

i) Does this statement convey the same impression as Alexander's speech of how emancipation affected the nobility? Why is this? (3 marks).
ii) Why might Alexander have felt it necessary to advise peasants how they must now behave? (3 marks).
iii) Does Alexander's recipe for prosperity look convincing? (2 marks).
iv) What vital supplement to royal authority is clearly identified in the edict? (2 marks)

C. Causation in history

C.1. Consider the following contemporary evidence about serfdom, and study chart 3.1. Then answer the questions below.

a) Catherine the Great (in her diary):
It is 'contrary to the Christian religion and to justice to make slaves of men, who are all free by birth.'
(Quoted by Christian, D. (1986), *Power and Privilege* p.63)

b) Doré 1854 cartoon (printed in Acton, E. (1986), *Russia* p.64).

'Gambling with Souls'

c) Picture of serf market, and advertisement for the sale of serfs.

'Serfs for sale 1832'

d) Slavophil landowner Koshelyov, 1858:
'This measure is more necessary for the welfare of our class itself than the serfs. The abolition of the right to dispose of people like objects or like cattle is as much our liberation as theirs: for at present we are under the yoke of a law that destroys still more in us than in the serfs any human quality.'
(Quoted by Seton-Watson, H. (1967), *The Russian Empire* p.334)

Continued on page 24.

Chart 3.1 Emancipation of the serfs

A. Reasons for emancipation

Crimea
- Crimean defeat discredited whole 'Nicholas system'.
- Military defeat showed Russia's backwardness compared with the West.
- Serf-based army generally fought bravely but there was always the danger of revolt.
- Army shown to be inadequate, and it was impossible to utilise it all.
- Soldiers poorly supplied as production, often by serf labour, of wool, linen, leather, and armaments was inadequate.
- Some soldiers had to be diverted to quell unrest.

Personal
- Accession of new tsar an opportunity for change.
- Alexander humane; had studied serf problem, and desired to help his subjects.

Moral
- Growing criticism of immorality of system based on degradation and ownership of people.

- Serfdom seen as a blot on Russia's international reputation.

General
- Army could not be reorganised (with shorter length of service, and trained reserve) whilst serfdom kept, as such a change would mean trained ex-soldiers and reservists going back to villages, still serfs, so a potential source of unrest.
- Need to reduce size of military forces to lessen the financial strain of a large, standing army.
- War Minister, D. Milyutin, was a firm supporter of emancipation.

Peasant unrest
- 1770s. Pugachov revolt; major serf rising inspired by rumours of liberation; thousands of lords killed; great fear of a recurrence.
- Growing incidence of serf unrest; Count Tolstoy spoke of a coming 'holocaust'.

Economic
- Growing criticism of harmful economic effects of serfdom which dissuaded both serfs and gentry from being enterprising.
- Benefits of free peasant labour in Siberia being realised.
- Growing tide (though small overall) of voluntary emancipation.
- Increasing famines as heavy state and noble exactions of grain left peasants with little food reserves.
- Railways were needed to boost Russia's economic and military might but the government was reluctant to encourage them whilst serfdom, based on serf's immobility, survived.

General
- Serfdom seen as the prime cause of Russia's inefficiency.
- Other major reforms were not possible whilst serfdom remained.

B. Key provisions

Land
- Key problem; if peasants were not given land this would cause mass destitution, vagabondage; but if given land on generous terms, this would upset gentry, the main prop of the state.
- All non-state land was declared to belong to nobles, so had to be bought by, not given to, serfs.
- Peasants had to buy land they had previously used and considered their own, but overall they lost 20-40% as 'cut offs'.
- Minimum and maximum plots set by commissioners.
- Peasants often lost rights to woods, commons now declared the lord's private property.
- Domestic serfs not given land.

- Basic principle behind the reform (land for peasants) was also its greatest weakness as not enough land was allocated to peasants.

Personal
- Peasants no longer owned by lords (or after 1866 by the state).
- Free to marry, trade, work as pleased (though see section on mir, and special courts for peasants also still existed).
- No longer forced to work for, or give money to, lords.

Compensation and finance
- Lords technically were not compensated for loss of serf labour or obrok (former cash payments from serfs), but just for land losses; there was hidden compensation as land overvalued.

- Peasants to pay for land via redemption payments to state for 49 years.
- State gave lords 80% of value of lost land in interest bearing bonds, and collected repayments from mir.

Mir
- Powers strengthened; took over much of former lord's role, ie tax collection, selecting army recruits, maintaining order.
- Mir collectively owned peasant land, and responsible for collecting redemption payments.
- Had to agree if peasant wanted to leave.

Chart 3.1 *continued*

C. Effects of emancipation

Social

- Peasant discontent continued as they were disappointed over terms.
- Desire for 'second emancipation' developed.
- Ministry of Interior reported 647 peasant riots in first four months; 70 peasants killed by troops at Bezdna in 1861.
- Peasants overall,
  - i) lost land to use,
  - ii) had to pay redemption (roughly equivalent to old payments to lord),
- Many peasants had to rent more land from nobles, often on similar terms as under serfdom.
- Peasants still had special courts, and did not possess full citizen's rights.
- Gentry decline continued and hastened, as lost about one third of previous land, and most of redemption payments used to pay off debts.
- Massive population rise put pressure on land.

Military

- Series of military reforms as nobles' power over conscription removed.
- Trained peasant reserve army now possible.

Economic

- Emancipation has been seen as a vital stage in the transition to a capitalist economy.
- Encouraged growth of railways, banking, industry, cities.
- Encouraged freer atmosphere, entrepreneurial initiative.

BUT, easy to exaggerate this impetus, as:

- Flow to towns restricted by mir.
- Agricultural production was not revolutionised, as many gentry were indebted, and peasants impoverished.
- Strong mir retarded agricultural change; primitive methods continued.
- Most peasant farms did not produce a natural surplus; in 1861 about ¼ of farms were not even self-sufficient; by 1900 over half.
- Peasants did not form a strong market for industrial goods as they were burdened by redemption and other payments.

Judicial

- Lords legal powers removed, so legal reforms were required.

Political

- Gentry's loss of power over their serfs caused some to demand compensation in the form of greater political power through an assembly.
- Their new role in zemstva not seen by some as sufficient.
- Growth of liberalism amongst forward looking gentry; keen for further reforms.
- Most gentry, however, were conservative; resentful of change; forced to rally to government threatened by revolt from below.

Administrative

- Old abuses now questioned.
- New local government structure necessary to replace lord's role.
- Elected zemstva created.
- Mir strengthened.

General

- New atmosphere of change and reform; momentum of reform developed.
- Old assumptions challenged; faults previously accepted, now criticised.
- Actual process, involving discussions with nobles, politically awakened some.
- Some nobles now questioned the autocracy.

Additional points

Operation

- Some serfs had already been freed (voluntarily, or by Alexander I in Baltic region).
- Initial proposals were modified to appease nobles, and were enacted by generally hostile bureaucrats.
- 1861 Emancipation Edict only gradually introduced.
  Stage one (1861-3). Serfs immediately free, given personal plots, but old dues remained.
  Stage two. Peasants 'temporarily obligated'; negotiated buying of land. Old land system kept.
  Stage three. Negotiations over, peasants began paying to state for land acquired. By 1881 over one million

peasants had still not reached this stage; then made compulsory.

Beggars allotments

- Optional scheme. Peasants could take one quarter of their old plot free.
  Take up varied, in some areas of Black Earth over 20% peasants took this option. Overall, about ¾ million did so.
- These allotments were not enough to live on, so most looked for alternative income, or sold their plots.

State peasants

- Liberated with land in 1866 on better terms.

Finance

- Peasants in theory had to pay 20% of cost of land direct to lord; terms varied; often not paid.

Land losses

- Both peasants and nobles 'lost' land:
  - a) Peasants, as the land peasant communities were now buying was usually less than the land they had worked when they were serfs; they lost 'cut offs'.
  - b) Lords, because all land before had been owned but not used by them; now they were forced to sell about one third to the peasants.

D. Typical* Russian village before and after emancipation.

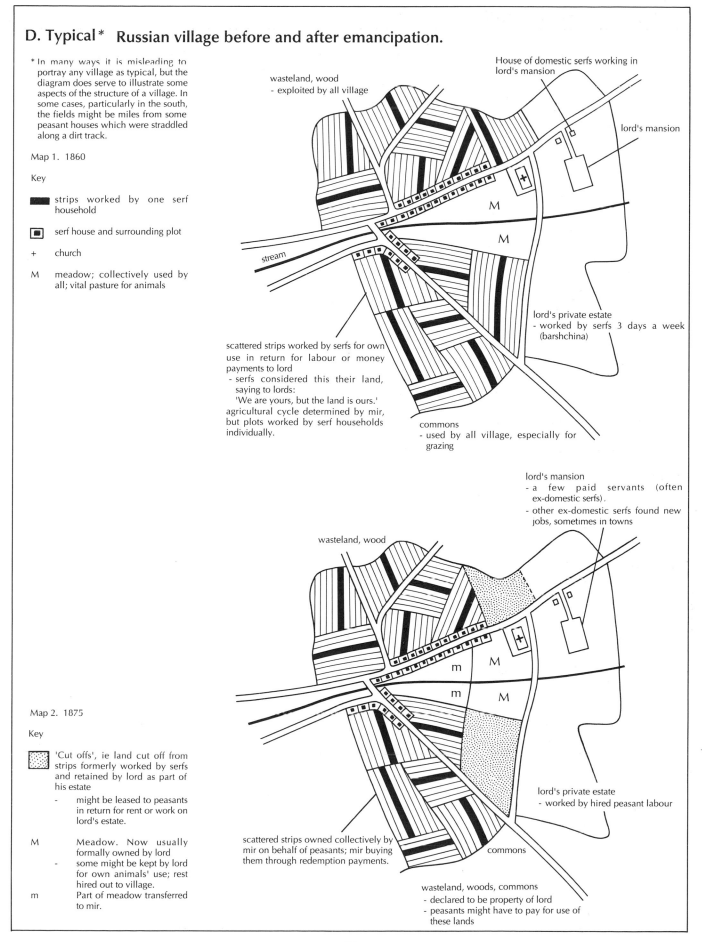

*In many ways it is misleading to portray any village as typical, but the diagram does serve to illustrate some aspects of the structure of a village. In some cases, particularly in the south, the fields might be miles from some peasant houses which were straddled along a dirt track.

Map 1. 1860

Key

▨ strips worked by one serf household

▣ serf house and surrounding plot

+ church

M meadow; collectively used by all; vital pasture for animals

wasteland, wood
- exploited by all village

House of domestic serfs working in lord's mansion

lord's mansion

M

M

stream

scattered strips worked by serfs for own use in return for labour or money payments to lord
- serfs considered this their land, saying to lords:
'We are yours, but the land is ours.'
agricultural cycle determined by mir, but plots worked by serf households individually.

lord's private estate
- worked by serfs 3 days a week (barshchina)

commons
- used by all village, especially for grazing

lord's mansion
- a few paid servants (often ex-domestic serfs).
- other ex-domestic serfs found new jobs, sometimes in towns

wasteland, wood

m m

M

M

Map 2. 1875

Key

▦ 'Cut offs', ie land cut off from strips formerly worked by serfs and retained by lord as part of his estate
- might be leased to peasants in return for rent or work on lord's estate.

M Meadow. Now usually formally owned by lord
- some might be kept by lord for own animals' use; rest hired out to village.

m Part of meadow transferred to mir.

lord's private estate
- worked by hired peasant labour

scattered strips owned collectively by mir on behalf of peasants; mir buying them through redemption payments.

commons

wasteland, woods, commons
- declared to be property of lord
- peasants might have to pay for use of these lands

e) Serfs mortgaged to the state by impoverished nobles:

Year	No. serfs (m)	% all serfs
1820	1.8	20
1830	4.5	37
1842	5.6	50
1855	6.6	61
1859	7.1	66

f) Winner of essay competition on serfdom organised by Catherine the Great:

'The best way to attract, arouse, and encourage the tillers of the soil is to give them ownership of the land they cultivate. Then each one will toil for himself, for his children, for his descendants; in a word, he will enrich the state while increasing his property . . . Two thousand peasants doing forced labour will be of less benefit to the state than one hundred husbandmen who see a sure path open to their own enrichment; for the former labour under duress and always seek ways of avoiding hard work.'
(Quoted by Christian, D. (1986), *Power and Privilege* p.60)

g) Provincial noble commenting to government official 1840:

'There is no doubt that free labour is better. It is wrong to suppose that once our peasants are free they will become even lazier. This is untrue! A free man knows that if he does not work he is not going to be fed for nothing, and as a result, he works hard. Here is my own experience . . . I have some unsettled land which I have worked using my own peasants, not under barshchina (serf-labour) but by hiring them under a free contract. The same peasants who idle about on barshchina work extremely hard there.'
(Quoted by Christian, D. (1986), *Power and Privilege* p.60).

h) Scottish visitor to Siberia 1864:

'It was probably the growing prosperity of Siberia and the marked superiority of the population there, that induced the government to emancipate the serfs of Russia proper.'
(Quoted by McManners, J. (1977), *Lectures in European History* 1789-1914 p.275)

i) Widespread famines in Russia:
1820 1833 1839 1845 1848 1855 1859

j) Alexander II 1856:

'The existing manner of serf owning cannot remain unchanged. It is better to abolish serfdom from above than to await the time when it will begin to abolish itself from below.'
(Quoted by Seton-Watson, H. (1967), *The Russian Empire* p.335)

k) Figures for serf revolts:
1825-34 148 outbreaks
1835-44 216 outbreaks
1845-54 348 outbreaks
1858-61 53 nobles, bailiffs killed.

l) Report of Third Section on rumours amongst serfs:

'They expect a liberator, whom they call Metelkin. They say Pugachov gave the masters a fright, but Metelkin will sweep them away.'
(Quoted by Seton-Watson, H. (1967), *The Russian Empire* p.227)

m) Benckendorff, Head of Secret Police, reporting to Nicholas I, 1840s:

'The whole mood of the people is concerned with one aim, emancipation. Serfdom is a powder keg under the state, and is the more dangerous because of the fact that the army itself consists of peasants. It is better to begin gradually, cautiously, than to wait until the process is started from below by the people themselves.'
(Quoted by Christian, D. (1986), *Power and Privilege* p.62)

n) War Minister D. Milyutin to Alexander II:

'Serfdom does not permit us to shorten the term of service nor to increase the number of those on indefinite leave so as to reduce the number of troops on hand.'
(Quoted by Kochan, L. /Abraham, R. (1983), *Making of Modern Russia* p.182)

o) Landowner Kavelin in 1856:

'The first thing is that we must emancipate the serfs, because this is the knot which binds together all the things that are evil in Russia.'
(Quoted by Seton-Watson, H. (1967), *The Russian Empire* p.335).

i) Note down the reason each extract suggests as to why serfdom was abolished. What other reasons were there?

ii) 'Serfdom was becoming a dire threat to both domestic and foreign security.' (Acton, E. (1986), *Russia* p.73). Referring to the above extracts, and chart 3.1.A, explain this comment.

iii) Look at chart 3.1.A. Rearrange the reasons for reform in a list in descending order of importance, and briefly explain your choice.

D. Effects of emancipation

D.1. Look at chart 3.1.B. List those features of emancipation which should have pleased serfs, and those they might have disliked. Give reasons for your answers.

D.2. Read page 18, and study chart 3.1. and the figures below (from Florinsky, M. (1971), *End of the Russian Empire p.172*)

Peasant Land Holdings (in dessyatins) before and after Emancipation.
(1 dessyatin = 2.7 acres)

Region	Before Emancipation	After Emancipation	% Change
Less fertile region (15 provinces)	13,944,000	13,390,000	−4
Black soil and eastern provinces (21)	14,016,000	10,709,000	−23.6
Russian Poland (9 provinces)	7,737,000	10,901,000	+40.9

i) Explain the reason for the great variations in the above figures.

ii) One estimate of the national average for peasant land losses after emancipation is 4%. What do these figures suggest about the value of such national averages?

D.3. Study chart 3.1.

i) Do you agree with the view that emancipation made little change to the lives of ex-serfs, merely replacing payments to the lord with payments to the state? (Consider the amount of land held, and its organisation, personal rights of peasants, financial burdens, position of mir etc.)

ii) It would be more appropriate to speak of the 'abolition of serfdom' than the 'emancipation of the serfs.' Explain this comment.

iii) Were the broader effects of emancipation greater than its effects on the lives of peasants?

E. Alternatives

Alexander II tried to satisfy both the peasants and nobles, whilst not weakening Russia's social and political system. This required a delicate balancing act which arguably failed.

i) Discuss emancipation with your group. Suggest an alternative form of emancipation which might have been more successful?

ii) From your knowledge of the U.S.A., which finally abolished slavery in 1865, did they do any better?

C Other reforms

Emancipation led to other reforms. Once the power of the nobles was removed, it affected the government's system of tax collection and conscription, both of which had operated through serfdom. Also the judicial and local government systems had depended on the nobility's control of the serfs, and so these now had to be changed. A new local administrative structure was needed to link up the scattered villages. Thus a whole series of reforms was passed. (See chart 3.2.)

Although these reforms covered social, economic and administrative issues, they were not supposed to affect the autocratic power of the tsar. Alexander II was as firm a believer in autocracy as his father, and indeed as his two successors were to be. However, many historians identify a potential contradiction between granting this whole series of reforms, whilst refusing to allow wider sections of the community to participate in the national political process. For example, having set up a form of elected local government, the zemstva, many considered this should naturally develop into what was called a 'parliamentary roof', ie a national consultative, and eventually legislative, assembly. But Alexander was determined to resist this.

In this respect, Alexander's reforms can be seen as actually serving to increase discontent, as he had whetted appetites. This possible effect can also be seen in his educational and legal reforms, which also served to introduce elements potentially critical of autocracy. Similarly, the weakness of the emancipation, combined with rapid population growth, meant that peasant land hunger increased, and the countryside remained prone to considerable discontent and periodic revolt, until the eventual eruptions of 1902-1906 and 1917.

Worksection 3 part 2

A. The military reforms

A.1. 1874 Statute on Military Reforms.

'Under present legislation the duty of military service falls exclusively on the lower class of town dwellers and on the peasants. A significant section of the Russian people is exempt from a duty which should be equally sacred for all. Such an order of things, which came into being in different circumstances, no longer accords with the changed conditions of national life; nor does it satisfy our military needs. Recent events have shown that the strength of armies is based not only on the number of soldiers but on their moral and intellectual qualities. These attain their highest development where the defence of the fatherland has become the common concern of the whole people and where all, without exception and without distinction of calling or estate, combine in this sacred task.'
(Quoted by Mosse, W. (1970), *Alexander II and the Modernisation of Russia* p.102)

i) What evidence is there of the way emancipation led to a whole new atmosphere, in which other reforms were necessary?
ii) What reasons for reform does the statute put forward?
iii) To what 'recent events' do you think it is referring?

B. The peasants' view of reforms

B.1. Which four of the following comments might you most expect a Russian peasant to have made in the 1870s? Explain your choice.

a) 'The Tsar is on our side. This so-called emancipation is not what he wanted. His true intentions have been twisted by our grasping lord.'

b) 'I agree with the Populist Revolutionaries. The terms of emancipation clearly show how the whole tsarist system oppresses us, and can only be changed by violent revolution.'

c) 'We're having to pay heavy taxes for land which is rightly ours.'

d) 'Although many of my lazy fellow villagers are as usual moaning, this emancipation means I am at last free to own my own land, and run it how I wish.'

e) 'These zemstva are just another burden; they're not for the likes of us.'

f) 'Alexander's reforms in the universities and of the censorship give us great opportunities to improve our lives.'

g) 'Though this emancipation has been disappointing, at least we've lost the fear of being removed from our families for life by being conscripted into the army.'

D The reign of Alexander II. Overall

Historians studying emancipation and Alexander II's other reforms are now modifying traditional interpretations of him as the 'Tsar Liberator'. Instead they stress the inadequacy of the reforms, and the extent to which initial reforms were not followed through (see chart 3.2). According to this view Alexander was not personally committed to reform. He was easily frightened and naturally happy to retreat into conservatism once the overhaul, necessitated by the Crimean defeat, was over. His refusal to allow the participation of the public in government meant potential supporters of reform were alienated, and reforming elements within the bureaucracy could not overcome its innate conservatism.

The partial nature of the Emancipation Edict aroused criticism. The relaxation in universities, followed by intensification of repression, served to assist the development of revolutionary groups amongst the intelligentsia. In 1862 St Petersburg was hit by a wave of arson attacks. In 1863 Poland revolted, and in 1866 a student attempted to assassinate Alexander. Such threats to the established order reinforced the position of reactionary influences at court.

It is clear that by the 1870s there was a considerable change of atmosphere, away from the liberal expectations of the early 1860s, to one where many felt a sense of frustration with the government. The gap between the educated public, or 'society' as it was known, and the government, was clearly seen in the Vera Zasulich case in 1878. This young radical had shot the hated General Trepov, but she was acquitted by a jury to much public rejoicing. Increasing discontent led Alexander to establish a special commission under General Loris-Melikov to inquire into discontent and to propose remedies. His suggestion of giving some elected representatives a chance to express their opinions to the government was accepted by Alexander II on the very day the inappropriately named 'People's Will' terrorist group (see chapter 8) finally succeeded in assassinating him. Their first bomb missed the chief target, but killed some of his attendants. He went back to see how they were and a second bomb severely wounded him. He eventually died in agony. It was a sad finale to a reign which had started with so much promise.

Worksection 3 part 3

A. The pattern of the reign

A.1. Read the following contemporary evidence.

Extracts from reforming minister D. Milyutin's diary:
a) 1873:
'Everything is done under the exclusive influence of Count Shuvalov, who has terrified the emperor with his daily reports about frightful dangers, to which allegedly the state and sovereign himself are exposed. All Shuvalov's strength is based upon this bogey . . . He has surrounded the emperor with his people; all new appointments are made at his instructions . . . Such is the milieu in which I am condemned to operate. Is it possible for one man to fight against a whole powerful gang? What a devastating and disgusting contrast with the atmosphere in which I entered government thirteen years ago! Then everything was striving forwards: now everything is pulling backwards. Then the emperor sympathised with progress, himself was moving forwards: now he has lost confidence in everything he created, in everything that surrounds him, even in himself.'
(Quoted by Seton-Watson, H. (1967), *The Russian Empire* p.387).

b) 1879:
'It is impossible not to recognise that our entire state structure demands fundamental reforms from the top to the bottom . . . Everything ought to be given new forms in agreement with the Great Reforms carried out in the 1860s. It is highly lamentable that such a colossal work cannot be taken on by our present-day statesmen, who are not in a condition to raise themselves above the point of view of a police chief . . . The higher administration is frightened by the audacious appearances of socialist propaganda

Continued on page 29.

Chart 3.2 Other reforms

Details	Limitations	Effects
(Zemstva) – Form of elected rural local councils, at district and provincial level. – Wide suffrage, with 40% of members chosen by peasants. – Powers to levy taxes, to appoint officials, and improve local community, eg roads, prisons, public health, poor relief, education. – Seen partly as compensation to nobles for loss of their power over serfs. – Also DUMAS established in 1870 (similar elected councils for towns).	– Seen by central government as partly an agent for them, rather than local self government; took financial burden from central government. – Only slowly introduced; many provinces never affected; by 1914 still only 43 of 70 provinces with zemstva. – Voting system weighted to favour nobles who dominated assemblies, so local affairs still run by gentry. – Largely manned by traditional elite most of whom showed little interest in the job. – Chaired by local marshall of nobility. – Provincial governors had powers to reverse zemstva decisions they considered 'contrary to the laws and to the general welfare of the state.' – No power over police who supervised them. – Publicity, tax powers restricted and reduced; taxes were an extra burden on peasants. – Attempts at national organisation stopped.	– Though seen by central government as their agents, zemstva did for the first time allow initiative from below so ending the administrative monopoly of officialdom. – Members often came into conflict with the bureaucracy, and were critical of unresponsive regime. – New local organisations which could respond to local needs far better than central bureaucracy. – Impact varied, but in many places despite later restrictions, they did important work in education and public health, especially from the 1890s onwards. – Created 'Third Element' by appointing often liberal minded professionals, eg teachers, doctors, scientists. – Became 'seedbeds of liberalism'. – Created desire to extend zemstva into national assembly, to form a 'parliamentary roof'. – Aroused government hostility.
(Legal Reforms) – Cumbersome, secretive, formalistic old system replaced by new structure based on open trials in public, argued out by lawyers, in front of jury. – Clear hierarchy of courts and appeals system. – System of separate courts for separate estates (classes) ended. – Defence counsel allowed. – JPs established, chosen by zemstva. – More independent judiciary separated from administrative bureaucracy. – Judges better paid, trained, irremoveable by government. – New lower courts to replace serf owner as local magistrate. – Legal flogging curtailed.	– Only slowly introduced because shortage of lawyers. – Some courts outside new system, eg peasant, church, military courts. – In the 1870s series of special courts used against terrorists. – Government retained power of administrative (arbitrary) arrest. – Judges still influenced by government (eg by promotion prospects), and increasing government pressure from 1866 onwards. – Government officials could only be tried under special rules. – Arbitrary police action continued. – Secret police remained; Third Section only abolished in 1880, and soon replaced.	– Have been described as most thorough and remarkable of all the reforms. Readily accepted, and great success, despite breaking with Russian tradition. – Legal machinery modernised, and new atmosphere of rule of law. – Justice now not dispensed by government, but administered by society for its benefit. – JP courts very popular, and poor given sympathetic hearing. – Court debate revealed injustices, and these reported by press. – Established atmosphere of debate, and increased the number of lawyers, potentially critical of tsarist regime.

Chart 3.2 *continued*

Details	Limitations	Effects
(Education) – 1863 University Statute gave autonomy (self-rule). – Primary and secondary education extended. – Class bias against poor students reduced.	– Guidelines laid down by government; it still had the power to veto appointments; student organisations banned. – 1866. Liberal Education Minister Golovnin replaced by reactionary Count Tolstoy. – Led to new stress on traditional subjects; tighter government control over schools. – Periodic prosecution of students throughout reign, eg in 1861 many universities closed.	– Initial expectations of major reforms not fulfilled, and student criticism grew, leading to greater restrictions, which then led to greater unrest. – Students grew from 3,600 to 10,000. – Increase in the number educated, therefore potentially more people critical of, and dangerous to, tsarism.
(Censorship) – Initial relaxation, and 1863 regulations codified; prepublication codes reduced. – Infringements taken through courts. – 1865. Press allowed to discuss government policy.	– Relaxed atmosphere varied, especially as criticism grew. – 1866. Journal 'Contemporary' suppressed. – 1870s. Increased government pressure.	– Beginning of Russian political journalism and educated public opinion. – Vast increase in number of publications. – Relaxation encouraged criticism of tsarist abuses, which led to tightening up, which led to increased criticism etc, so overall discontent grew.
Military – Series of post-Crimean reforms, the work of Dimitri Milyutin, culminating in 1864 with the reorganisation of conscription. – Conscription extended to all, not just peasants. Partial exemptions for educated. – Service reduced from 25 to 6 years, plus 9 years in reserve. – Military colonies, and conscription as a punishment were ended. – Better officer training, more open promotion. – Broad system of army education. – Administration reorganised. – New military code. – Similar reforms in navy.	– Considerable noble opposition delayed major reforms till Prussia's successes in 1866-71 showed value of a modernised army. – Substitutes could be provided by people conscripted. – Low educational standards of recruits limited effectiveness of training. – Officers still mainly aristocratic.	– Reduced financial burden of massive, inefficient standing army. – Smaller, better trained army. – Great move towards weakening class privilege. – No overwehelming success against weak Turkish troops in 1877 ('the one-eyed beat the blind', as Moltke said). Severe supply problems. – Russia defeated by Japan, 1904-5. – Reduction of 25 years conscription lifted threat of virtual life sentence; great burden removed from life of ordinary peasants. – Helped spread literacy; army educated 2-3 million soldiers 1870s-90s. – Only major reform which posed little threat to autocracy, (apart from increased literacy).
National minorities – Poland. Initial relaxation. – Finland. Concessions. Diet accepted; Finnish language encouraged. – Early liberalisation of controls on Jews.	– Liberal policy to Poland reversed after 1863 revolt, and Russification imposed. Name 'Poland' replaced by 'Vistula Province'. 10,000 exiled. – Liberal policy towards Jews also halted.	– Early Polish reforms whetted appetite for even more which were rejected; inspired revolt, and then repression. Poles potentially rebellious till 1917. – Finnish policy successful till Russification policies of Alexander III.

Chart 3.2 *continued*

Details	Limitations	Effects
Finance – 1862-78. Reutern rationalised treasury. – Public budget established; better auditing. – Improved banking, credit facilities.	– Government still dependent on taxing peasants highly, via poll tax, indirect taxes, and new redemption payments. No real tax reform; two thirds of revenue still from indirect taxes. – Published budget of limited value, given lack of a parliament to scrutinise it. – Budget only balanced five times.	– Financial stability of the government re-established after Crimean defeat.
Economic – Reutern adopted more liberal trade policies; tariffs lowered till 1877. – Growth of railways continued (1,100km to 22,000km,) helped by government subsidies. – Industrial expansion, esp. cotton (helped by American Civil War, and improved transport); beginnings of Donets coal-iron industry.	– Lack of Russian entrepreneurial spirit, and limited domestic market.	– Beginnings of industrial transformation that speeded up in the 1890s.
Political – 1881. Loris-Melikov proposals for consultation on national decisions with respresentatives from zemstva.	– Not a constitution, just an opportunity for wider involvement. – Part of reaction to increased unrest, not purely voluntary. – Never implemented. – Alexander determined to uphold, and strengthen, the autocracy.	– Might have developed into a form of constitutional monarchy, but proposals dropped and Loris-Melikov dismissed by Alexander III.

Worksection 3 part 3 *continued*

during recent years and thinks only of defensive police measures, instead of acting against the very root of the evil.'
(Quoted by Lincoln, W. '*Dimitri Milyutin and the Russian Army*', History Today, Vol.26 p.47)

Comments by the composer Tchaikovsky (who was not involved in political affairs):
c) 1878:
   'We are living through terrible times, and if one stops to think about the present one is terrified. On one side a completely panic-stricken government . . . on the other side, ill-fated youths, thousands of them exiled without trial to lands where not even a crow flies; and between them the masses, indifferent to everything, waist deep in the mire of their egoistic interests, watching everything without a sign of protest.'
(Quoted by Crankshaw, E. (1976), *Shadow of the Winter Palace* p.299)

d) 1879:
   'So long as all of us, the citizens of Russia, are not called upon to take part in our country's government,

there is no hope for a better future.'
(Quoted by Crankshaw, E. (1976), *Shadow of the Winter Palace* p.301)

   i) What problems, from both left and right, does Milyutin identify for reforming ministers like himself?
   ii) What approach does Tchaikovsky advocate which would remedy one of the problems identified by Milyutin?
   iii) Make a list of all the ills afflicting Russia which the extracts reveal.
   iv) What impression do they give of the success of Alexander's reforms?
   v) How valuable is the evidence contained in these sources?

B. The Alexandrine thaw and Russian history past and present

Mosse has argued that the reign of Alexander II fits into a broader pattern in Russian history. 'The Tsar was fated to preside over one of the recurring and normally abortive 'liberal' interludes in the history of Russia. After the reign of Nicholas, as after those of

Peter I, Paul I or Stalin, a 'thaw' had become an imperative necessity . . . Yet as soon as Alexander lifted the tight lid of repression, the compressed steam began to escape with powerful effect. Conditions developed enough to frighten even a ruler less naturally insecure than Alexander . . . By 1862, the dangers of the 'thaw' were clearly apparent to all, and repression, never completely abandoned, again came into its own.' (Mosse W. (1970), *Alexander II and the Modernisation of Russia* pp. 177-78)

Mikhail Gorbachev's reforms in the Soviet Union have also been seen as part of this pattern, though some argue that by broadening the basis of government, Gorbachev may succeed where other Russian reformers have failed.

Do you consider such a comparison is valuable:
a) in helping one understand the reign of Alexander II,
b) in helping one understand current developments in the Soviet Union.

Give reasons for your answers.

C. Views on Alexander II

C.1. Read the following extracts about Alexander II, and answer the questions which follow.

Statements by Alexander II.

a) Alexander to Nicholas Milyutin, chief architect of emancipation, 1861:
    'I am sorry to part with you, but I must: the nobility describe you as one of the reds.'
(Quoted by Mosse, W. (1970), *Alexander II and the Modernisation of Russia* p.81)

b) Alexander to a group of peasants 1861:
    'Reports have reached me that you expect a new emancipation. There will be no emancipation except the one I have given you. Obey the laws and the statutes! Work and toil! Obey the authorities and the landowners!'
(Quoted by Mosse, W. (1970), *Alexander II and the Modernisation of Russia* p.80)

c) Alexander reacts to the Address of the Assembly of Moscow Nobility, 1865, asking the Tsar 'to complete the structure of the state by convoking a general assembly of elected persons of the Russian land for the consideration of needs common to the whole state.'
    Alexander said the task of reform was his alone, and rejected any group speaking for the others. 'Such deviations from the order of things established by the laws in force, can only make it more difficult for me to fulfil my plans; in no case can they assist the achievement of the purpose to which they may be directed.'
(Quoted by Seton-Watson, H. (1967), *The Russian Empire* pp. 351-2)

d) Alexander II explains his views to a member of the St Petersburg Zemstvo:
    'I suppose you consider that I refuse to give up any of my powers from motives of petty ambition. I give

you my imperial word that, this very minute, at this very table, I would sign any constitution you like, if I felt that this would be for the good of Russia. But I know that, were I to do so today, tomorrow Russia would fall to pieces.'
(Quoted by Mosse, W.(1970), *Alexander II and the Modernisation of Russia* p 133)

e) Alexander in the 1870s, when told that someone had spoken ill of him: 'I don't remember ever having done him a favour; why then should he hate me . . . All I have to do to make an enemy is to do someone a favour,'
(Quoted by Mosse, W. (1970), *Alexander II and the Modernisation of Russi* p. 163)

Other contemporary evidence.

f) Granville, Britain's representative in Russia, described Alexander II:
    'well-intentioned but weak as water . . . intelligent and amiable . . . (little) strength either of intellect or character.'
(Quoted by Mosse, W. (1970), *Alexander II and the Modernisation of Russia* p.163)

g) Novelist Tolstoy proposes a toast to Alexander II, the 'Tsar Liberator':
    'I drink this toast with particular pleasure. No others are needed, for in reality we owe Emancipation to the Emperor alone.'
(Quoted by Mosse, W. (1970), *Alexander II and the Modernisation of Russia* p.81)

Either,

i) Briefly comment on what each of the above extracts shows about Alexander II.
    Or,
ii) Explain what the above evidence suggests about:
    a) his character,
    b) his attitude to his own authority,
    c) his concern for his people.

C.2. Historians' assessments.

Read these assessments by historians, then answer the questions which follow.

a) Grenville:
    'In view of Alexander's character — he was rather indolent and indecisive and despite public displays of emotion and kindheartedness capable of maintaining a severe police regime with all its attendant cruelties — it is surprising that it was especially his reign that became associated with the period of great reforms in Russian history. To the extent that in an autocracy good deeds are credited to the autocrat personally, he earned the title 'Tsar Liberator'. Nevertheless, his personal contribution to reforms was less positive than his more admiring biographers would have us believe. In many ways his influence impeded the practical realisation of reforms which had become law. He was indecisive and throughout his reign alternated between reforming impulses and reaction. As his advisers he selected both true reformers such as Dimitri Milyutin and extreme conservatives, men

such as Dimitri Tolstoy, and kept both in office simultaneously. It was only with reluctance that Alexander took up the root cause of Russia's social ills, the problem of the serfs. Once a programme for emancipation had been devised, the other practical reforms of his reign followed from that . . .

The 'great reforms' of the 1860s did not liberate the Russian people. That process was so gradual, and the contrast between aspirations, the laws of the state, and the realities of the situation were so stark, that the degree of discontent was raised more by the hope of reform than satisifed by their application.'
(Grenville, J. (1976), *Europe Reshaped* pp.262-3)

b) Crankshaw:

'He was to preside over an epoch of radical change, now initiating change, now resisting it; but, even though he is celebrated in history as the Tsar Liberator, he left no personal stamp on the age; he gave it no colour. He could, and did, assert himself and fight hard to secure the emancipation of the serfs, the reform of the judiciary, the revival of local government after centuries of neglect; but to these remarkable achievements he brought a curiously negative approach. He insisted and he decreed; but the creative drive came from others . . .

There was no hard centre to the reign. There was no discernible pattern. In the end everything turned sour. The reforms, spectacular as they were, lost their impetus . . .

During all his twenty five years as Tsar he was to display that inconsequence, that lack of a cutting edge, that alternation between enthusiasm and apathy, stubborness and defeatism, vision and myopia, which in early days had so disconcerted his well-meaning tutors. He was consistent in only three particulars, and these were at odds: he seriously desired the good of his people and was ready to make radical changes in the interest of the common welfare; he was a convinced imperialist; and he was an autocrat in intention no less absolute than his father.'
(Crankshaw, E. (1976), *Shadow of the Winter Palace* pp.179, 210)

c) Mosse:

'The prince had a natural inclination to what was good. He had, however, a disposition to vagueness and hesitation when faced with obstacles or difficulties . . .

Alexander lacked the firmness, the vision, and the statesman like grasp of detail to be completely successful . . .

Alexander proved himself not only a disappointing 'liberal', if indeed that term can be applied to him, but, more seriously, an inefficient autocrat. While he would not give his educated subjects the constitution for which they clamoured, he failed to use to advantage the autocratic powers which he felt impelled to retain. He merely succeeded in proving that a pseudo-liberal autocrat is an unhappy hybrid unlikely to achieve political success. The narrow principles of Nicholas I or Alexander III, for whom Alexander's problems did not exist, proved, on a short term view,

more effective than the unsuccessful attempt to combine authority and freedom.'
(Mosse, W. (1970), *Alexander II and the Modernisation of Russia* pp.30, 106, 176)

d) Stephenson:

'Nothing Alexander did altered, or was intended to alter, the fundamental political fact of a God-created autocracy. On the contrary, all that he did was conservative in intention. By rearranging the social relations of the classes he planned to restore the full power of the autocracy.'
(Stephenson, G. (1969), *History of Russia* 1812-1945 p.105)

e) Westwood:

'With the possible exception of Khrushchev, no Russian ruler brought so much relief to so many of his people as did Alexander II, autocratic and conservative though he was.'
(Westwood, J. (1973), *Endurance and Endeavour* p.72)

f) Leroy-Beaulieu:

'The emancipation was followed by numerous reforms, administrative, judicial, military, even financial; yet all these reforms, prepared by different commissions subject to rival or hostile influences, were undertaken in isolation, in an incomplete manner, without coherence and without a definite plan. The task was to build a new Russia; the edifice was constructed upon the old foundations. Building operations were carried out without a blue-print, without a general plan, without an architect to co-ordinate the different operations. By introducing here and there particular innovations while neglecting near-by indispensable repairs: by incorporating everywhere his innovations into the ancient structure, Alexander in the end succeeded after immense labours in making of the new Russia an incomplete and uncomfortable dwelling where friends and opponents of innovation felt almost equally ill at ease.'
(Quoted by Mosse, W. (1970), *Alexander II and the Modernisation of Russia* p.105)

g) Schlözer:

'No despot can make happy a country which his predecessors have made unhappy. The traces left by centuries of oppression cannot be wiped out by imperial decree. That is the tragedy of Alexander II.'
(Quoted by Mosse, W. (1970), *Alexander II and the Modernisation of Russia* p.8)

h) Rieber:

'Alexander II measured out doses of freedom to his subjects in relation to their ability to understand exactly how he wanted them to use it. Like his other reforms, the extension of civil liberties was meant to increase the opportunities of the people to serve him . . . A great distance separated the idea of voluntary acceptance of the will of the tsar from the liberal ideal of the inalienable rights of the individual.'
(Rieber, A. (1971), *Alexander II, a Revisionist View, Journal of Modern History*)

Continued on page 33.

Chart 3.3 The reign of Alexander II

A. Character

i) **Upbringing**
- Educated by humane, liberal tutors Zhukovsky and Merder.
- Well prepared by Nicholas I to be ruler; travelled widely in Empire.
- Involved in committees.

ii) **Personality**
- Gentle, charming.
- Most intelligent, humane of Romanovs.
- Less attracted to military than most Romanovs.
- Somewhat indolent, weak, indecisive.
- Mood varied from enthusiasm to apathy.

B. Alexander as Tsar

i) **Alexander's role.**
- Alternated between reforming and reactionary tendencies.
- This was reflected in his appointment of ministers.
- Lacked grasp of detail.
- Historians still debate his importance in reforms, but he did help overcome resistance to emancipation.
- Increasingly gave no clear lead in government; had to be kept up to the mark by his family.
- Worried by assassination attempts.
- Upset by criticism which continued despite reforms, and also by demands to extend them.
- Became infatuated with his mistress Catherine Dolgoruky; alienated most of court.

ii) **Other key individuals**
- Several other members of royal family, and ministers, made vital contribution to reign, especially:

- Grand Duke Constantine (brother); convinced reformer, major role as Chairman of Chief Committee on Emancipation, Viceroy in Poland, Minister of Navy; major naval reforms.
- Duchess Elena Pavlovna (aunt); with Constantine, helped convince Alexander to accept form of emancipation overriding nobles' opposition; helped secure position of reforming Milyutin.
- Major reforming ministers:
  Rostovtsev; very influential in drawing up emancipation details but died 1860.
  Nicolai Milyutin; major influence on emancipation but dismissed 1861 due to conservative pressure.
  Dimitri Milyutin (Nicolai's brother); War Minister for 20 years.
  Reutern; reforming Finance Minister.
  Golovnin at Education.
- So Alexander used many able, reforming ministers, but also appointed reactionaries like Panin, Count Tolstoy (not the writer), and increasingly influential Shuvalov. Reactionary Pobedonostsev as tutor to heir Alexander.

C. Domestic policy

Major series of reforms (details see Charts 3.1 and 3.2.), ie

Emancipation
Zemstva
Judicial Reforms
Relaxation of Censorship
Education Reforms
Military Reforms
Financial Reforms

but also **Repression, Retraction,** especially
- 1866. Prosecutions; 1870s. Virtual war against revolutionaries.
- Retraction of zemstva powers.
- Reduction of university autonomy.
- Use of administrative arrest.
- Increased censorship.

and **Growth of dissent**
- In universities.
- Revolutionary groups, eg 'To the People', 'People's Will'.
- Peasant discontent.

D. Foreign policy

1856 Peace of Paris ended disastrous Crimean War. Russia lost mouth of Danube; Black Sea neutralised.
Afterwards, Russia was largely passive in Europe, as a major redrawing of boundaries took place at Austria's expense, especially German Unification which was ultimately fatal for Tsarist Russia.
1863 Polish Revolt eventually crushed; name

Chart 3.3 *continued*

'Poland' replaced by Vistula Province; 100,000 exiled to Siberia.	1860 Amur region. 1961, Vladivostok. 1875, Sakhalin. But 1867 sold Alaska to U.S.A. for $8m.

1871 Black Sea Clauses of Paris Treaty renounced.

1877 War against Turkey over atrocities in Balkans; Russian success. Alexander's forward policy influenced by Panslav public pressure.

1878 March, Treaty of San Stefano. Large gains for Bulgaria, Russia's client state.
June, Congress of Berlin. Previous gains largely lost; seen as diplomatic humiliation.

1878 Also Expansion in East. Throughout reign, after failure in Europe, Russia vastly expanded east, eg

E. Overall assessment

- Period of great reforms, but failed to establish firm base for a modernised autocracy.
- Emancipation 'too little, too late?' Failed to tackle major agrarian problems.
- Other reforms created elements potentially critical of autocracy.
- Missed opportunities over a) emancipation b) the establishment of some form of national representative assembly.

Worksection 3 part 3 *continued*

i) Kemp:

'The efforts of Tsarism to survive, and reform in order to conserve, inevitably increased the numbers of the educated and potentially critical.'
(Kemp, T. (1969), *Industrialisation of Nineteenth Century Europe* p.134)

j) McManners:

'Tocqueville's famous dictum, that the most dangerous moment for a bad government comes at the point when it tries to reform, was proved right again. Half measures aroused the demand for full measures, and a glimpse of the shadow whetted the imagination which yearned for reality. By dabbling in freedom, the autocracy had demonstrated its own obsolescence without being able to adapt itself to the new age.'
(McManners, J. (1977), *Lectures on European History 1789-1914 p.281)*

k) Seton-Watson:

'The reign of Alexander II which began with bright promise, and changed to dreary stagnation, ended in tragedy. The Tsar-liberator was a victim of the unsolved conflict between social reform and the dogma of political autocracy.'
(Seton-Watson, H. (1964), *Decline of Imperial Russia* p.73)

In preparation for the debate and essay which follow, discuss the views the above historians hold on the following questions:

(Identify similarities and differences in their analyses.)

i) How well intentioned was Alexander II?

ii) How appropriate is the description of Alexander II as 'the Tsar Liberator'?

iii) To what extent did Alexandrine reforms suffer from contradictions?

iv) Were the inadequacies of the reforms chiefly due to circumstances or Alexander's personal failings.?

v) How successful were the reforms?

C.3. Study the above quotations and chart 3.3, then draw up two lists, or write two paragraphs, covering points criticising, and defending, Alexander II as tsar.

C.4. Group debate.

Use all the available information to debate the statement: 'Alexander II got what he deserved.'

D. Concluding essay

'A period of remarkable reforms, for which the credit must be given largely to Alexander II.' Do you agree with this view?

Advice. This essay addresses the question of the nature of the reforms, ie were they 'remarkable', and to what extent was Alexander II responsible for them? The term 'remarkable' conveys a sense of surprise, unusualness as well as significance, impressiveness, and so as well as assessing the nature and impact of the reforms, one should discuss the extent to which they were necessitated by the state of Russia in the mid 1850s. (The idea of a reforming tsar could be discussed; by no means unusual in Russia, as the reigns of Peter and Catherine the Great suggest.)

This angle naturally leads on to consideration of the degree of Alexander's responsibility for the reforms. Here one needs to consider whether reform was likely regardless of who was tsar; then, the extent to which Alexander personally shaped the nature of the reforms, and also the extent of his actual involvement in them. As a counter to this implication, one could argue that as supreme autocrat Alexander must take the credit as well as the blame for all the government's actions. One could also refer to certain weaknesses in Alexander's character.

With regards to the essay's structure, it would probably be most effective to adopt a Yes/No approach to this discursive-type essay. Thus one could argue reforms were remarkable, and then make counterpoints. Next consider the case for giving credit to Alexander, then modify this. Or one could first argue in favour of both parts of the quotation, then discuss counterpoints. Alternatively, one could discuss the reforms one by one, relating them to the question, but the danger here is that one might not be sufficiently selective, and fail to highlight the central issues of 'remarkable' and the personal role of Alexander II.

As with many essays, this one can be tackled more effectively after studying later events to help assess significance, but you should be aware of the twentieth century unrest which led to two revolutions against tsarism, and this might suggest a cautious approach to assessing the success of Alexander's reforms.

4 The Reign of Alexander III

A Introduction

The reign of Alexander III is briefly covered in the accompanying chart. It was generally a period of successful repression presided over by the formidable tsar. The revolution which the 'People's Will' had hoped to provoke by the assassination of Alexander II failed to occur. Instead there was a general revulsion against the radicals. Reformers in the government such as D. Milyutin and Loris-Melikov were dismissed, and severe repression succeeded in crushing the revolutionary movement. Russia settled down to political calm. There was, however, considerable economic change as, during the 1880s, Russia embarked on rapid industrialisation.

Worksection 4

A. Assessing the reign

A.1. Look at chart 4 on the reign of Alexander III. Use this and other information to answer the following questions:

  i) Did Alexander III's policy provide a strong basis for the survival of tsarism, a) in the short term, b) in the long term?
  ii) Suggest reasons why Alexander III was prepared to accept economic and social reform, whilst standing strongly against political reforms.
  iii) To what extent did Alexander III's reign mark a major change from that of his father?

A.2. Read the following extracts:

'The era of the great reforms marked the high-water mark of the Russian autocracy as a creative force. There were to be no more revolutions from above. For the next fifty years the dynasty was to conduct a holding operation, only spasmodically intervening in a drama played out by forces beyond its control: the bureaucracy itself; imperially minded soldiers; the rising class of capitalist entrepreneurs; nationalist or Panslav journalists and agitators; these forces, and more besides, interacting against the background of a sullen peasantry and a rapidly growing proletariat
. . .

  With the accession of Alexander III Imperial Russia entered a new phase of her history. It was not simply that all effective revolutionary activity ended for many years to come: more importantly, it was the end of serious reform from above; when 25 years later, certain reforms were at last, belatedly, undertaken they were forced upon a desperately resisting monarch from below . . .

  Although he was to march his country steadily towards catastrophe, he was a more able ruler, in the sense of management and political finesse, than is usually believed. He was not against pragmatical reforms in principle, but was determined to stop anything that smelt of liberalism dead in its tracks, and did so with a minimum of fuss. For eleven years he achieved what so many of his predecessors had aspired in vain to achieve, peace and tranquility of the grave, without extravagent bloodshed or spectacular cruelty.'
(Crankshaw, E. (1976), *Shadow of the Winter Palace* p.233, pp.321-2)

  i) Crankshaw uses a series of striking phrases, but historians must make sure they are historically sound as well as stylish. Discuss the appropriateness of the following phrases:
  a) 'revolution from above'
  b) 'peace of the graveyard' (the title of Crankshaw's chapter on the reign of Alexander III).
  ii) In what sense could Alexander be said to have marched 'his country steadily towards catastrophe'?
  iii) Given the points made by Crankshaw, could late nineteenth century Russia still be called an autocracy?

A.3. Trotsky commented 'Alexander III bequeathed Nicholas II a revolution.'
(Quoted by Pearson, R. (1974), *Russia in Revolution* p.8).

  i) How justified do you consider this view?
  ii) In order to assess fully the validity of this analysis, what else would you need to consider apart from the reign of Alexander III?

B. Concluding essay

How successful was Alexander III in tackling the problems facing the tsarist regime?

Chart 4 Alexander III

A. Character

- Honest, unimaginative, sincere.
- Narrow intelligence, slow.
- Stern, ruthless, strong willed.

B. Alexander as Tsar

- Trained for the army rather than as tsar because he only became heir when 20 on death of elder brother.
- Firm believer in autocracy.
- Natural autocrat; impressive in appearance (6′ 3″) and manner.
- Conscientious devotion to duty.
- Arguably restored monarchical office to some respect, affection.
- Natural conservatism enhanced by brutal death of his father.
- Anti-semitic.
- Healthy, vigorous then suddenly died aged 49 of nephritis.

C. Domestic policies

Overall, reaction and repression, and industrial development.

REPRESSION

Emergency powers
- 1881. Statute Concerning Measures for the Protection of State Security and the Social Order; wide government powers, eg special courts, increased repression of critics, removal of elected officials. Used in some areas until 1917.
- New secret police, the Okhrana, established.

Censorship
- Tightened into rigid system; maintained throughout reign.

Law
- Increased government interference in law courts.
- Judges' security of tenure ended.
- JPs abolished.

Land Captains 1889
- New government agent, chosen from gentry by Provincial Governor (supervised by Interior Minister) to control peasants; could overrule mir; replaced JPs' functions.
- Greatly resented by peasants.

Revolutionary groups
- Weakened for a decade. Plot to assassinate tsar led to execution of Lenin's brother and four others in 1887.

REACTION

Ministers
- 1881. Loris-Melikov and D. Milyutin resigned.
- Reactionary Pobedonostsev had great influence, together with Tolstoy and Katkov.

Zemstva
- Powers further reduced.
- 1890 Zemstva Act, 1892 Municipal Government Act; increased power of Interior Minister over zemstva officials and decisions. Intensified bureaucratic control and administrative centralisation. Vote further restricted.
- Government officials interfered in elections.
- Meetings of zemstva presidents restricted.

Education
- 1884. University Statute (1863) replaced; now tighter government control; chief appointments made by Minister of Education.
- Stress on religion; barrack-like atmosphere.
- Fees quadrupled to restrict entry to secondary and higher education.
- Church schools favoured; zemstva schools discouraged.
- 1887. Decree to prevent children from humble backgrounds being 'encouraged to abandon the social environment to which they belong.'

Russification
- 1881. Series of anti-Jewish pogroms, tacitly encouraged by the authorities.
- Over 600 decrees against Jews, eg prevented from voting in zemstva; entry to education restricted; residence restrictions tightened.
- Increased attempts to impose Russian culture on national minorities, (eg Finns, Poles, Ukrainians, Armenians, Tatars), and to deny them their own.

Chart 4 *continued*

but also **REFORMS**

Social

- Poll tax ended (though indirect taxes increased).
- Redemption payments lowered; work of finance Minister Bunge.
- 1883. Peasants Land Bank (and 1885 Nobles Land Bank) to provide cheap loans to buy land.
- Factory Legislation.
- Hours, employment of women and children restricted; inspectorate established.
- Zemstva.
- Despite government restrictions, zemstva continued to improve local areas, especially primary education.

Economic development

- Beginning of major spurt in industrialisation, under Finance Ministers Bunge, Vyshnegradsky, Witte.
- Alexander III as a realist prepared to support industrialisation, and Witte's policy.
- Economy grew 8% p.a. in 1890s.
- Agriculture was exploited as source of export earnings; this helped cause a series of famines, especially in 1891.

D. Foreign policy

- Overall pattern. Russia kept out of war. Broadly traditionalist, cautious policy, but changes in Germany eventually forced a radical change of alliance.
- 1881. Conclusion of Dreikaiserbund with Austria, Germany; old Holy Alliance system.
- 1887. Russia estranged from Austria over Balkans; Dreikaiserbund not renewed; replaced by Reinsurance Treaty with Germany.
- 1890. Bismarck dismissed, and Germany did not renew Reinsurance Treaty.
- 1891. Loose Russo-French agreement.
- 1893. Russia reluctantly accepted formal French alliance.
- Russia's expansion in Asia slowed.
- 1880s onwards. Major naval building programme.

E. Overall assessment

- Preserved peace throughout reign (apart from a few skirmishes in Central Asia); virtually unique amongst tsars.
- Bleak period of counter-reform and repression; appeared to work and bring stability; but did it provide a secure basis for tsarism's longterm survival?

5 The reign of Nicholas II, 1894 — 1905

A Introduction

In 1894 the massive, dominating Alexander III died unexpectedly. He was succeeded by his diffident son Nicholas, who admitted he did not want to be tsar and was unprepared for the task. Despite this he was determined to uphold the autocracy. In this, what he believed to be his God given duty, he failed. Although the dynasty survived the revolutionary turmoil of 1905, twelve years later it collapsed and was replaced by a democratic republic, which itself was soon replaced by a communist regime.

B The early years of the reign

Nicholas's reign got off to a bad start. Due to drunkenness and poor crowd control, over a thousand people celebrating his coronation were killed in a stampede. Nicholas, greatly disturbed, overruled his own instincts and continued with a banquet at the French Embassy, advised that he could not afford to alienate these important financial backers. He only visited the injured later, after the impression of being uncaring had spread.

Far more significant was Nicholas's alienation of those who hoped for some broadening of the governing system. Guided by his former tutor, Pobedonostsev (see chart 9.3), he rejected zemstva representatives' moderate requests for some opportunity to express their views to the government as 'senseless dreams'.

Instead, Nicholas continued his father's repressive policies. After a virtual general strike by 13,000 students over police use of whips, all universities were temporarily closed, and many striking students were drafted into the army. The 1881 Emergency Decrees were maintained, and Russification increased, particularly at the expense of the Jews. However, the enforced quiescence of Alexander III's reign could not be maintained. Zemstva demanded a greater role, students protested at government controls, and strikes increased in the growing industrial cities. Revolutionary groups tried to exploit this, and some resorted to assassination. Rather than tackle the root causes of the discontent, the government tried various expedients. Interior Minister Plehve tried to control worker discontent by establishing police run trade unions. He also hoped to divert discontent by encouraging pogroms (violent attacks) against Jews (as at Kishinev in 1903), and he favoured 'a short victorious war to stem the tide of revolution'.

In the background peasant discontent increased as the government tax burden grew, and the continuing rise in population exacerbated peasant land hunger. Continued rapid industrial growth, followed by a major slump after 1900, added further strains to the fabric of tsarist society.

Worksection 5 part 1

A. Russia at the turn of the century

A.1. Primary evidence on Nicholas II's actions and views.

On his accession the Tver provincial zemstvo addressed Nicholas:

'Sire, we await the opportunity and the right for public institutions to express their opinion on questions which concern them, so that the expression of the needs and thought not only of the administration but also of the Russian people may reach to the very height of the Throne.'

Nicholas let his response be known at a meeting of nobles and zemstvo representatives, January 1895:

'I am informed that recently in some zemstvo assemblies voices have made themselves heard from people carried away by senseless dreams about participation by representatives of the zemstvo in the affairs of internal government; let all know that I, devoting all my strength to the welfare of the people, will uphold the principle of autocracy as firmly and unflinchingly as my late unforgettable father.'
(Quoted by Seton-Watson, H. (1967), *The Russian Empire* p.549)

i) For what reasons did the Tver zemstvo want the chance to express their opinions to the Government? Might this have strengthened the Government's position? Was it a demand for parliamentary government?

ii) How diplomatically did Nicholas refuse such requests? Was this wise? What other responses might he have made?

iii) How might members of the zemstva react to such a rejection?

iv) Can Nicholas' refusal be reconciled with his stated concern for the welfare of his people? Explain your answer.

A.2. The state of Russia in the early twentieth century.

The view of Leo Tolstoy. Extract from an open letter to Nicholas II, 1902:

'A third of the whole of Russia lives under emergency legislation, and that means without any lawful guarantees. The armies of the regular police and of the secret police are continuously growing in numbers. The prisons and penal colonies are overcrowded with thousands of convicts and political prisoners, among whom the industrial workers are now included. The censorship issues the most meaningless interdictions (prohibitions), as had not even been done in the worst times of the 1840s. At no previous time have the religious persecutions been so frequent and so cruel as they are today, and they still grow more frequent and more cruel. In all cities and industrial centres soldiers are employed and equipped with live ammunition to be sent out against the people. In many places fratricidal blood has been shed; everywhere, new and even more cruel events are irresistibly in preparation. Yet this strenuous and terrible activity of the government results only in the growing impoverishment of the rural population, of those 100 million souls on whom the power of Russia is founded, and who, in spite of the ever increasing budgets, or perhaps on account of the increases, are faced with famine which has become a normal condition. A similar normal condition is the general dissatisfaction of all classes with the government and their open hostility against it . . .

Autocracy is a superannuated form of government that may suit the needs of a Central African tribe . . . but not those of the Russian people, who are increasingly assimilating the culture of the rest of the world. That is why it is impossible to maintain this form of government except by violence.'

(Quoted by Kohn, H. (1957), *Basic History of Modern Russia* pp. 165-6, and Rogger, H. (1983), *Russia in the Age of Modernisation and Revolution* p.133).

  i) Make a list of all the criticisms Tolstoy makes of Tsarist Russia.
 ii) What indications are there that Tolstoy considers the situation can't be sustained for long?
iii) Was Tolstoy correct in this view? Give reasons for your answer.

A.3. Gradovsky made the following comment on the tsarist governing system:

'In the hands of governmental offices and officials remained power without competence; in the hands of the zemstvo institutions was concentrated competence without power.'
(Quoted by Lee, S. (1982), *Aspects of European History* p.166).

Explain what Gradovsky might have meant by this comment.

C 1905 Revolution

(See charts 5.1 and 5.2)

Growing tensions came to a head with military defeat. Russian expansionary pressures in the Far East provoked Japan, who was similarly modernising, to attack. The initial loss of Port Arthur was the first of a series of military catastrophes for Russia. This military incompetence, and the government's refusal to broaden the basis of government, combined with growing economic hardship, provoked increasing criticism. The crisis erupted in January 1905 when, during a wave of strikes involving over 100,000 workers in St Petersburg, Father Gapon led a mass march to the tsar's Winter Palace. Nicholas, despite being warned of the growing tension, was away from his capital. He was held responsible when his troops fired at and repeatedly charged the peaceful, icon carrying crowd who had come to request help from their tsar.

Several hundreds were killed on 'Bloody Sunday', and the position of the dynasty was wounded, perhaps fatally. Just as the loss of Port Arthur had revealed the incompetence of the autocracy, so Bloody Sunday illustrated its cruelty. Even the conservative 'New Times' commented, 'It is no longer possible to live in this way.' The strike wave grew, accompanied by a growth in political organisation amongst zemstva and other middle class bodies.

Political assassination created further pressure. The murder of Nicholas's uncle Grand Duke Sergei, combined with further military defeat at Mukden, may have been the final precipitant for the tsar to make concessions. The consultative national assembly which Nicholas offered in February was, however, too little too late. Momentum had built up for major changes and this was not to be denied. By the summer, unrest had spread to the countryside, and over half Russia's provinces reported serious disturbances.

In October a rail strike originating in Moscow developed into a virtual national general strike. Print workers, factory workers, doctors, teachers, and even Imperial ballet dancers went on strike, virtually paralysing the governing system. Workers in some major towns set up liaison committees of factory representatives which developed into new councils called soviets. In October the St Petersburg Soviet probably exercised more authority than the Imperial Government. Revolutionaries rushed back from exile to try and exploit the situation. Liberals also utilised this unrest to press for major reforms. In addition, protests were spreading amongst the Empire's national minorities, particularly in Poland and Finland. Even more worrying, some isolated incidents of revolt were occurring in the armed forces themselves.

Nicholas at first favoured a military dictatorship, but his preferred choice to lead it, Grand Duke Nikolai Nikolayevitch, refused. Finally, he appointed Witte, recently returned from negotiating peace with Japan, as virtual prime minister, and promised a genuine parliament with legislative powers. This October Manifesto, accompanied the following month by promises to end redemption payments, succeeded in splitting the protest forces. The moderate Liberals, worried by the growth of mass unrest, formed the Octobrist movement to support the government. The latter, now strengthened by the return of troops from the Far East, took the offensive. It arrested the St Petersburg Soviet, and proceeded to suppress a second wave of industrial unrest, bloodily crushing a rising in Moscow in December. Order was gradually restored in the countryside. General Trepov ('Cartridges must not be spared'), and later Interior Minister Stolypin reinforced the pacifying effect of the news of the ending of redemption payments with mass executions.

With the peak of the crisis over, Nicholas began to modify his concessions. When in April 1906 the formal details of the new constitutional system were announced, the position of the elected Duma was weakened (see chart 6.1.), but the ending of redemption payments did lead to major agrarian reforms.

Tsarism had survived this first major threat, due to

weaknesses in the opposition forces, the tsar's granting of major concessions, and the rallying of key groups to the government. Rather than being a concerted attempt by revolutionaries to seize power, the events of 1905 can best be seen as a general but temporary collapse of authority, accompanied by scattered, sporadic outbreaks of protest and violence, both urban and rural. Tsarism had survived, and the reforms forced from it raised the possibility of a third alternative to that of autocracy or revolution, a reforming constitutional monarchy.

Worksection 5 part 2

A. Analysis of the nature of 1905

A.1. Read the following extract by the historian Pearson:

'By mid 1905 all the ingredients of revolution were present. The dynasty was weak and indecisive. The government was a victim of its own policies, whether the repression which raised the proletariat or the reforms which promoted the middle classes. War, another by-product of tsarist ineptitude, both united the elements of latent opposition as never before and put exceptional strain on the fabric of tsarist government. For the first time all classes of society were involved, albeit not as a unified coherent political alliance but as an expedient grouping, united by individual self-interests. The middle classes initiated the movement cautiously, the proletariat's precipitate entry added a new militancy, and the final opportunist affiliation of the peasantry added a daunting geographical and numerical scale to the confrontation.'
(Pearson, R. (1974), *Russia in Revolution* p.12-13).

i) Identify the 'ingredients' of revolution. Can you think of any more?
ii) Give examples of how 'repression raised the proletariat' and of 'reforms which promoted the middle classes.'
iii) How did discontent in 1905 vary from previous unrest?
iv) What did each group contribute?
v) What indication is given of why the revolution eventually failed?

A.2. Study charts 5.1 and 5.2 of the 1905 Revolution.

i) Why do you think that in chart 5.1 the various groups involved in the revolution are drawn in differing sizes? How accurate can such a representation be?
ii) Why was the government worried about the loyalty of some troops? Was this fear justified?
iii) Comment on the role and performance of the Russian military (army and navy) in 1904-05.
iv) Which quotations in chart 5.1 suggest reasons why tsarism survived the revolution? Explain your answers.
v) What do you consider were the three main reasons why the tsarist government survived the crisis of 1905?
vi) The events of 1905 are normally portrayed as a revolution which failed. It has, however, also been suggested by some historians, eg by Mendel, that the revolution succeeded. In contrast, Wood argues that the events of 1905 hardly amounted to a revolution at all. Discuss these alternative viewpoints.

B. Primary evidence on 1905

B.1. Study the cartoons from Punch in chart 5.3, and the following written evidence on the revolutionary crisis of 1905, and answer the questions which follow. (The numbers in brackets by the headings for the quotations identify the questions referring to that extract.)

a) Extracts from Witte's Diary (i):
'A general feeling of profound discontent with the existing order was the most apparent symptom of the corruption with which the social and political life of Russia was infested . . .

The students recognised no law. As for the workers they were concerned with filling their stomachs with more food than had been their wont . . . Finally, the peasantry, the majority of the Russian people, were anxious to increase their holdings . . .

The government had lost its power to act, everybody was either doing nothing or moving in different directions, and the authority of the regime and of its supreme bearer was completely trampled down.'
(Quoted by Taylor, J., (1974), *Russia in Revolution* p.28, and L. Kochan, (1967), *Russia in Revolution* p.104)

b) Extracts from the Workers' Petition Jan 1905 (i,ii):
'Sire,
We working men and inhabitants of St Petersburg, our wives and children, and our parents, helpless and aged men and women, have come to you, our ruler, in quest of justice and protection. We have become beggars, we have been oppressed . . . we are not recognised as human beings; we are treated as slaves . . . We have no strength at all, O Sovereign. Our patience is at an end. We are approaching that terrible moment when death is better than the continuance of intolerable sufferings. We have left off working and have declared to our masters that we shall not begin to work again until they comply with our demands. We beg but little . . . ' (the right to discuss grievances with employers, wage increases).

'Sire, here are many of us, and all human beings in appearance only. In reality in us, as in all Russian people, there is not recognised any human right, not even the right of speaking, thinking, meeting, discussing our needs . . . We have been enslaved . . . under the auspices of Thy officials. Every one of us who dares to raise a voice in defence of working class and popular interests is thrown into gaol or is sent into banishment.

Is this, O Sovereign, in accordance with the laws of

39

God by whose grace you reign?

We are seeking here the last salvation. Do not refuse assistance to Thy people . . . Give their destiny into their own hands. Cast away from them the intolerable oppression of officials. Destroy the walls between Thyself and Thy people, and let them rule the country with Thyself . . .'
(There follows a series of political demands, including a national assembly elected by universal suffrage, basic civil liberties, improved working conditions, tax changes, transfer of land to the people, and an end to the war.)

'Order and take an oath to comply with these requests, and Thou wilt make Russia happy and famous, and Thou wilt impress Thy name in our hearts . . . If Thou wilt not order and will not answer our prayers, we shall die here on this place before Thy Palace. We have nowhere to go further, and nothing for which to go. We have only two ways, either towards liberty and happiness or into the grave . . .'

(Quoted by Kertesz, G.(1968) *Documents in the Political History of the European Continent* p.297)

c) Extract from the October Manifesto (i, ii, iv, v):

'The rioting and agitation in the capitals and many localities of Our Empire fills Our hearts with great and deep grief. The welfare of the Russian Emperor is bound up with the welfare of his people, and its sorrows are His sorrows. The turbulence which has broken out may confound the people and threaten the integrity and unity of our Empire.

The great vow of service by the Tsar obligates Us to endeavour, with all Our strength, wisdom and power to put an end as quickly as possible to the disturbances so dangerous to the Empire . . .

We lay upon the Government the execution of Our unchangeable will:
1. To grant to the population the inviolable right of free citizenship, based on the principles of freedom of person, conscience speech, assembly and union.'
2. (to extend the right to vote in the already promised Duma to those excluded).
3. 'To establish as an unbreakable rule that no law shall go into force without its confirmation by the state Duma . . .
We call on all true sons of Russia to remember their duty to their homeland, to help put a stop to this unprecedented unrest and, together with this, to devote all their strength to the restoration of peace to their native land.'
(Quoted by Kertesz, G. (1968), *op cit* p.301)

d) Extract from the Manifesto to better the conditions of the peasant population (i, ii, iv, v, vi):

'The troubles that have broken out in the villages . . . fill Our heart with deep sorrow. Violence and crime do not, however, help the peasant and may bring sorrow and misery to the country. The only way to better permanently the welfare of the peasant is by peaceful and legal means; and to improve his condition has always been one of our first cares.'

(Series of reforms, including abolition of redemption payments after 1907, and cheap loans to buy land.)
(Quoted by Kertesz, G. (1968), *op cit* p.301)

e) Extract from a letter by Nicholas to his mother describing discussion with Witte about possible solutions (i, v, vi):

'We very often met only in the early morning to part only in the evening when night fell. There were only two ways open: to find an energetic soldier to crush the rebellion by sheer force. There would be time to breathe then but, as likely as not, one would have to use force again in a few months, and that would mean rivers of blood and in the end we should be where we started.

The other way would be to give the people their civil rights, freedom of speech, and press, also to have all the laws confirmed by a State Duma or parliament, that of course would be a constitution. Witte defends this energetically. He says that while it is not without risk, it is the only way out at the present moment.

Almost everybody I had an opportunity of consulting is of the same opinion . . . He drew up a Manifesto. We discussed it for two days and in the end, invoking God's help, I signed it . . . My only consolation is that such is the will of God and this grave decision will lead my dear Russia out of the intolerable chaos she has been in for nearly a year.'
(Quoted by Pearce, M. (1986), *Sources in Twentieth Century History* p.62).

f) Article in 'Izvestia', newspaper of the St Petersburg Soviet, 17 October 1905 (v, vii):

'We have been given freedom of assembly yet our meetings are surrounded by troops. We've been given freedom of speech, yet censorship remains inviolate. We've been given freedom to study, yet our universities are occupied by soldiers. We've been given personal immunity, yet our prisons are overflowing with prisoners. We've been given Witte, yet we still have Trepov. We've been given a constitution, yet the autocracy remains. Everything has been given and nothing has been given. The proletariat knows what it wants. It wants neither the police hooligan Trepov nor the liberal stockbroker Witte, neither the wolf's jaw nor the fox's tail. It doesn't want a whip wrapped in the parchment of a constitution.'
(Quoted by Trotsky, L. (1973), *1905* p.141)

g) Extract from '1905', a book written in 1909 by Trotsky a leader of the St Petersburg Soviet, and later organiser of the Bolshevik Revolution (vii):

'Summoning up the courage to initiate some constitutional reform, he (Witte) doesn't actually pronounce the word 'constitution' since his power rests on those who cannot bear to hear its name. But to do this he needs a period of calm. He declares that although arrests, confiscations and shootings will continue on the basis of the old laws, they will henceforth be carried out 'in the spirit' of the Manifesto.'
(Trotsky, L. (1973), *1905* p.138)

Causes and nature of the 1905 revolution

i) What evidence do extracts (a), (b), (c), (d) and (e) contain of the failure of the tsarist regime, and the forms and extent of unrest? (4 marks)

ii) 'There is a remarkable coincidence in the view of Nicholas II and the petitioners as to the correct relationship between tsar and people.' On the basis of extracts (b), (c) and (d), do you agree with this statement? Whom did the petitioners blame for their problems? (4 marks)

iii) What does cartoon (c) suggest could have happened as a result of this relationship? Why did that not occur in 1905? (4 marks)

Nicholas II as tsar

iv) Consult documents (c) and (d). How does Nicholas portray the power of the monarch, and the way social reforms would occur? Was he correct in these views? (4 marks)

v) 'Nicholas II was primarily concerned with the welfare of his people.'
'Nicholas only made concessions in order to restore order in the Empire.' On the basis of documents (c), (d), (e), and (f) with which of these statements do you most agree? Give reasons why you agree. (6 marks).

vi) To what extent does document (e) support the impression of Nicholas II given in cartoons (b) and (c)? Give your reasons. (3 marks)

Effects of the revolution

vii) What evidence is there in documents (f) and (g) as to the prospects for the reforms granted in 1905? Do the reasons why the reforms were granted also suggest this? Which cartoon seems to share a cautious or pessimistic outlook? (5 marks)

Nature of the evidence

viii) Consider any five of the documents, and discuss how reliable and useful they are as sources of historical evidence. (Consider, for example, who the authors are, the date, form and purpose of the evidence.) (10 marks).

ix) Study the four Punch cartoons in chart 5.3. Do you consider any of them unfair? Of what value are cartoons to historians? (10 marks).
(Total 50 marks).

B.2. Study the other cartoons on Russia in chart 5.4.

Unrest in Russia
Study cartoons (a) and (b)

i) What problem facing the Government do cartoons (a) and (b) show?
Do you think such acts had any effect on the Government? (3 marks)

ii) Cartoon (b) was on the front of the radical magazine *Raven* in 1906. Can you detect any members of the government? (Chapter nine will help here.) What attitude to assassination does the magazine seem to hold? (3 marks)

iii) For what actions does cartoon (a) hold Plehve responsible? (2 marks)

iv) In which country was cartoon (a) drawn? Does it, nevertheless, seem to share the same attitude as the Russian cartoon? (2 marks)

Nicholas in 1905
Study cartoons (c), (d), (e) and (f).

v) What event is being portrayed in cartoons (c) and (d)? (1 mark)

vi) How responsible do cartoons (c), (d), (e) and (f) suggest Nicholas was for what happened in 1905-6? What differences between the cartoons are there in this respect? (3 marks)

vii) How justified do you consider these views? (3 marks).

Aftermath of revolution. Repression

viii) What do cartoons (f), (g) and (h) show about the way Russia was restored to calm after the 1905 revolution? (2 marks)

ix) With which minister were the events drawn in (f) and (g) most associated? (Chapter nine will help here) (1 mark)

x) What does cartoon (g) suggest about possible uses by the government for railways? Might they, however, as Nicholas I's Finance Minister Kankrin had argued, also serve to help the cause of revolution? (2 marks)

General

xi) 'The Russian cartoons in chart 5.4 are far more reliable and valuable pieces of evidence than the Punch cartoons.' Explain whether you agree with this statement. (3 marks)
(Total 25 marks).

C. Overall view

C.1. Simulation on 1905. Empathy.

Split up into groups to represent the following participants in the events of 1905:
a) workers b) peasants c) bourgeoisie d) soldiers e) minority groups, eg Finns, Poles or Jews.
   You might like to subdivide the groups, eg moderate liberals (to become Octobrists), radicals (Kadets).
   Examine charts 5.1 and 5.2 on the 1905 revolution. In your groups, write a brief speech explaining your role in 1905. Cover the following points:

i) What your grievances were.
ii) What you did.
iii) What you achieved from the revolution, and how you now (1907) view the regime.

C.2. Analysis. The survival of the regime.

You could argue that the tsarist government survived by adopting the following tactics:

a) immediate concessions to reduce discontent,
b) splitting the revolutionary coalition,
c) moving onto the offensive.

What evidence is there to substantiate this analysis?

D. Concluding essay

Why did tsarism survive the crisis of 1905?

Chart 5.1 1905 Revolution

A. CAUSES

Long Term
- Industrialisation
- Population growth
- Peasant poverty and land hunger
- Repression and arbitrary action by government
- Lack of political reforms
- Alienated intellectuals
- Russification

Medium Term
- Economic slump
- Weak tsar

Catalyst
- Unsuccessful war

Sparks/Precipitants
'Bloody Sunday' (first wave of protest Jan)
Moscow print strike (Oct wave of protest)

B. EVENTS

POLITICS	DATE	WAR
Plehve assassinated	1904 Feb	War v Japan
	July	
	Dec	Loss of Port Arthur
Bloody Sunday Massacre	1905 Jan	
Grand Duke Sergei assassinated	Feb	Mukden retreat
Consultative Duma granted		
Union of Unions formed	May	Fleet lost at Tsushima
Zemstva rebuffed	Jun	Potemkin mutiny
Bulygin Proposals; University autonomy	Aug	Peace of Portsmouth
General strike	Oct	
St. Petersburg Soviet		
Imperial Manifesto		
Peasant reforms	Nov	
Moscow rising	Dec	

C. THE REVOLUTIONARY MIX CHART

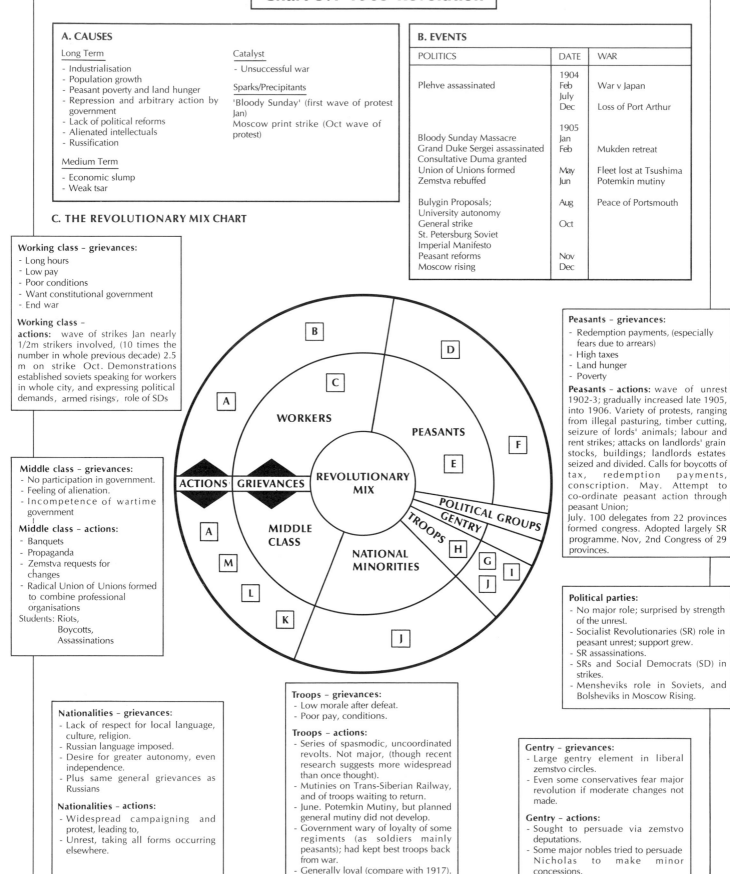

Working class – grievances:
- Long hours
- Low pay
- Poor conditions
- Want constitutional government
- End war

Working class – actions: wave of strikes Jan nearly 1/2m strikers involved, (10 times the number in whole previous decade) 2.5 m on strike Oct. Demonstrations established soviets speaking for workers in whole city, and expressing political demands, armed risings; role of SDs

Middle class – grievances:
- No participation in government.
- Feeling of alienation.
- Incompetence of wartime government

Middle class – actions:
- Banquets
- Propaganda
- Zemstva requests for changes
- Radical Union of Unions formed to combine professional organisations

Students: Riots,
Boycotts,
Assassinations

Nationalities – grievances:
- Lack of respect for local language, culture, religion.
- Russian language imposed.
- Desire for greater autonomy, even independence.
- Plus same general grievances as Russians

Nationalities – actions:
- Widespread campaigning and protest, leading to,
- Unrest, taking all forms occurring elsewhere.

Troops – grievances:
- Low morale after defeat.
- Poor pay, conditions.

Troops – actions:
- Series of spasmodic, uncoordinated revolts. Not major, (though recent research suggests more widespread than once thought).
- Mutinies on Trans-Siberian Railway, and of troops waiting to return.
- June. Potemkin Mutiny, but planned general mutiny did not develop.
- Government wary of loyalty of some regiments (as soldiers mainly peasants); had kept best troops back from war.
- Generally loyal (compare with 1917).

Peasants – grievances:
- Redemption payments, (especially fears due to arrears)
- High taxes
- Land hunger
- Poverty

Peasants – actions: wave of unrest 1902-3; gradually increased late 1905, into 1906. Variety of protests, ranging from illegal pasturing, timber cutting, seizure of lords' animals; labour and rent strikes; attacks on landlords' grain stocks, buildings; landlords estates seized and divided. Calls for boycotts of tax, redemption payments, conscription. May. Attempt to co-ordinate peasant action through peasant Union;
July. 100 delegates from 22 provinces formed congress. Adopted largely SR programme. Nov, 2nd Congress of 29 provinces.

Political parties:
- No major role; surprised by strength of the unrest.
- Socialist Revolutionaries (SR) role in peasant unrest; support grew.
- SR assassinations.
- SRs and Social Democrats (SD) in strikes.
- Mensheviks role in Soviets, and Bolsheviks in Moscow Rising.

Gentry – grievances:
- Large gentry element in liberal zemstvo circles.
- Even some conservatives fear major revolution if moderate changes not made.

Gentry – actions:
- Sought to persuade via zemstvo deputations.
- Some major nobles tried to persuade Nicholas to make minor concessions.

A Report by French consul in Kharkov in October

'Work stopped everywhere: on the railways, in all factories, workshops, in shops of all types, in the University, and all schools, in all administrative offices, even the telegraph offices...the whole population was on the streets, either as sightseers or demonstrators.. People began to ransack arms stores and to smash the windows of the large stores and conservative journals... Students, directed by lawyers, doctors and teachers and helped by workmen and Jews... set up barricades.. The rioters seized the law courts where the archives were and threw them into the streets.'

B Witte describes mass urban unrest in October:

'The press came out without any supervision or respect for the law. The municipal railways were on strike , almost all traffic on the streets had ceased, street lighting was no more, the inhabitants of the capital feared to go out on the streets at night, water supplies were cut off, the telephone network was out of action, all railways to St Petersburg were on strike.

C St Petersburg metal factory strike call Oct 1905:

'We proclaim a political strike, and we will fight to the last for the summoning of a constituent Assembly on the basis of universal, equal, direct and secret suffrage to introduce a democratic republic in Russia.'

D Grand Duke Alexander comments in his diary on rural unrest;

'Spring and Summer 1906, the so called 'illuminations'. In the whole of European Russia the peasants burn the landlord's houses. A number of Governors and police are killed.'

E July Peasant Union Congress:

'Private property in land should be abolished... The land should be considered the common property of the whole people.'

F Newspaper report of rural disturbances:

'Hundreds of buildings worth several millions of roubles have been destroyed. All the building have been razed to the ground in (some) enormous estates. Many houses have been burnt down without reference to the relations which had existed between the peasants and the landowners or the latter's political views. The farms of ... well-known zemstvo liberals have suffered along with the rest.'

G Yermolov, Agriculture Minister, discusses with Nicholas the use of troops, January 1905:

'On 22 January the soldiers certainly carried out the very difficult task which fell to their lot, to fire on a defenceless crowd. The unrest which started in Petersburg has now spread to most of the towns of Russia, and everywhere they have to be put down by force of arms.
So far this is proving possible and the soldiers are doing their duty. But..

what shall we do when disorder spreads from the towns to the villages, when the peasants rise up and when the slaughter starts in the countryside? What forces and what soldiers shall we use then to put down a peasant revolt, which will spread across the whole country? And in the second place, Your Majesty, can we be sure that the troops who have now obeyed their officers and fired into the people, but who come from that very same people, and who even now are in contact with the population, who have heard the screams and curses hurled at them by their victims, can we be sure that they will behave in the same way if such incidents are repeated? '

H Russian Seaman describes conditions in navy.

'Sailors were beaten for all kinds of reasons, and often... There was no way of complaining... We were compelled to eat rotten biscuits and stinking decaying meat while our officers fatted themselves with the best food.'

I Witte spoke of his:

'fear that when the army returned home after all its failures it would join the revolution and then everything would really collapse.'

J Witte reports on actions of non-Russian peoples:

'Seeing this great upheaval, (they) lifted their heads and decided that the time was ripe for the realisation of their dreams and desires. The Poles wanted autonomy, the Jews wanted equal rights, and so on. All of them longed for the destruction of the system of deliberate oppression which embittered their lives. And on top of everything, the army was in an ugly mood.'

K Liberal leader Struve late in 1905:
'Thank God for the Tsar, who has saved us from the people.'

L May Union of Unions:
'All means are admissible in the face of the terrible menace contained in the very fact of the continued existence of the present government: and every means must be tried. We appeal to all groups, to all parties, all organised unions, all private groups.. and we say with all our strength, with all the means at our disposal, you must hasten the removal of the gang of robbers that is now in power, and put in its place a constituent assembly.'

M Student congress in Vyborg 1905:
Students must mobilise their forces in the powerful towns and create the possibility of using higher education institutions for revolutionary agitation and propaganda in the broad masses of the people and undertake measures to organise student fighting squads so that the students, when necessary, can join the general political strike and armed uprising.'

Sources;
A. Christian D. (1986), *Power and Privilege* p.111
B. Kochan L. (1967), *Russia in Revolution* p.103

D. ROLE OF GOVERNMENT

- Helped provoke revolution, by
  Refusal to involve 'society' in administration, yet unable to organise country for war.
  Hard line against protest, and brutality of Bloody Sunday.
- Nicholas made a series of mistakes:
  Absent for Bloody Sunday demonstration.
  Failed to realise seriousness of situation.
  Offered too little too late, eg Feb reforms.

E. EFFECTS

- Major political concessions; granting of Duma.
- Peasants lost redemption payments, and further reforms promised.
- Basic civil liberties promised.
- Workers gained experience.
but,
- Doubt over whether reforms would be consolidated.
- Power still lay with autocracy.
- Wave of fierce repression, executions and exile.

F. REASONS FOR FAILURE OF REVOLUTION

- Troops generally loyal, as seen in suppression of Moscow Rising. Disloyal elements isolated.
- After Peace, troops returned to quell unrest.
- Division in opposition forces; widespread opposition elements divided after October Manifesto; many middle class (Octobrists) accepted reforms.
- Socialists disagreed over violence. Violence isolated, eg Moscow. Middle class fear of masses (as in 1848 European revolutions) therefore reluctant to go too far.
- Peasant risings part of generalised discontent, more prominent in 1902-3 than 1905: now an added worry to government, but not a major threat.
- Protests generally unco-ordinated, lacking in clear purpose, and powerful leadership.
- Mass protests were more outbreaks of rage rather than revolutionary actions; sufficient to force concessions, but not replace government.
- Revolutionary forces, especially strikes, spent themselves.
- Government concessions bought off many opponents.
- Upsurge of frightened right wing forces, eg Black Hundreds, attacking dissidents and Jews.

RESILIENCE OF TSARISM

REASONS FOR FAILURE

WEAKNESS OF OPPOSITION

C. Trotsky L. (1973), *1905* p.124
D. Halpern A. (1954), *History Today* p.109
E. Kochan L. (1967), *Russia in Revolution* p.100
F. Floyd D. (1969), *Russia in Revolt* p.78
G. Floyd D. (1969), *Russia in Revolt* p.68
H. Westwood J. (1973), *Endurance and Endeavour* p.157

M. Kochan L. (1967), *Russia in Revolution* p. 95
I. Christian D. (1986), *Power and Privilege* p. 111
J. Floyd D (1969), *Russia in Revolt* p.81
K. Stone N (1983), *Europe Transformed* p.226
L. Kochan L. (1967), *Russia in Revolution* p. 98

Chart 5.2 Russia in war and revolution 1904-5

1 POLAND
- Jan 1905. beginning of series of major strikes, especially in Warsaw.
- Over 1/4 million Russian troops needed to keep order.

2 LODZ
- Textile centre; most serious Polish disturbances.
- June. 5 days of street fighting.

3 FINLAND
- Oct. General strike forced concessions.

4 BALTIC
- Series of meetings demanding greater autonomy for Estonians, Latvians, Lithuanians.
- Unrest, virtual civil war. Peasants and workers against German landlords.
- Placed under martial law.

5 RIGA
- Nov. 1000 local officials at meeting demanded autonomy.
- Centre of disturbances, spread to countryside.

6 REVAL
- Nov. All-Estonian Congress of 800 demanded official acceptance of Estonian language.

7 JEWS
- Feb. At Vilna, Union for Attainment of Equal Rights for Jews founded.
- May. Joined Union of Unions.
- Played active role in unrest.
- Summer onwards victim of right-wing pogroms, especially by Union of Russian People (Black Hundreds), supported by the Government.

8 DOGGER BANK INCIDENT, 21 Oct
- Nervous Baltic fleet fired on Hull fishing boats as suspected Japanese torpedo boats.
- Nearly caused war with Britain, Japan's ally.

9 VYBORG
- July 1906. Kadets called on Russians to refuse to pay taxes as a protest at the dissolution of the 1st Duma.

10 KRONSTADT
- Oct. Naval mutineers controlled base for 2 days.
- Eventually 1200 arrested by loyal Guards.

11 PARIS
- Sept 1904. Paris bloc of Liberals and Socialists combined to try to end autocracy.

12 ZURICH
- Lenin and other revolutionaries in Switzerland; faction struggles; Lenin briefly returned to Russia in Nov 1905, too late.

13 KIEV
- Centre of liberal meetings and strikes.

14 ODESSA
- June. Serious fighting between revolutionaries and authorities.
- City bombarded by battleship Potemkin; 2000 killed.
- Oct. Rightwing rampage, and 300 Jews killed.

15 UKRAINE AND BLACK EARTH
- massive unrest, initially urban then also rural.
- Social and national grievances intermeshed.
- June. At Kiev, demands for Ukrainian assembly.
- Over 3/4 of all peasant outbreaks were in Black Earth areas; required major deployment of troops 1906.

16 BLACK SEA FLEET AND POTEMKIN MUTINY
- Black Sea fleet only one remaining (after loss of Pacific and Baltic fleets in Japanese war).
- Russia at peace with Turkey so Fleet bottled up in Black Sea under Straits agreement.
- June. Crew seized ship in spontaneous protest over conditions.
- Admiral concerned at mutiny spreading, so put sailors on leave.
- Potemkin sailed to Rumania where scuttled by mutineers.

17 ARMENIA
- Armenian religious groups demanded All-Russian Assembly, and autonomy for Armenia.
- Government encouraged Muslim Tatars of Azerbaizhan to attack Christian Armenians; hundreds killed in Baku.

18 GEORGIA
- Influential Social Democrats.
- Guria province briefly became virtual independent socialist republic.
- Cossacks fiercely repressed disorder.

19 ST PETERSBURG
- 1904. Growing criticism of government incompetence over war.
- Nov 1904. Over 600 liberals held banquet and declared for constitution.
- Growing strikes.
- Jan 1905. Bloody Sunday Massacre.
- Oct. General Strike; Soviet established.
- Nov. Second strike wave failed.
- Dec. Soviet arrested.

20 MOSCOW
- Wave of strikes.
- Oct 1905. Print strike spread to railways; became general throughout Russia.
- Nov. Soviet formed of 180 members representing 80,000.
- Dec. Armed uprising by 800; controlled city centre for over a week; local troops wavered.
- Crushed by loyal St Petersburg troops. 1000 insurgents killed.

21 BJORKO
- July 1905. Nicholas met Kaiser William II on the tsar's yacht in Bjorko Bay and agreed an alliance with Germany, but France hostile, and soon the alliance was rejected by both governments.

22 IVANOCO-VOZNESENSK
- Major textile centre.
- May 1905. First Soviet formed as a strike committee; system spread to 40 cities.

23 NIZHNY NOVGOROD
- Aug. All-Russian Muslim League demanded equal rights.

24 TRANS-SIBERIAN RAILWAY
- Only single track; took 6 weeks to transfer troops to East.
- After August used to transport troops back from east to quell unrest.
- Strikes, mutinies along its path disrupted communications; had to be cleared by loyal troops from east and west, meeting at Chita.
- Line around Lake Baykal only completed during the war; before then the train had to go by ferry.

25 PEACE OF PORTSMOUTH (USA)
- Negotiated by Witte Aug 1905.
- Korea recognised as Japan's sphere of influence.
- Japan gained South Sakhalin, lease on Port Arthur and South Manchurian railways.
- Russia kept control of North Manchuria (and Chinese Eastern Railway).

26 KOREA
- Competing Russian and Japanese interests.
- Russian involvement with Yalu River annoyed Japan.

27 MANCHURIA
- Occupied by Russia 1900-1905

28 MUKDEN
- Long, bloody defensive battle; 100,000 Russian casualties.
- Feb 1905. Russians retreated.

29 PORT ARTHUR
- Port leased from China 1898, with railway rights to Harbin.
- Feb 1904. Japanese torpedoed Russian warships and besieged port.
- Dec 1904. Surrendered to Japanese.

30 TSUSHIMA
- May 1905. Russian Baltic fleet, after seven month journey round world, attacked by Japanese in Tsushima Straits and lost 24 of 27 warships in 90 minutes.

31 TAMBOV
- One of many provinces in Central Russia where there was widespread revolt.
- 10,000 troops sent to keep order. 1906. Returning put down widespread industrial unrest.

✂ ---- Military defeat by Japanese

Route of Baltic Fleet Oct 1904 - May 1905

M Navy or Army mutiny

I Major industrial unrest

U Armed uprising Dec 1905

BALTS Unrest amongst National Minorities

P Pogroms; anti-Jewish violence encouraged by government to deflect unrest

⧄ Rural unrest, esp strikes and violence against lords' estates.

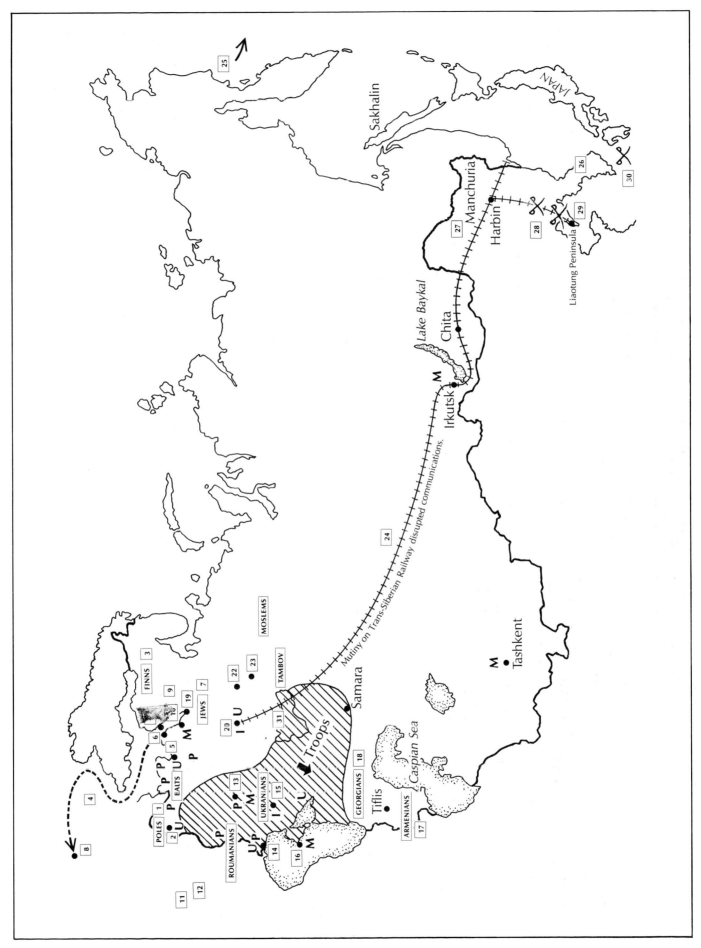

Sakhalin

JAPAN

25

26

30

Manchuria

Harbin

27

28

29

Liaotung Peninsula

Lake Baykal

Chita

Irkutsk M

24

Mutiny on Trans-Siberian Railway disrupted communications.

MOSLEMS

M Tashkent

FINNS 3

9

23

22

TAMBOV

JEWS 7

19

M

Samara

20

I U

31

P

Troops

Caspian Sea

6

5

P U

EALTS

U

18

M

13

P M 15

UKRANIANS

GEORGIANS

Tiflis

POLES 1 P

2 U

P

ROUMANIANS

U P

14

16 M

ARMENIANS 17

4

8

12

11

45

Chart 5.3 Punch on Russia in 1905

THE CZAR OF ALL THE RUSSIAS.

SPORT OF THE WINDS.

THE RELEASE.

THE ELEVENTH HOUR.

Chart 5.4 Cartoons on Russia 1904-6

a) *Cartoon on the assassination of Interior Minister Plehve.* Cover of French periodical, Purin Satirique, no 27, 1904.

b) Russian Magazine, Raven, no 1, 1906.

c) British cartoon, 1905.

d) *'The Blind Tsar'.* German cartoon, January 1905.

e) *The tsar as the 'Angel of Peace'.*

f) *'Now at last my people and I are at peace', says the tsar.*

g) *'Nightmare. Aftermath of a Cossack punitive expedition'.* Russian magazine, Leshii, no 1, 1906.

h) *'He seems to have purified her'.* Russian magazine, Vampire, no 1, 1906.

6 The reign of Nicholas II, 1906 — 1917

A Introduction

The following section consists of a detailed discussion of the prospects for the survival of the newly reformed tsarist state after the turmoil of 1905. Some historians argue that, but for the First World War, Tsarist Russia might have gradually progressed into a modern industrialised, parliamentary state. Others argue that the overthrow of tsarism was inevitable.

Worksection 6 part 1

A. The prospects for tsarism – a debate

Compilation of a chart

Use the material below and chart 6.1 to draw up your own chart about the prospects for tsarism. It should have two columns. The first should include all 'optimistic' points, (ie evidence that tsarist Russia might have continued to develop peacefully in a more modern direction, but for the First World War. The second column should contain 'pessimistic' ones, (ie evidence that the reforms of 1905 were insecure, perhaps 'too little and too late', and that in reality autocratic Russia had not really changed. In this view revolution is seen as likely even if Russia had not been put under the tremendous stress of world war).

Virtually all the information that follows can be used to help assess Tsarist Russia in this way. An example of how this can be done is taken from points made in section B, and chart 6.1.

You may find it difficult to fit some points into the chart. For example, was the June 1907 change in the electoral system a promising development as it created a more moderate Duma which was more likely to survive? Alternatively, can it be seen a step back from genuine representative government? Such issues can be discussed when the chart is completed.

The chart can then be used as a basis for a debate and essay (see p.59).

Optimistic	Pessimistic
Nicholas granted a parliament. The Duma had legislative powers. The tsar had to call a new Duma to replace a dissolved one.	He only did so under pressure. The State Council, and tsar needed to approve all new laws. The tsar could dissolve the Duma.

B Political developments

At the beginning of his reign, Nicholas II had dismissed zemstvo requests for some participation in central government as 'senseless dreams', and as late as 1904 he had rejected demands for an elected assembly. However, with revolt spreading throughout Russia, Nicholas finally granted an elected Duma with legislative powers in October 1905.

This major concession helped split the opposition, and stem the tide of revolution. In the calmer atmosphere of April 1906 he issued a new set of Fundamental Principles limiting the powers of the new Duma (see chart 6.1). The Duma had the right to question ministers (interpellation), but had no real control over them as they were responsible solely to the tsar, (ie they could only be appointed and dismissed by Nicholas). Nicholas even forbad use of the word constitution. Witte, the chief minister, tried to entice some liberals into his government, but they were suspicious of the sincerity behind the new system and refused. Nicholas had, with Witte's help, secured a large French loan. Just before the Duma met however, he dismissed his chief minister, the architect of the new system, blaming him for the radical nature of the peasant dominated Duma.

The First Duma called for an extension of its powers, and confiscation of some landlords land. The new chief minister Goremykin first tried to ignore the Duma, then proceeded to lecture it on its proper role. He bluntly dismissed its proposals as 'inadmissable'. After three months it was dissolved. The liberal Kadets protested at this. From Vyborg in Finland they issued a manifesto calling on Russians to refuse to pay taxes as part of a non-co-operation campaign. Their call met with little response.

The next Duma was just as radical, and refused to accept the agrarian reforms of the new chief minister Stolypin. In June 1907 it too was dissolved. Stolypin then, infringing the Fundamental Laws, issued a decree altering the electoral system for the duma, by giving the nobles far more representation at the expense of the peasantry and national minorities. Such a limited franchise was, however, fairly normal in other European countries. The resultant Third Duma was dominated by moderates and the Right, and lasted its full five years (1907-1912), as did the Fourth Duma.

Stolypin tried to co-operate with the Duma, and developed good relations with the Octobrist leader Guchkov. However, as the Nationalist Right took more control of the Duma, Stolypin's System began to weaken as his measures aroused opposition from all quarters. Crucially, his relations with Nicholas also deteriorated, and his dismissal was likely even before he was assassinated in 1911. From 1910 reactionary influences at court

Chart 6.1 Political concessions 1905-1907

A. Introduction

The details of the various political changes made between 1905 and 1907 can be confusing. They are, however, important for understanding the process and nature of political reform, particularly the extent to which reforms granted under pressure in October 1905 were later modified. The following chart is designed to illustrate the various fluctuations.

	Details	Effects
Feb/Aug 1905 Bulygin Proposals 1905	– Feb 1905. Nicholas told Interior Minister Bulygin to draw up plan to create elected assembly, composed of 'the most worthy persons, with the confidence of the people, elected by the population, to take part in the preliminary consideration of projects of law.' – Details announced 6 Aug; ie consultative assembly, elected on indirect and restricted franchise, excluding most workers, all jews and women. Peasants electing 43%, landowners 33%, towns 23%.	– Failed to reduce discontent as too little too late.
October Manifesto 1905	– Earlier proposals extended by: a) Duma now to have legislative power, ie would have to agree to new laws, and to supervise legality of government. b) Franchise broadened so as to include 'those classes which are now completely deprived of electoral rights.' c) Promised civil rights, ie free meetings, free speech, liberty of conscience.	– Split revolutionary forces; moderate liberals accepted it and formed Octobrist Party.
Spring 1906 Details of Constitution	– Dec 1905, and February 1906. Details given of electoral system promised in October. – Power of Duma weakened as: Now two chambers to agree new laws, ie Duma and reformed State Council, half of whom were appointed by the tsar, the other half elected by the Church, nobles, zemstva, universities and business groups. – Duma elected in separate electoral colleges depending on class/property. Mainly indirect elections, especially for peasants. Colleges roughly corresponded to population, so peasants would predominate. Complicated arrangements meant about half urban workers had no vote. Women still excluded. – March 1906. Details of Duma's powers over budget announced. Duma only had control of one third of government income. – April 1906. Fundamental Laws. Tsar still had 'supreme autocratic power . . . (and) submission to His power, not only from fear but as a matter of	– Framework set up within which Duma had to work. Duma's powers clipped even before it met. – Formal constitution, but not parliamentary government; (similar system to the Second Reich in Germany). – Basis on which 1906 elections proceeded. – Meant peasants dominated first two Dumas, (30% members were peasants or workers), and surprised government by their radical demands. – Great gulf between government and Duma.

Chart 6.1 *continued*	Details	Effects
	conscience is enjoined by God himself.' — Tsar appointed and dismissed ministers who were not responsible to Duma. — Article 87. Tsar could issue decrees 'in exceptional circumstances' when Duma not sitting. Such decrees had to be submitted to Duma within two months of its new session. — Tsar could dissolve Duma, but had to call another.	
June 1907 Electoral Law Change	— Stolypin used Article 87 to alter electoral system; broke Fundamental Laws which said Duma and State Council had to approve electoral changes. — Franchise restricted to favour gentry and urban rich, at the expense of peasants, workers and nationalities; so now it took the following to elect one member of the Duma: 230 landowners, 1000 rich businessmen, 15,000 lower middle class, 60,000 peasants, 125,000 urban workers.	— Alienated many liberals by breaking constitution. — Only 3.5 million (of population of 140m) voted in 1907; only 16% of adult male population. Turnout averaged about 50%. — Secured far more moderate Third Duma which lasted full five years.

B. Clarification of terms

Three different types of elected assembly were discussed during these years.

Consultative Assembly

An assembly able to express opinions to government, but with no real power as its advice could be rejected. Could be first step to eventual representative government. This had been the hope of moderate liberals since Alexander II's reforms, ie a parliamentary roof for the zemstva, but it had been rejected out of hand by tsars (except 1881 Loris-Melikov proposals). In 1905 Nicholas forced to offer a consultative Duma, but by then too late.

Legislative Assembly

An assembly with powers to make laws, ie with real power (but details of how laws made would be important). Nicholas granted this October 1905, and won moderates' support.

Constituent Assembly

Classic demand of radical liberals and socialists, ie an assembly popularly elected (by direct, equal, secret, universal suffrage) to draw up (constitute) a new constitution for the country. Never conceded by tsars. One was elected late in 1917, and then dispersed by the Bolshevik Government January 1918.

Form of election

Indirect election. An election where voters do not directly choose their member of parliament, but instead choose a representative who then chooses the MP. More stages could be introduced. Normally designed to reduce real power of masses. Already used for some groups in zemstva elections, and also used for lower classes in Duma.

increased, and in 1912 and again in June 1914 Nicholas considered reducing the powers of the Duma to make it purely consultative, but his ministers unanimously advised against this.

There had earlier been signs that the Duma was becoming more accepted. Its control over the budget increased, and several ministers consulted with the Duma committees, a move which can be seen as the beginning of ministerial responsibility to parliament. However, two Ministers of War were dismissed for co-operating with the Duma, and others refused to submit to questioning by deputies. The government interfered in the 1912 elections to ensure satisfactory candidates were elected. Though the Third and Fourth Dumas passed a series of major reforms, several others were blocked by the State Council, eg bills to extend the Duma's budget rights, and on religious freedom.

Nicholas was unable or unwilling to provide clear government. There was no real cabinet, and ministers carried out their policies almost in isolation of those of others. Criticism grew as the quality of Nicholas's appointments deteriorated. With the able Witte an outcast, and Stolypin dead, Nicholas appointed a series of nonentities to government posts. The most notorious was the aged Goremykin, re-appointed as Chairman of the Council of Ministers in January 1914. This was indicative of the growing strength of reactionary elements within the government after 1913.

The success of the Duma system would not totally depend upon the attitude of the government (especially as the various ministers were divided on the issue), but also on the strength of political parties trying to consolidate a parliamentary system. After 1905 political parties were legal, though their activities could be restricted. In addition, legalisation of politics could not compensate for the historic weakness of liberalism in Russia. The moderate groups distrusted each other, were all weak in the later Dumas, and lacked a truly national party structure. They generally only represented the educated elite in Moscow and St Petersburg. They also faced a dilemma. Although they wanted further reforms from the government, many were reluctant, after the turmoil of 1905, to seek support from the masses. However, by 1912, even the Octobrists were becoming concerned about the course of events and there was increasing criticism of the government in the Duma. Many were alienated by the growing influence of Rasputin, and it has been argued that more and more former reformists were reacting against a government they considered incompetent and intolerable.

C The development of agriculture

The peasant unrest of 1902-3 and 1905-6 finally forced the government to address the agrarian problem, neglected since emancipation. In November 1905, at the height of the Revolution, Nicholas had promised to cancel redemption payments. This was the first part of a major reform programme designed to improve agriculture by liberating enterprising peasants from the restrictions of the commune. (see chart 7.8).

The impact of Stolypin's reforms has been the subject of much debate. The confusing array of statistics available, as well as the political implications of the debate, mean that it is unlikely to be finally resolved. This is even more the case as the First World War broke out before the reforms had had the twenty years of peace which Stolypin considered necessary for them to become established.

The period 1909-14 saw a vast movement of peasants away from the commune, although there were considerable regional variations. The least change occurred in the most overpopulated areas like Tambov. The incidence of leaving also changed (see chart 6.4). The reforms were largely suspended on the outbreak of war, and in the 1917 Revolution most peasants opted to return to the mir. This evidence has led some commentators, especially Shanin, to argue that Stolypin's reforms were fundamentally ill-conceived. This was because they assumed a Western style desire for private property amongst a peasantry which would thus become increasingly differentiated between the prosperous, enterprising larger owners, and the landless. Such a view failed to recognise the strong communal traditions of the Russian peasantry. These were based on the belief that the land should belong to all tillers.

On the other hand between 1907 and 1916 two and a half million households (about 20%) left the commune. By 1916 approximately one quarter of all peasant land was privately owned outside the commune, though most of this was still in strip form (see chart 7.8). Lenin was worried that the reform was succeeding, and agricultural prosperity was increasing, with both production and prices rising.

There was also a growth in co-operative farms, and a series of model farms tried to convince the peasantry of the advantages of improved techniques. The death rate, which had been rising during the second half of the 19th century, now began to fall. This, however, worsened the massive population rise, which put more pressure on resources, especially land. Over the period 1908-1914 production, helped by good harvests, increased, culminating in the record harvest of 70m tonnes in 1913. However, productivity is estimated to have only risen by 1% per annum, and Russian agriculture was still characterised by wooden ploughs, few animals for draft and manure, and low productivity. In 1917 half of all peasant households did not have their own plough, and less than 5% of farming land received artificial fertilisers.

Helped by State Bank loans, the land held by the peasantry continued to increase as they bought land, often from frightened gentry. Peasant ownership also increased due to migration to set up new farms in Siberia. Between 1900 and 1913, 5 million voluntarily went east, though 1 in 6 returned. Half a million peasants lost the new land they had acquired through inability to pay their loans. However, Trebilcock estimates that the ending of redemption payments increased the potential purchasing power of 160 million peasants by about 15% and peasant deposits in Post Office Savings banks increased dramatically.

It is difficult to assess the political effects of the reforms. Stolypin hoped his reforms would create a prosperous, conservative peasantry, but in the meantime he reduced peasant representation in the Third Duma. Official statistics show a decline in peasant riots from over 3000 in 1905 to only 128 in 1913, but police statistics can not fully convey the true temper of the peasantry. There is considerable evidence that the Stolypin reforms did not bring peace to the Russian countryside. Gatrell has described them as 'conflict-ridden', as they fostered new bitterness, now directed at those 'separators', who took advantage of the reforms and government support, to set up as individual farmers. Those peasants remaining in the mir took out their resentment in various ways, from bullying separators' children at school, to burning down their houses. In his opinion, far from solving agrarian problems, Stolypin created new ones.

D Industrialisation

The period 1906 to 1914 saw tremendous developments in industry. In contrast to agriculture, this was a resumption of the earlier trend which had been disrupted by the general economic depression of 1902-6. Though impressive growth was achieved, the low base from which it started made it comparatively easy to achieve large percentage increases.

Although the chief features of Russian industrialisation remained (see chart 7.3), the economic historian Gerschenkron has argued that there was a change of emphasis in this period which augured well for the future development of Russia. He contrasts the early dependence on state backed railway development in the late 19th century, with the more self-sustained economic growth of the last years of tsarism, which was based on a growing natural internal market. This was mainly due to the benefits of Stolypin's agrarian reforms. These, together with a rise in agricultural prices, produced a growing domestic market, and a more consumer-based, Western style of industrialisation, with the state playing a far smaller role than in the initial stages. Gatrell and others, however, have disputed this interpretation. Although agreeing that state supported railways were far less important in this period, they argue that the state still played the dominant role in industrialisation through its armaments programme. Though the production of consumer goods did rise, its proportion of total industrial output actually fell from 52% to 45%, and it was heavy industry that was still central to the pre-war economic boom.

Kemp has argued that Russia's continued dependence on foreign capital embroiled her in foreign entanglements, culminating in the First World War. Thus the war was not an unfortunate accident that ruined a promising development. However, though foreign capital invested in Russia rose during this period, its proportion compared to domestically raised capital fell. On the other hand, Russian industrialisation still did not have a secure, widespread base. Provincial towns served more as centres for administrative and social functions rather than production and marketing ones. The comparative lack of medium sized factories, with large scale works of over 1000 coexisting with a mass of small handicrafts, indicated the unbalanced nature of Russia's industrialisation, and probably contributed to increased social tension.

As well as creating discontent amongst urban workers, Russia's rapid industrialisation, by putting burdens on the peasantry, also caused discontent in the countryside. Another potential adverse effect of industrialisation was the growth of a middle class. Here, however, the peculiar nature of Russian industry meant that industrialists did not add significantly to the political muscle of liberal parties. The one attempt by industrialists to become more involved politically, the establishment of the Progressist Party, was made by the Russian dominated Moscow textile industry, and received little support from other industrial sectors.

Trebilcock concludes his discussion of the Russian economy by emphasising its dualistic nature. In agriculture, a modern sector of integrated farmsteads opposed a traditional sector of dirt-scratching cultivation; in entrepreneurship, a modern sector of trained technologists opposed a traditional sector of corruption and incompetence; in business structure, cartel opposed kustar (craft manufacture); in markets,the spread of urban demand opposed the persistent tastes of the rural 80 per cent.' (Trebilcock, C. (1981), *Industrialisation of the Continental Powers* p.275). The optimists stress the first features, and the pessimists the second.

E Revolutionary groups and protest

The prospects for tsarism did not just depend upon its own strengths, but also on the extent of opposition. The changes made after the 1905 Revolution, combined with 'Stolypin's necktie', seemed to have restored calm to the countryside. However, by 1909, troops were increasingly used to quell unrest, and the inexorable population rise increased peasant covetousness for the nobles' estates which they eventually seized in 1917. These peasant revolts were largely stimulated by news of the overthrow of the tsar in February.

Unrest in the growing towns was always likely to be more politically significant than rural discontent, and here too the same pattern seems evident. The concession of some basic rights, such as trade unions, and wage increases, combined with repression, had ended the dangerous urban unrest of 1905. Industrial recovery reinforced the return to order. Employers then began retracting some of the concessions forced out of them in 1905. Hours were lengthened and piece rates used. However, the rapid development of large scale industry inevitably produced social tension, due to overcrowding and long hours, low pay, fierce discipline and numerous accidents. The Duma's 1912 Insurance scheme, however, established some protection from the hardships of industrial life.

Cowed by the repression of 1905-6 the proletariat, at least before 1912, remained sullenly passive, though potentially highly volatile. This was seen in 1912 when troops were called into a strike in the Lena goldfields, and 270 strikers were killed. There was a wave of sympathy strikes, and the Okhrana warned that the situation was similar to that in January 1905. From 1912 a growing number of strikes were classifed by the inspectorate as political, such as in protest at previous repression, at the arrest of strikers, and at press censorship. The rapidity with which the police and troops were called into industrial disputes, as well as the agitation of political groups, served to politicise the Russian workers. In various trade union and other working class institutions, radical Bolsheviks were replacing their more cautious fellow Marxist Mensheviks. In July 1914 a general strike broke out in St Petersburg, with virtually all workers striking. It was, however, largely confined to that area, and unlike 1905, it aroused no support from the other sectors of society. The strike ended just before the outbreak of war which inspired a mass patriotic rallying to the government.

The trade union movement only had influence in a few major industrial cities, such as Moscow, St Petersburg and Riga. It is estimated that in 1913 there were only 114 unions, with about 31,000 members, out of an industrial workforce of two and quarter million. Initially the more moderate Menshevik wing of the Marxists, with their stress on legal campaigns to improve conditions, were more influential. There was, however, growing Bolshevik influence, directed into more political and revolutionary directions. In the Duma and in elections for workers' representatives the Bolsheviks were gaining over the Mensheviks, and their 'Pravda' newspaper reached a circulation of about 40,000. On the other hand, the revolutionary groups only had real influence in the few major industrial centres. They had no effective national organisation, were penetrated by police spies, and as the July St Petersburg strike showed, the Bolshevik leadership could not control the rank and file. Soviet historians tend to stress the importance of the Bolsheviks in working class militancy from 1912 to 1917, but few Western historians consider they, or any other revolutionary party, posed much of a threat to tsarism.

On the other hand, relative passivity should not be confused with support for the regime. Stability had been secured on the basis of coercion, not contract and consent. This might not suffice if the regime were put to new tests.

F Social and other reforms

The period of constitutional monarchy has been seen as one of remarkable social advance, making the overthrow of tsarism within a decade more ironic, and for some tragic. The Duma's plan for universal, free primary education by 1922 was well on target by 1914, and literacy was increasing. Spending by zemstva and the government on education greatly increased, though this was more due to Duma pressure than government enthusiasm, some of whose members were suspicious of the effects of extended education. A critic described the Ministry of Education as 'less a ministry of public instruction than a ministry for the prevention of it.' The concession of greater university autonomy granted in 1905 was gradually withdrawn, and in 1910 Stolypin ordered a new wave of repression against universities, and non-academic meetings were banned. Student strikes were countered by mass expulsions. However there was great progress in techological and agricultural colleges.

A similar mixed picture is seen over the civil rights granted in 1905. The scope of the civil liberties which existed on paper really depended on the arbitrary whim of officials; there was still no fundamental acceptance of the rule of law. JPs, however, were reintroduced to replace the hated land-captains. Whereas trade unions were now legal, many were stamped out. Whilst the number of newspapers grew rapidly, nearly a thousand publications were closed, and others suffered from deletions by the censor and the threat to editors of being fined or arrested. The emergency legislation of 1881 could still be used, and in 1912 only 5 million people did not live under the jurisdiction of some form of 'exceptional measures'.

G Nationalism and the minorities

The last years of tsarism saw a growth of aggressive nationalist feeling, both amongst large sections of the population and more ominously within governing circles as well. This was combined with widespread anti-semitism, the worst expression of which was a series of pogroms to which the authorities turned a blind eye, and to which their anti-Jewish laws gave tacit encouragement. This reached a peak with the notorious Beilis Case where the bureaucracy exerted great pressure to gain a conviction against the Jew Beilis for the ritual murder of a Christian child.

The Finns, too, became victims of Russian chauvinism. Supported by the Duma, the government began to retract the concessions made in 1905, and even to undermine Finland's special status granted on her acquisition in 1809. Poles, Armenians, Baltic Germans, Georgians and the vast range of minority groups suffered similarly. Such policies served to discredit tsarism in liberal circles abroad, and also to stimulate the growth of revolutionary parties amongst the national minorities. A disproportionate number of Social Democrats, for example, were Jews or from other subject races. In Central Asia thousands of Muslims were dispossessed of 'surplus' land by Russian migrants, backed by the army. The resultant resentment led to a massive rebellion in 1916 in which thousands were killed.

H Foreign policy

In this field it did seem that lessons were learnt from the humiliation of 1904-5. The government came to agreements with Japan and Britain over spheres of influence in the Far East. This however, was accompanied by a renewed concentration on Balkan affairs. This was partly due to increased nationalist pressure in the Duma, but chiefly due to the growth of tensions in that area as Slav nationalism grew, and Austria-Hungary became more concerned. During a series of crises (1908-9, over the Austrian annexation of Bosnia-Herzegovina and 1912-13, during the Balkan Wars) Russia, aware of her military weakness after 1905, backed down to Austrian and German pressure. The wise advice of chief minister Kokovtsov against mobilisation of the army had then been accepted. However, these diplomatic humiliations made Russia less prepared to accept a further setback in 1914. For when an Austrian ultimatum to Serbia after the assassination at Sarajevo provoked a new crisis, Nicholas eventually, reluctantly, mobilised his troops which triggered off war with Germany.

I Nicholas II

(See Chapter 9 for a more detailed discussion of Nicholas.)

Many historians have stressed the importance of Nicholas II in determining the fate of Tsarist Russia. There is little disagreement over Nicholas's inadequacies, but some historians consider them unimportant compared to other weaknesses in Russia at the time. Instead they stress the institutional factors making it unlikely that a governing system trained under autocracy could truly convert itself to a form of democracy in which initiative was allowed from below, in contrast to Russia's tradition of all power coming from above. Other historians, such as Kennan and Crankshaw, however, lay more stress on the 'imbecilities' of Nicholas in causing the collapse of the system. They point to his indecisiveness (for example regarding the troubles of 1905), his deceitfulness towards ministers, and his lack of support to able ministers like Witte and Stolypin. In contrast they stress the confidence he placed in such nonentities as Goremykin and the way in which he allowed himself to be dominated by Alexandra and consequently influenced by Rasputin. His anti-semitism and political naivety in openly approving the extreme right-wing Union of the Russian People, his stubborn belief in upholding the autocracy and his military adventurism have also been viewed as disastrous for the monarchy.

Chart 6.2 Contemporary comments on Russia 1906-1914

A. Comments by Nicholas and his ministers

i) 1906. 'Damn the Duma, it's Witte's work.'

ii) 1908. 'I created the Duma not to have it instruct me, but to have it advise me.'

iii) 1909 to his mother. 'One thing is difficult: to persuade Kokovtsov to get money without the Duma; but we will do it one way or another, never fear.'

iv) 1909 to Stolypin. 'This Duma cannot be reproached with an attempt to seize power and there is no need at all to quarrel with it.'

v) 1912. 'The Duma started too fast. Now it is slower, but better and more lasting.'

vi) 1912 to Kokovtsov: 'I have decided to part with Makarov. He has let the press get completely out of hand, and has absolutely refused to proclaim a law which would give the government authority to check the excesses in which newspapers have been indulging.'

vii) Witte to the historian Pares: 'I have a Constitution in my head, but as to my heart, I spit on it.'

viii) Stolypin 1908: 'If you took an assembly which represented the majority of the population, sane ideas would not prevail in it . . . We want not Professors but men with roots in the country, the local gentry and such like.'

ix) Stolypin 1909: 'Give the state twenty years of quiet at home and abroad, and you will not recognise the Russia of that day.'

x) Stolypin in 1911: 'Every year of peace fortifies Russia not only from the military and naval point of view, but also from the economic and financial . . . Russia is growing from year to year: self-knowledge and public opinion are developing in our land. One must not scoff at parliamentary institutions. However imperfect, their influence has brought a radical change in Russia.'

xi) Interior Minister Makarov's speech to the Duma on the Lena massacre 1912: 'It has always been so; it always will be so.'

xii) Justice Minister Shcheglovitov's comment on the cabinet meeting, June 1914: 'We were asked to give our judgement on whether to return to the unrealised situation of August 1905, namely whether the State Duma could be changed from a legislative to a consultative institution.'

B. Politicians' views

i) Kadet Nabokov Oct 1905: 'We do not believe that yesterday's wolves can be miraculously transformed into today's lambs.'

ii) Kadet Milyukov 1909 in a speech in London: 'We representatives of the Opposition would like the Duma's rights greatly enlarged, the electoral law democratised, and the system of political institutions brought into harmony, to make productive legislative work possible. But so long as Russia has a legislative chamber with the right to control the budget, the Russian Opposition will remain His Majesty's Opposition, and not opposition to his Majesty.'

iii) Kadet Maklakov 1909: 'Confidence is a tender plant. Perhaps the Government is better than its deeds, perhaps it is merely powerless. But having gained a reputation for insincerity, it has lost the confidence of the country and therein lies the tragedy of its fate.'

iv) Octobrist Golitsyn 1910: 'The inviolability of the person promised by the October manifesto appears now as a simple myth.'

v) Octobrist Guchkov in a speech to his party conference Nov 1913 argued that 'the attempt made by the Russian public, as represented by our party, the attempt to effect a peaceful, painless transition from the old condemned system to a new order, has failed.' He warned of 'an inevitable and grave catastrophe . . . Let those in power make no mistake about the temper of the people; let them not take outward indications of prosperity as a pretext for lulling themselves into security. Never were those revolutionary organisations which aim at a violent upheaval so impotent as they are now, and never were the Russian public and the Russian people so profoundly revolutionised by the actions of the government, for day by day faith in the government is steadily waning, and with it is waning faith in the possibility of a peaceful issue of the crisis.'

vi) Moderate paper Jan 1914: 'The Government is leaving society, just as society is leaving it.'

vii) Progressive Riabushinskii May 1914: 'Our government is not talented. If this goes on, even the broad masses will lose respect for authority. This will be sad, this is intolerable, this can lead to unfortunate consequences . . . A blind state, an orphaned people. One can only hope that our great country will outlive its petty government.'

viii) Resolution of the Fourth Duma May 1914: 'The Ministry of the Interior systematically scorns public opinion and ignores the repeated wishes of the new legislature. The Duma considers it pointless to express any new wishes in regard to internal policy. The Ministry's activities arouse dissatisfaction among the broad masses who have hitherto been peaceful. Such a situation threatens Russia with untold dangers.'

Chart 6.3 Pictorial evidence on prospects for reform

a) 'Will he strangle them?' Punch cartoon.

b) *Cartoon on the prospects for a new constitution.*

c) 'Interpellation' in the Duma. Russian magazine, Leshii, no 1, 1906.

d) *Russia in chains is surrounded by Church, State and the Black Hundreds. Figures demand 'A brake on Reforms'.* Russian magazine, Nagaechka, no 3, 1906.

e) *A satirical cartoon entitled 'Freedom of Meetings'.*

g) *Typical pages of Petrograd newspaper 'Den' containing verbatim report of a Duma debate.*

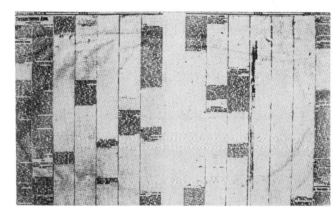

f) Russian cartoon, in magazine, Zarevo (Dawn), no 3, 1906.

h) *'The Imperial couple during the tercentenary celebrations for the Romanov dynasty in March 1913 . . . The royal tour was not a success: crowds were thin and unenthusiastic'.* E Acton, Russia, p.137.

Chart 6.4 Statistics on Russia 1906-1914

A. Composition of the Dumas

	Duma	1	2	3	4
Extreme Left					
Social Democrats		18*	65	14	14
Socialist Revolutionaries		*	34	*	*
Trudoviki (allies of SR)		94	101	14	10
Moderate Left					
Kadets		179	92	52	57
Progressists				39	47
National Minorities					
(mainly on the left)		120	130	26	21
Conservatives					
Octobrists		17	32	120	99
Right-wing and Russian		15	63	145	152
Nationalist Groups					

* official boycott (though some members stood)

The complexity of the new party system and of elections means that historians give slightly differing figures for parties depending on their interpretations of candidates.

B. Repression

	Executions by field court martials	Political exiles
1906	1000+	
1908	782	
1909	543	22,568
1910	129	10,972
1911	58	5,682

C Industrial Unrest

Year	No of strikers	No of strikes	No of strikes listed political
1905	13,995	2,863,173	6,024
1906	6,114	1,108,406	2,950
1907	3,573	740,074	2,558
1908	892	176,101	464
1909	340	64,166	50
1910	222	46,623	8
1911	466	105,100	24
1912	2,032	725,491	1,300
1913	2,404	887,096	1,034
1914	3,574	1,337,458	2,401

Figures published by the Ministry of Trade and Industry for strikes in workplaces covered by factory inspection.

D. Agrarian Reforms

Peasants separating from the Commune.
i) By region
Parts of Ukraine 1 in 2. Black Earth about 1 in 4. Tambov 1 in 20
ii) By Year

1908	1909	1910	1911
508,000	580,000	342,000	145,000
1912	1913	1914	1915
122,000	135,000	98,000	30,000

E. Social Reforms

i) Expenditure
Government spending on elementary education:
1905 19 million roubles 1.8% of budget
1914 76 million roubles 4.2% of budget

ii) Number of schools and students:
1900-1914 enrolments in primary schools doubled, in secondary quadrupled, and in higher education tripled.
Proportion of children of peasants and workmen in universities:
1880 15.7% 1914 38.8% (This figure reached 54% in higher technical institutions)

Number of Primary Schools under the Ministry of Education, 1905-1914 (from McCauley, M. 'Octobrists to Bolsheviks' p.187)

Year	No. of schools	% growth
1905	43,551	
1906	45,629	4.8
1907	47,838	4.8
1908	50,876	6.4
1909	54,726	7.6
1910	59,000	7.8
1911	64,318	8.9
1912	69,318	7.8
1913	76,416	10.2
1914	80,801	5.7

iii) Literacy
Rural literacy (average of 12 European provinces 1908-1912)

39.8% Men   24.8% Women

Urban Literacy, 1897-1912 (from McCauley, M. Op.cit. p.181)

Town	Years of census	literate %
St Petersburg	1897	52.6
	1910	66.9
Moscow	1897	52.3
	1912	64.0
Kharkov	1897	52.5
	1912	66.6
Voronezh	1897	52.1
	1911	61.2
	1916	65.8
	1897	32.4
Baku	1913	38.8

A. Interpreting historical evidence

A.1. Pictorial evidence on tsarism's prospects.

Study chart 6.3.

i) What impression do the cartoons give of the success of the reforms granted in 1905?
ii) Analyse four of the cartoons in detail, (eg consider the point which each cartoonist is making).
iii) Study picture (g). What does this show about the nature of the tsarist regime at this time? (Try to suggest two points.)
iv) Study photograph (h). What does this suggest about the popularity of the dynasty? Do you agree with Acton's comment about the crowds at the tercentenary celebrations?

A.2. Nature of evidence.

Study charts 6.2, 6.3 and 6.4.

i) Identify all the evidence in chart 6.2 that could be used to support an optimistic view of the period.
ii) Most of the primary evidence seems to support the pessimistic view of the regime's survival. Why might this be so? Does it necessarily prove the optimists wrong?
iii) Consider the value of the various types of primary sources in the charts, ie extracts from comments by contemporaries, cartoons, photographs and statistics. For each type of source, identify its advantages and disadvantages to the historian. Substantiate your views with specific examples from the charts.
iv) Which would you consider the most valuable type of source? Why?

B. Historical controversy

A class debate.

Use the chart drawn up in part 1 of the worksection, and the evidence in charts 6.2, 6.3 and 6.4, to hold a debate about the prospects for the survival of tsarism. One group should be 'optimists', the other 'pessimists'. One person in each group could specialise on one particular area.

C. Concluding essay

Using the above material, write one of the following essays.

i) How successful were the attempts to carry out reforms in Russia between 1905 and 1914?
ii) 'Too little, and too late to save Tsarist Russia.' Consider this view of the reforms initiated during the reign of Nicholas II.'
iii) To what extent in the period 1906-1914 did the Russian monarchy succeed in removing the primary causes of internal tension, and in creating a wider basis of support?

J   The impact of the First World War

The future of Russia was, arguably, finely balanced when the assassination of Archduke Ferdinand set off a crisis in Austro-Serb relations. This quickly escalated to involve Tsarist Russia in a World War, from which she was not to emerge intact. The war put great strains on Russia's social and political fabric which in the end she could not stand (see chart 6.5). The government refused to take heed of, and co-operate sufficiently with, the public's attempts to assist the war effort. Yet it was incapable of organising the country to face the strains of war. Some in the Duma, army and aristocracy were already considering a forced change of government when the people of Petrograd, facing severe economic hardship, erupted in revolt. The government was faced with mass protest, where workers were joined by rebellious troops. The forces of authority were now divided, as ministers reigned and several generals and members of the court aristocracy refused to support Nicholas. In these conditions, he was forced to abdicate on March 2 1917, and a Provisional Government was established to lead the new republic.

Historians still debate whether the war caused a revolution which might otherwise not have occurred, merely speeded its coming, or actually delayed it by diverting the tide of discontent building up by 1914. The view one adopts partly depend on one's analysis of the semi-constitutional regime considered earlier.

Chart 6.5 identifies the most significant developments during the war, and worksection 6.3 includes a range of evidence illustrating the impact of the war.

A. Russia in the First World War

A.1. Interpretation of statistical evidence.

Study chart 6.5, and the following evidence of developments in Russia during the First World War.

Comment on the significance of ten of the pieces of statistical evidence. Try to explain why the situation arose, and its effects.

Statistical evidence

i) Military figures.
   a) By 1917 0.8 million Russian troops killed, 4.6 million wounded, 3.3 million captured.
   b) Dec 1914 Russia had 4.7m rifles to issue to 6.5m front line troops.
   c) Peacetime army 1.4m. 1914 4m more mobilised. By 1917 another 10m.

d) By 1916 over half soldiers were in urban barracks, not at the front.
ii) Economic-social developments
a) Size of towns

	Petrograd	Moscow
1914	2.1m	1.6m
1917	2.65m	2.0m

b) The amount of gentry-owned land which was cultivated fell by half.
c) 1916 production of agricultural implements fell to 15% of that in 1913.
d) 1914 25% of harvest brought to market: 1917 15%
e) Ordinary goods conveyed by rail 1913 30 million tonnes, 1917 19 million tonnes. Military stores conveyed by rail 1913 2.5 million tonnes, 1917 43 million tonnes
f) Railway engines in working order late 1914 20,071, 1917 9,201.
g) By 1916 only half the necessary supplies were reaching cities.

iii) Government finances, and inflation.
a) 1914 the government banned the sale of alcohol (a state monopoly).
b) War costs (in roubles) 1915 1655m, 1916 14573m, 1915 8818m, 1917 13603m (first 8 months)
c) 1914-1916 inflation was nearly 400% Average wages doubled

iv) Industrial unrest.
(Figures from factory inspector reports, covering 70% of industrial workers.)

	Number of strikes	Number of strikers
1914 (Jan-Jul)	1560	413972
(Aug-Dec)	61	31907
1915	819	397259
1916	1167	776064
1917	1330	676286

Chart 6.5 Russia in the First World War

A. Military

a) **Events**

1914
– Aug. Two Russian armies invaded Germany, as promised to France.
– Initial success, but Germans switched 9 divisions from West (this allowed French to hold Germans at the 'miracle' of Battle of the Marne); Germans defeated the Russians who were forced to retreat.
– Russia had greater success in invasion of Austrian Galicia.

1915
– Disastrous year. Russian retreat after major German offensive.

1916
– June. Brussilov offensive. Russians made great advances, and relieved French at Verdun, but GHQ errors allowed Germans to concentrate against Brussilov and gains lost.
– Front largely stabilised into 1917.

b) **Organisation**
– Generals, officers generally aristocratic, inefficient, held position through favouritism not merit.
– Military given great powers, even away from front. Quarrel with civilian authorities.
– Large scale conscription; eventually 1 in 3 of all suitable males.
– Great losses of officers and men, weakened morale of army; training of troops and quality of officers deteriorated.
– Morale low; desertions, but army at front survived largely intact till after February Revolution.
– Supplies initially poor, despite taking priority over civilian needs, but improved by 1916.

B. Political

a) **Role of Nicholas II**
– Indecisive in 1914; wanted to avoid war, but under pressure, especially from Duma, to stand up for Russia. Others, eg Durnovo, Witte, Rasputin, warned of the political danger if war occurred.
– Inadequate grasp of complex diplomacy, yet he was determined to preserve his authority in diplomatic affairs. Cabinet was discouraged from discussing such issues.
– Failed to co-ordinate clear government line; sent contradictory signs to other countries.
– Confusion over mobilisation, a key decision as likely to lead to war.
– Nicholas initially ordered partial mobilisation only against Austria; then when told by generals this was unworkable, he ordered general mobilisation. He then cancelled it, then let it stand.
– Aug 1915. Despite the opposition of his ministers, Nicholas took over from Grand Duke Nicholas as Commander in Chief. He

Chart 6.5 *continued*

B. Political

moved to military head-quarters at Mogilev, leaving Alexandra (and Rasputin) in virtual control in Petrograd. Nicholas made this decision partly influenced by jealousy of the Grand Duke's power, but he also felt it was his duty to put himself in charge at a moment of crisis.

b) Duma

– Welcomed war Aug 1914; all except Social Democrats voted war credits; then the Duma was prorogued (suspended).

– Rarely met during war. In Aug 1915 it expressed concern at government's handling of war. Formed a 'Progressive Bloc', calling for a 'government of confidence'. This was rejected by the government, and Duma again prorogued.

– Met briefly in 1916. Challenged competence of the government. Due to meet again in Feb 1917. Members secretly considered abdication plans. Prorogued, but formed a Committee which became the Provisional Government during the Revolution.

c) Government

– Nicholas rejected Duma requests for a Government of confidence; but he made some wiser appointments till 1915 then he went to front, and appointments largely depended on Rasputin. Led to 'ministerial leapfrog' ie constant changes, eg 1914-17 4 Minister Presidents, 6 Interior Ministers.

d) Organisational

– After fifty years of government control, zemstva were allowed to form All Russian Union to supplement the bureaucracy, but,

– Government still suspicious of, and so restricted activities of, non-governmental organisations, eg Unions of Zemstva, War Industry Committees. Government and bureaucracy determined to preserve their own power, and were jealous of other organisations.

– Wide areas under military control where civilian access was restricted.

e) Political opinion

– Initially, all rallied to government except Bolsheviks.

– Bolshevik anti-war propaganda gradually made impact as morale fell.

– 1915 defeats encouraged rumours of treason; some generals began turning against the government.

– Opposition grew as failures continued. Allied pressure for government changes. Growing feeling of imminent chaos.

– Opposition elements eventually accused the government of treachery rather than mere incompetence, and some liberals resorted to conspiracy.

C. Economic

a) Industrial

– Production geared to war needs, but initially dependent on imports.

– Massive expansion of war production (artillery 1916 4 times that of 1914), but other industries declined.

– Production hit by supply problems, eg fuel and labour shortages.

b) Agricultural

– Production initially maintained, helped by good harvests, but gradually problems emerged.

– More efficient gentry farmers hit by shortages of labour, animals, equipment, fertiliser.

– Peasants initially benefited from higher prices, but increasingly kept grain back from market as the value of money fell, and as there was a lack of goods for purchase. The distribution, not the production, of food was the key problem.

c) Financial

– Government revenue (from tariffs, railways, vodka sales) fell.

– Expenditure rose; government resorted to borrowing, and money printing.

– Rapid inflation.

d) Transport

– Major problems, partly due to inadequate network, but chiefly due to poor administration.

– Rail network hit by loss of routes in West. Military authorities controlled west region, civilians the east, so lack of co-ordination. Military held on to vital rolling stock.

– Amount and quality of rolling stock fell.

– Supplies were stocked and food rotted whilst shortages elsewhere, especially in cities.

e) General

– Germany's mining of Baltic, and Turkey's closure of Straits prevented 80% of Russia's foreign trade.

D. Social

– Increasing strain on social fabric.

– Civilian population evacuated from occupied lands; scorched earth policy. Massive refugee problem.

– Threefold growth of proletariat. More heterogenous and volatile.

– Growing tension in cities, especially Petrograd. 1916 Police reports warned of great crisis and anarchy.

– Wage rises well below inflation; severe shortages.

– Returning wounded and deserters spread defeatist feelings.

– Bread queues. Growing strikes.

Chart 6.6 Causes of the Russian Revolution, February 1917

Nicholas II
- Narrow vision, poorly prepared to face problems of rule.
- Indecisive but obstinate.
- Firm belief in autocracy and his duty to uphold it.
- Greatly influenced by Pobedonostsev.
- Personal anti-semitism.
- Refused to grant political reforms during the 1890s.
- Did not really accept the role of the Duma after 1905.
- Political naivety; support for Union of Russian People.
- Bad judgement in the appointment and dismissal of ministers.
- Ordered general mobilisation July 1914.
- Left Petrograd 1915 for front.
- Refused to appoint government which had the confidence of the public during the war.

Alexandra and Rasputin
- Alexandra strong influence on husband; reinforced his belief in autocracy.
- German origins inspired rumours of treason during war.
- Influenced by Rasputin, who then influenced Nicholas, eg over appointments.
- Rasputin alienated aristocracy, the traditional supporters of tsarism.
- Rasputin more illustrated the ills of tsarism, than caused them.

Aristocracy and elite
- Traditional upholders of system, but many at court alienated by Rasputin's influence, and incompetence of Nicholas, and considered replacing him in Feb 1917 in order to avert mass revolution.
- Refused to rally to Nicholas, February 1917

Army
- Ultimate upholders of system, but mass disaffection in rank and file, especially in garrisons at rear, eg Petrograd.
- Feb 1917. Troops in Petrograd refused to fire on demonstrators and fraternised with crowds.
- Generals increasingly critical of incompetence of government; considered need for changes, and by Feb 1917 not prepared to defend Nicholas.

Causes of the Russian Revolution

First World War
(see chart 6.5)
- 3 years of little success, inefficient organisation, massive casualties, put great strain on military machine, economic strength, administrative efficiency, social cohesion and political structure of Tsarist Russia.
- Caused mass discontent in cities; growing criticism by Duma of government.
- Revealed incompetence of governing system.
- Undermined loyalty of army to tsarism.

Industrialisation and the role of the working class
- Increased proletariat, working in poor conditions, living in overcrowded cities; susceptible to socialist ideas.
- Also industrialisation increased pressures on peasantry, who were highly taxed to pay for industrialisation via 'surplus' grain.
- Growth of middle class; initially beneficiaries of system, but increasingly critical of incompetence of tsarist regime.
- Increased significance of Straits (of Constantinople), as trade route, and closer financial / diplomatic ties with France, contributed to Russia's entry into first World War.
- Working class organised a series of strikes and demonstrations, especially in Feb 1917. Revealed collapse of system.

Land question and peasantry
- Growing land hunger due to inadequacy of emancipation, and population rise.
- Desire for gentry lands, (but peasant land seizures more a consequence than a cause of February Revolution).
- Land question still unsolved despite Stolypin's reforms, but some argue these might have made most peasantry loyal.
- Most soldiers were peasants so did play role in crucial disaffection of army.
- Failure to supply sufficient grain during war led to urban discontent.

Failure of reform
- Potentially promising reforms of 1905-6 not sincerely supported by government; Duma not fully accepted within autocracy.
- No genuine acceptance of liberal freedoms.
- Stolypin's agrarian reforms did not solve key problem, and were too late.

Chart 6.6 *continued*

Causes of the Russian Revolution

Revolutionary parties	Growth of political opinion and middle class	Political system
– Debate over their import-ance, but usually seen as playing little role in largely spontaneous February Revol-ution. – Broad propaganda role helped undermine loyalty to regime, especially amongst workers and soldiers. – By attracting able, youthful idealists away from corrupt government machinery, oppo-sition groups may have re-duced quality of bureaucracy. – By frightening government into repression they may have increased chances of eventual explosion, but also frightened cautious middle class so latter became less hostile to status quo.	– Despite autocracy, 19th cen-tury saw growth of political debate, involvement of non-government officials in organ-isation, eg zemstva, and gene-ral belief in need to widen basis of tsarist regime. – Development of professions, commerce, industry pro-vided basis for growing desire for modernisation of governing system. – Spread of education, although limited, served to increase cri-tical opinion, especially in universities. – Growth of primary education, esp via zemstva, increased literacy and potential for spread of opposition prop-aganda.	– Russia still semi-autocratic; Duma had no real control over government, clearly seen during First World War. – Opportunities for gradual political reforms missed dur-ing 1860s and in 1881. – Bureaucratic system inflexi-ble, outdated; inefficient, centralised system inadequ-ate in provinces, and lacked. co-ordination at centre. – Strongly entrenched reac-tionary views at court, eg Pobedonostsev. – Repressive Okhrana and gov-erning machine.
Russification and discontent amongst minorities – Attempt to impose Russian culture, language, religion on national minorities was counter-productive.	– Increased desire for auton-omy or independence, seen in 1905 and re-emerged in 1917. – Strong Russian/Pan Slav feel-ing one factor behind Gov-	ernment's refusal to accept further diplomatic humilia-tion in 1914 and consequent involvement in First World War.

A.2. Primary evidence on Russia during the First World War.

Read the following contemporary accounts, and answer to questions which follow.

a) Extracts from a Police Department report in October 1916:

'In the opinion of the spokesmen of the labour group of the Central War Industries Committee* the industrial proletariat of the capital is on the verge of despair and it believes that the smallest outbreak, due to any pretext, will lead to uncontrollable riots, with thousands and tens of thousands of victims. Indeed, the stage for such outbreaks is more than set: the economic position of the masses . . . is distressing . . . Even if we assume that wages have increased 100%, the cost of living in the meantime has risen by an average of 300%. The impossibility of obtaining, even for cash, many foodstuffs and articles of prime necessity, the waste of time involved in spending hours waiting in line in front of stores, the increasing morbidity due to inadequate diet and insanitary lodgings (cold and dampness as a result of lack of coal and firewood) etc, all these conditions have created such a situation that the mass of industrial workers are quite ready to let themselves go to the wildest excesses of a hunger riot.

In addition to economic hardships the 'legal disabilities' of the working class have of late become 'intolerable and unbearable', the denial of the mere right to move freely from one factory to another has reduced labour, in the opinion of the Social-Democrats, to the state of mere cattle, good only for 'slaughter in the war'. The prohibition of all labour meetings . . . the closing of trade unions . . . and so on make the labour masses, led by the more advanced and already revolutionary-minded ele-ments, assume an openly hostile attitude towards the Government and protest with all the means at their disposal against the continuation of the War . . . A saying by one of the speakers at a meeting . . . 'You must end the War if you do not know how to fight' has become the war-cry of the Petrograd Social-Democrats.

The close relations between the workers of Petrog-rad and the army also indicate that the atmosphere at the front is disturbing, not to say revolutionary. The high cost of living and the shortage of foodstuffs from which soldiers' wives are the first to suffer have been made known to the army by soldiers returning from leave . . .

Revolutionary circles, then, have no doubts that a

revolution will begin soon, that its unmistakable precursors are already here, and that the Government will prove incapable of fighting against the revolutionary masses, which are the more dangerous because they consist largely of soldiers or former soldiers.'
(Quoted by Florinsky, M. (1961), *End of the Russian Empire* pp. 165-6)

* Footnote. Non-governmental body set up in 1915 to help armaments production. Wide membership, including representatives from industrialists, zemstva and workers.

b) Liberal Duma Leader Milyukov, Nov 1916:
'The gulf between us and the government has grown wider and has become impassable . . . We are telling this government, as the Declaration of the Bloc stated: We shall fight you; we shall fight with all legitimate means until you go . . . When the Duma . . . insists that the rear must be organised for a successful struggle . . . the government . . . prefers chaos and disorganisation; what is this: stupidity or treason?'
(Quoted by Christian D. (1986), *Power and Privilege* p. 131)

c) Ministerial report, late 1916:
'The army in the rear and at the fighting line is full of elements, some of whom may become an active force of rebellion, while others may refuse to participate in punitive measures against the mutineers. Should the former succeed in organising themselves properly, there would hardly be enough units in the Army to constitute a strong counter-revolutionary force to defend the government.'
(Quoted by Cash, A. (1967), *Russian Revolution* p. 46)

d) General Krymov to Duma members, 1917:
'The spirit of the army is such that news of a coup d'etat would be welcomed with joy. A revolution is imminent and we at the front feel it to be so. If you decide on such an extreme step, we will support you. Clearly, there is no other way.'
(Quoted by Kochan L./Abraham R. (1983), *Making of Modern Russia* p. 285)

e) General Brussilov, 1917:
'If I must choose between the Tsar and Russia, I shall march for Russia.'
(Quoted by Robottom, J. (1972), *Modern Russia* p. 57)

f) Duma leader Rodzianko's telegraph to Nicholas, 27 Feb 1917:
'The situation is serious. The capital is in a state of anarchy. The government is paralysed; the transportation system has broken down; the supply systems for food and fuel are completely disorganised. General discontent is on the increase. There is disorderly shooting in the streets; some of the troops are firing at each other. It is necessary that some person enjoying the confidence of the country be entrusted immediately with the formation of a new government. There can be no delay. Any procrastination (delay) is fatal. I

pray God at this hour the responsibility not fall upon the sovereign.'
(Quoted by Christian, D. (1986), *Power and Privilege* p. 132)

g) Nicholas's brother-in-law Grand Duke Alexander, Jan 1917:
'The Government is today the body which prepared the revolution; the people do not want it; but the Government does everything it can to increase the number of discontented, and succeeds admirably. We are witnessing an unprecedented scene; a revolution not from below, but from above.'
(Quoted by Halpern, A. in *Russian Themes* ed. Kochan, M and L p. 124)

h) British Ambassador Buchanan to Nicholas, January 1917:
'"Your Majesty, if I may be permitted to say so, has but one safe course open to you, namely to break down the barrier that separates you from your people and to regain their confidence." Drawing himself up and looking hard at me, the Emperor asked, "Do you mean that I am to regain the confidence of my people, or that they are to regain my confidence?"'
(Quoted by Massie, R. (1968), *Nicholas and Alexandra* p. 373)

Read extract (a).

   i) Identify the reasons why the Police Department considered a revolution might occur. Why were the workers' grievances becoming politicised? (5 marks)
  ii) Why, according to the report, was the atmosphere at the front alarming? Was it primarily due to military reasons? (3 marks)
 iii) How reliable do you consider this source? (5 marks)

Consult extract (g).

  iv) Comment on Grand Duke Alexander's view that a 'revolution from above' was occurring. Do any of the other extracts lend any support to this view? Explain why. (3 marks)
   v) How does extract (h) help explain why so few people were prepared to support Nicholas by 1917? (3 marks)

Consult all the extracts.

  vi) Referring closely to specific extracts, explain what they reveal about the extent of criticism and opposition to Nicholas and his government by 1917. (6 marks)
      (Total 25 marks)

B. The 1917 Revolution. Causation

B.1. Study chart 6.6 Causes of the Russian Revolution.

This is one way of presenting factors contributing to the revolution. Other ways might be to establish a list of points in order of importance, or to divide points up into long term, medium term and immediate causes (precipitants or triggers) of revolution. A further way would be to organise points thematically, eg political, economic, social, military causes.

Rearrange the points (and any others you consider relevant) into one of these structures, or devise your own. Consider the advantages and disadvantages of the various methods of analysis.

B.2. Comparative analytical chart. 1905 and 1917 Revolutions.

It is often useful in history to make comparisons between similar events, for this helps one appreciate broad patterns and themes, as well as highlighting contrasts. It can also help deepen understanding of each event. An interesting question sometimes asked by examiners is why tsarism survived the revolution of 1905, but not that of 1917.

Probably the most important determinants of the outcome of any revolutionary crisis are:
a) the strength of the forces of unrest, and
b) the actions of the government and its normal supporters.

The context of such actions could also be crucial. In addition to these broad factors, there might be particular occurrences which spark off or precipitate a revolution.

i) Draw up and complete a comparative chart like that below.
ii) Use it as a basis for discussion, and for the concluding essay.

C. Concluding essay

Write one of the following essays:

i) How important was the First World War in causing the Russian Revolution of February 1917?
ii) Why did the tsarist regime survive the revolution of 1905 yet fall in 1917?

Advice In the first essay you must concentrate on a detailed discussion of points identified in the material above, especially charts 6.5. However, other issues, such as the state of Russia in 1914, and the contribution of other factors to revolution (chart 6.6), also need brief discussion.

The second essay is more challenging. In many ways, particularly if you take an 'optimistic' view of the 1906-14 period, you might have considered tsarism more deserving and more likely to be overthrown in 1905 than in 1917. On this view the First World War seems the crucial factor, but also consider the inadequacy of post 1905 'reformed' tsarism, and how this might have made Russians less prepared to give it another chance. Alternatively, some historians have suggested that if the various upper class conspirators of 1916-17 had been more organised they might have been able to preserve monarchical rule under a different tsar, and that the republic was set up almost by default. Such modifications to a more determinist interpretation (ie one that assumes that what did happen was bound to happen) can often be effective in essays.

Determinants	1905	1917
a) **Potential Revolutionary Forces** (identify grievances and actions) Workers Peasantry Middle classes National minorities Army Revolutionary parties		
b) **Behaviour, Actions of Government Forces** Nicholas II Government Ministers Aristocracy Army generals		
c) **General Situation** Military context (incl. length, nature, location of war) Economic context Political context		
d) **Precipitants**		

65

7 Economic Development

A Introduction

A study of economic development is vital to understand Tsarist Russia in the nineteenth century. The question of serfdom was a major issue during the first part of the century, and emancipation left many problems unsolved. From the 1880s, the government embarked on a policy of rapid industrialisation, which was seen as vital to maintain Russia's great power status. The strains arising from this combination of agrarian backwardness and industrial advance played a major part in the regime's eventual overthrow.

B Key areas to study

a) Industrialisation. Reasons for industrialisation. Its nature, and especially the role of the state and foreign capital.

b) Agricultural development. The effects of emancipation and the connection between industrialisation and agriculture.

c) The social and political effects of economic changes, especially against a background of rapid population growth.

d) The work of Witte and Stolypin, Tsarist Russia's two most notable modernisers (see chapter 9).

C Industrialisation. Problems of interpretation

This topic is a particularly controversial one for several reasons. Firstly, it is a political issue. Soviet historians tend partly to justify the later Communist Revolution by highlighting the inadequacies of tsarist government, and how it was incapable of developing Russia's economic or social potential. Conversely, some Western historians are nostalgic about Tsarist Russia before what they see as the tragedy of Lenin's usurpation of power, and the horrors of Stalin's forced economic transformation. Such historians are inclined to stress the promising features of tsarist industrialisation.

Secondly, the issue of modernisation, whether it is desirable and the best way of achieving it, is facing many Third World countries today. Various models can be constructed from Russian experience to justify particular current policies. Lastly, the nature of the available evidence is such that no definitive conclusions are likely to be reached. One must understand the sheer size of Russia, the diverse experience of various regions, and the problem of collecting accurate statistics and then interpreting them. This means that even if the topic had not been politicised, there would always be evidence that could be interpreted to substantiate differing conclusions. This should not discourage the student from entering the debate, but just make him or her more cautious about coming to firm conclusions.

The key aspects of the topic are illustrated in the accompanying charts, but here some central issues are briefly discussed.

D Industrialisation. The government's attitude

It was only in the 1880s that the government changed its initial attitude of hostility to industrialisation, being by then convinced that Russia's great power status could not be upheld without economic modernisation. Industrial development, slightly stimulated by emancipation and, far more so, by the growth of the railways, was already occurring, but it was the government's commitment to that process which helps explain the big upsurge of the 1880s.

Here it is important to realise that we are not dealing with the sort of coherent government policy that we may be accustomed to in other countries. There was no clear cabinet until Stolypin, and even he faced considerable opposition from within the government. The tsar appointed and dismissed ministers at will, and they frequently pursued policies in isolation from that followed by fellow ministers. There was, then, no collective ministerial agreement on issues such as industrialisation. Broadly, it can be said that whereas Ministers of Finance tended to favour industrialisation as a means of boosting the economy and eventually government revenue, Ministers of the Interior, concerned about the effects of such policies on social unrest, were more hostile. In addition, any minister favouring changes within Russia was likely to arouse opposition from the many reactionaries at court. It only needed a minor setback in a reformer's programme for them to influence the tsar into changing his ministers. The chief advocates of industrialisation in all reigns from Alexander II to Nicholas II were ousted in such a manner.

E Industrialisation. The role of the state

Tsarist Russia's industrialisation was much shaped by the traditions of Russia, even if inspired by the need to emulate Western Europe. Initiative in Russia traditionally came from the tsar rather than from below. This had been true of the first great Russian moderniser, Peter the Great, and was to be true of Russian industrialisation, both under the tsars, and later the communists. This was largely a reflection of the backward nature of the Russian economy, with little stimulus from below. The middle classes were weak, and the non-professional sectors were more interested in trade and commerce (often with foreign goods), than in production itself. The political considerations determining the nature of emancipation meant that the Russian peasantry was still largely controlled by the mir and tied to the countryside. This hindered the movement of surplus population into the towns. In addition, few prosperous estates developed, thus little capital for industrial investment was easily available, and there was a poor market for potential industrial goods. This meant that industrialisation developed under the auspices of the state rather than

Chart 7.1 Background to economic development

A. PROBLEMS HINDERING MODERNISATION

Economic

- Inefficient agriculture.
- Small home market.
- Lack of investment capital.
- Unstable currency (till 1880s).
- Scattered mineral resources.

Political

- Government dominated by conservative aristocracy.
- Elements in tsarist bureaucracy hostile to industrialisation as 'un-Russian', and afraid of proletariat.
- Unfavourable climate in government and administration; corrupt, inefficient bureaucracy.
- Ruling elite, concerned to prevent surplus rural population drifting to towns, were keen to preserve mir.

Geographical

- Scattered location of resources.
- Vast distances, poor communications.
- Harsh climate.
- Potential of rivers as trade routes reduced by freezing.

Social/Cultural

- Weak middle class, and lack of vigorous, enterprising attitude within it.
- Widespread scorn for trade. Capitalist ethic alien.
- Low commercial honesty, and underdeveloped regard for property rights.
- Charging interest on loans still regarded as usurious by some.
- Many businessmen more attracted to the quick profits from trade (often of foreign goods) than to the risks of production.

B. FACTORS BEHIND MODERNISATION

Diplomatic, military

a) Crimean Defeat
- Showed backwardness of Russia compared with France and Britain.
- Revealed need to modernise to maintain great power status.
- This reinforced by diplomatic defeat at Berlin Congress, 1878.

b) Rivals' Strength
- Rapid economic development of Britain and especially neighbouring Germany, showed need to match rivals.

Economic

a) Utilisation of Resources
- Need to develop own resources rather than rely on imports.
- Agricultural depression showed need to develop alternative sources of wealth.
- Railways vital to organise resources (exports, and military), but they needed development of industrial, banking structure.

b) Financial
- Economic advance would lead to increased wealth, and thus greater potential government revenue.

ie RUSSIA CONCERNED TO MAINTAIN HER GREAT POWER STATUS.

---

autonomously (ie in its own way, without artificial stimulation). In addition, given the low base from which railway and industrial development had to commence, and the perceived need for speed, great dependence had to be put on non-Russian resources.

F Industrialisation. Tariff and tax policy

The government helped industrialisation by its tax policy (see chart 7.2). High tariffs on imports, and high indirect taxes helped raise revenue to balance the budget to inspire confidence in Russia abroad, and attract foreign loans. These were needed as the government could not afford to spend much directly on industry as other demands were so high, eg defence, administration, railways and interest payments on previous debts, especially those incurred during the 1855, 1877 and 1904 wars.

These high taxes also served to force peasants to bring their grain to the market to sell to meet their tax burden. Much of this grain would then be exported to help pay for imports of machinery, and to service Russia's foreign loans.

The cost of such a policy, however, was not just social in terms of the excessive burdens placed on the Russian people, it also served to limit their capacity to buy goods, ie it harmed the domestic market.

G Industrialisation and the middle class

As a result of the large role of the state in the economy, Russian industrialisation did not, as it did in the rest of Europe, particularly Britain, lead to the growth of a powerful, commercial, industrial middle class. This was to have tremendous political consequences. For it meant that the liberal element within Russia remained centred on the professions in the universities and zemstva, and was not greatly deepened by commercial, industrial interests. The use of large numbers of foreign experts, and of Western financial resources slowed the rate of development of an indigenous (native) bourgeoisie. The political aspirations of those Russian industrialists who did exist were further deadened by the heavy dependence of their growing enterprises on the state. This made them less critical of tsarist absolutism, a trait reinforced by their frequent dependence on the state's forces to maintain their workers' acceptance of poor living conditions.

H Industrialisation and agriculture

In contrast to the dramatic development of Russia's industry, her agriculture in the nineteenth century was characterised by considerable continuity, despite the apparently major change of emancipation (see chapter 3). This had failed to solve the rural question, and agriculture remained backward and poor. Yet it still had a major part to play in Russian industrialisation; for though this was not to be built upon the ground of rural prosperity, it was to be financed at the cost of rural misery. Given the need for the state to attract foreign capital, agriculture had a vital role to play as a source of tribute. With the brief and partial exception of Bunge who reduced direct taxes and tried, but failed, to stimulate agricultural prosperity, Russian Finance Ministers saw peasants as, chiefly, a source of revenue. Put bluntly, the peasant was forced to pay for industrialisation. His 'surplus' grain was needed for export, and his 'wealth' for taxation. Both were equally illusory, but the state apparatus extracted grain and money payments from the peasant population, even at the cost of starvation.

Even the timing of payments to the state was harmful to the peasantry. They were collected in autumn when grain was plentiful and prices low (so the amount of grain needed to raise the money for tax payments was thus high). This often meant that by the spring the peasants had run out of grain, and now had to buy some (when shortages made prices high). The position of the peasantry was further worsened by the depressed grain prices of the late nineteenth century (due chiefly to the opening up of the American prairies) which limited the income of those peasants who did produce a surplus, and meant more grain had to be sold to meet tax demands.

Russian industrialisation, designed to buttress the autocracy, thus directly contributed to the growing pressure on the peasantry that finally erupted in 1905. The government had tried to prevent unrest from peasants drawn into industrial cities, but instead created it on a more massive scale in the countryside itself. It was only then that the government under Stolypin was forced to address the peasant question (see p52).

I Industrialisation. The contradictions

Several historians have identified what they see as major contradictions in tsarist industrialisation. Firstly, the policy was designed to buttress tsarism, both domestically and internationally. However, the process of industrialisation created forces potentially threatening to its position. For it created a discontented, volatile proletariat, an increasingly impoverished peasantry, and lastly, though least importantly for reasons explained above, a middle class. All these groups were in 1905 and 1917 to challenge autocracy. In addition, industrialisation required, and indeed was accompanied by, an increase in educational provision at all levels, and this too served to foster groups and attitudes potentially critical of tsarism.

Christian has talked of the terrible dilemma facing the government: 'industrial growth was needed if Russia were to remain an independent nation, yet industrial growth seemed bound to generate revolutionary upheavals. During its final decades, the tsarist government tried but failed to find a safe path between the twin dangers of backwardness and revolution.'
(*Power and Privilege* pp.78-79)

Secondly, and this point is not universally accepted, Kemp and other Marxists have argued that Russia's reliance on European capital for funds for industrialisation constrained her freedom in international affairs, (rather than strengthening her diplomatically, as intended). This eventually served to bind her more closely to France which helped lead to Russia's disastrous involvement in the First World War.

Worksection 7 part 1

A. Factors behind, and requirements for industrialisation

A.1. Group debate on whether to industrialise.

i) Divide into groups.

ii) Draw up a list of points for and against Russia industrialising, from the view point of the tsarist government in the 1880s.

iii) After completing this, compare your ideas with chart 7.1 which covers this issue.

iv) Next allocate roles, and hold an imaginary discussion within the Russian ruling group as to whether Russia should industrialise or not.
Possible roles:
Minister of the Interior
War Minister
Finance Minister
Head of Holy Synod
Tsar.
(You might want to be particular ministers, eg Witte, Pobedonostsev.)

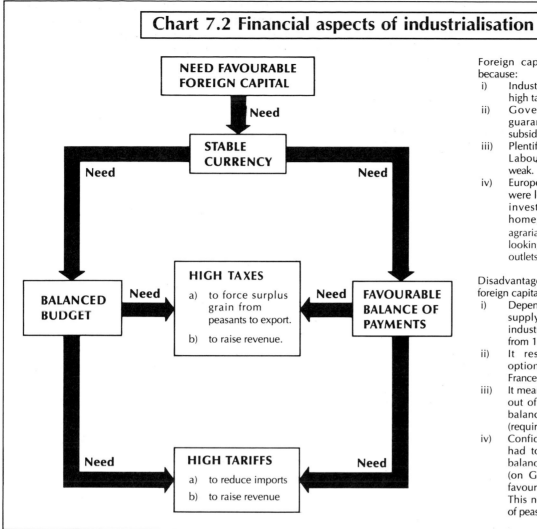

Chart 7.2 Financial aspects of industrialisation

NEED FAVOURABLE FOREIGN CAPITAL

↓ **Need**

STABLE CURRENCY

Need ← → **Need**

BALANCED BUDGET → **Need** → **HIGH TAXES**
a) to force surplus grain from peasants to export.
b) to raise revenue.

Need ← **FAVOURABLE BALANCE OF PAYMENTS**

Need **HIGH TARIFFS** **Need**
a) to reduce imports
b) to raise revenue

Foreign capital attracted to Russia, because:
i) Industry could develop behind high tariff barriers.
ii) Government support, eg guaranteed dividends, profits, subsidies, orders etc.
iii) Plentiful, cheap labour in Russia. Labour organisations initially weak.
iv) European domestic interest rates were low, and there were limited investment opportunities at home, especially in largely agrarian France. So money was looking for alternative investment outlets.

Disadvantages of Russia's reliance on foreign capital:
i) Dependence on European money supply fluctuations, eg Russian industry hit by money shortages from 1899 onwards.
ii) It restricted her diplomatic options, eg diplomatic ties to France.
iii) It meant dividends had to be sent out of Russia, causing potential balance of payments problems (requiring massive grain exports).
iv) Confidence of foreign investors had to be maintained, by, eg, balancing budget, secure rouble (on Gold Standard 1897), and favourable balance of payments. This necessitated heavy taxation of peasants.

A.2. Construction of an analytical chart on requirements for industrialisation.

Here is a list of some of the possible vital requirements for a country attempting to industrialise:

raw materials
prosperous agriculture
labour force
capital
entrepreneurial talent

sympathetic government
technology
growing home market
good communications
political stability

  i) Add any more aspects you consider important.
  ii) Draw up a chart as shown below, briefly indicating whether Russia possessed the requirements identified above, and if she didn't, how she overcame this handicap.

Requirement	Present in Russia	Action taken

A.3. Re-read section F above and study chart 7.2, Financial Aspects of Industrialisation, then answer the following questions.

  i) Why did Russia need foreign capital?
  ii) Why would foreign capital be more readily available if Russia had a stable currency?

  iii) Explain in what two ways confidence in a strong rouble could be maintained.
  iv) In what two ways could Russia's balance of trade be improved? (How could high taxes on peasants help Russia's exports?)
  v) What two sources of revenue could be used to help the government balance its budget?
  vi) Explain how the peasantry was adversely affected by the government's strategy.

B. Nature and effects of economic developments

B.1. Contemporary views.

Read pages 66-68, and the following comments on economic developments.

  i) Explain each statement. (For extract (b), consider: Why would peasants be taking grain to market in autumn? Why would they be buying some back in spring? Why would prices then be higher?)
  ii) What is the connection between the statements?

a) Finance Minister Vyshnegradsky:
'Let us go hungry, but export.' (Quoted by Willets, in ed. Katkov, G. (1972) *Russia enters the Twentieth Century* p.123). **Continued on page 71.**

Chart 7.3 Russia's economic development

A. Trends

1850s. Early growth, especially of railways, stimulated by the shock of Crimean defeat.

1860s. Free trade policies helped expansion, using imported raw materials and machinery.

1870s. Growth disrupted by general European economic problems.

1877. End of liberal tariffs; move to high tariffs, culminating in 1891 in the very high 'monster tariff.'

1890s. Great spurt, ie 8% p.a., associated with Witte. State played major role.

1900s. Slump, due to
- i) general European depression, and retraction of foreign investment,
- ii) government limited its involvement due to financial difficulties,
- iii) exhaustion of tax-paying capacity of the peasantry,
- iv) series of bad harvests,
- v) lack of internal market.

1906 onwards. Renewed spurt, with expanding domestic market. 6% growth p.a.

B. Key Ministers in Russian economic development

Bunge. (Finance Minister, 1881-87). Reduced tax burden on peasantry to try and stimulate economy. Tried to balance budget, but failed due to high military expenditure.

Vyshnegradsky. (Finance Minister, 1887-1892). Boosted industry by establishing budget surplus and strong gold reserves to encourage investment in industry. Meant squeezing peasantry, especially by very high tariffs. This contributed to 1891 famine, and his dismissal.

Witte. (Finance Minister, 1892-1903). State played great role.

Stolypin. (Interior Minister, 1906-1911). Introduced major agrarian reforms.

C. Chief characteristics of Russian industrialisation

i) Role of state.
- Government played key role, as a substitute for natural pressures for economic development which were lacking due to Russia's backwardness.
- Role in
  a) direct investment, ownership to provide capital,
  b) loans, subsidies to industry,
  c) guaranteed profits to private investors and companies,
  d) government orders for products,
  e) economic policies to maintain budget surplus and a favourable balance of payments to attract foreign loans and investment.

ii) Role of foreign capital.
- Needed as substitute for lack of sufficient indigenous investment capital.
- Foreign private investment in companies in Russia. eg in the 1890s foreigners invested on average 100m. roubles p.a., compared to 36m by Russians. In 1910 over 50% of capital invested in heavy industry was foreign.
- Foreign loans to Russian state to help finance government expenditure. In 1914 nearly half of Russia's debts of 8,800m roubles were foreign.

iii) Squeezing of peasantry.
- Grain squeezed from peasantry (via state tax burden, ie poll tax till 1885, redemption payments, land tax, and especially high tariffs and indirect taxes on necessities):
  a) to provide 'surplus' for export to maintain favourable balance of payments, and pay for needed machinery imports,
  b) to raise revenue needed for government financial assistance to industry, and to balance budget,
  c) to feed growing urban population.
- Role of peasantry as potential market neglected (except by Bunge) till Stolypin reforms 1906 onwards.

iv) Large scale, modern industry.
- The most modern technology could be used, as:
  a) large state and foreign capital available,
  b) foreign equipment imported.
- Thus Russia benefited from the 'advantage of backwardness'.
- Large scale units, eg in 1900 30% of factories had over 1000 workers, 43% of coal was produced from 4% of all mines.
- BUT, these large, modern plants co-existed with a mass of small, handicraft industries.

v) Role of railways.
As elsewhere, railways played a major role:
- Boosted industry generally, especially coal, iron, steel.
- Greatly helped by government, via grants, orders, guarantees.
- But strategic considerations also influenced their location.

vi) Role of banks and cartels.
- Helped channel middle class savings into industry.
- Assisted, with the state, the development of cartels (combinations of firms), eg Prodameta in metallurgy, Prodvagon in rolling stock.

Chart 7.3 *continued*

D. Effects of industrialisation	Linked to state, but still possible friction with auto-cracy. – Exploitation of peasantry worsened rural misery, and population rise exceeded flow into industry. iii) Political. Above developments had dangerous political implications. – Increased number potentially hostile to tsarism, especially socialist inclined proletariat. Also liberal minded bourgeoisie, and discontented peasantry. – Modernising economy called into question the maintenance of an outdated political structure.	iv) Military. – Growth of industry and railways boosted Russia's military capacity. – Allowed her to resist might of industrial Germany 1914-17 (contrast to Crimea); but, – Financial precedence given to industrialisation may have diverted some resources from military. v) Diplomatic. – Need for French financial resources influenced Russia's foreign policy; – The 1905 attempted Bjorko Treaty with Germany was unworkable as it upset France. – Factor behind growing commitment to France and entry into war 1914, but arguably not a major one.
i) Economic. Massive growth in industry led to: a) increased production, b) increased growth rate, c) raised Russia's status in world. ii) Social. – Proletariat doubled between 1865 and 1890. By 1900, over 2 million. Volatile mixture of 'hereditary proletarians' and recent peasant recruits. – Poor conditions in rapidly expanding cities, with few social amenities. – Growth of middle class, but due to role of state and foreigners, less powerful than one might expect.		

Worksection 7 part 1 *continued*

b) A peasant taking grain to market in autumn:
   'Don't be sorry, Mother Rye, that my path is city-wards. In the spring I will overpay; but I will take thee back.'
(Quoted by Christian, D. (1986), *Power and Privilege* pp. 90-91)

c) Prince Kropotkin:
   'Misery and famine have become the normal state of society . . . It is the peasant of one third of Russia dying of diphtheria, typhus, of hunger from hardship, amidst piles of grain making their way abroad.'
(Quoted by Kochan, M and L. (1967), *Russian Themes* p.15)

iii) Tolstoy commented that Russia 'was the only country in the world where Ghengis Khan enjoys the use of the telephone'.
(Quoted by Wood, A. (1987), *Origins of the Russian Revolution* p.8). Explain what he meant by this.

B.2. Study chart 7.4

i) How vital was the South West to Russia's economic development?
ii) How effective was the Trans-Siberian railway in opening up the Far East? What criticism could be made of it?
iii) What evidence does the map provide of the role of foreigners in Russia's development?

B.3. Contemporary evidence on Russian industrialisation.

Read the following sources, and then answer the questions which follow.

Extracts (a) and (b) are from Witte's Memorandum on Industrial Development 1899:

a) 'The economic relations of Russia to Western Europe are fully comparable to the relations of colonial countries with their metropolises. The latter consider their colonies as advantageous markets in which they can freely sell the products of their labour and of their industry, and from which they can draw with a powerful hand the raw materials necessary for them . . . Russia was, and to a certain extent still is, such a hospitable colony for all industrially developed states, generously providing them with the cheap products of her soil and buying dearly the products of their labour. But there is a radical difference between Russia and a colony: Russia is an independent and strong power. She has the right and the strength not to want to be the handmaiden of states which are more developed economically.'
(Quoted by Christian, D. (1986), *Power and Privilege* p.83)

b) 'Of all the charges against the economic policy of Russia, the minister of finance is most keenly aware of the following: that because of the tariff, a Russian pays for many items considerably more than the subjects of other countries . . . that the cost of living also grows for both rich and poor; and that the paying powers of the population are strained to the utmost, so that in many cases consumption is directly curtailed. The minister of finance recognises that the customs duties fall as a particularly heavy burden upon the impoverished landowners and peasants, particularly in a year of crop failure. These imposts are a heavy sacrifice made by the entire population, and not from surplus but out of current necessities.'
(Quoted by Christian, D, (1986), *Power and Privilege* p.90)

Continued on page 74.

Chart 7.4 Economic development

1 GERMANY
- Neighbouring state, undergoing massive economic advance.

2 POLAND
- Major industries, ie. coal, iron, textiles, chemicals.

3 ODESSA
- Major expanding port for grain exports.
- 1890 - 1910. Population quadrupled.

4 STRAITS
- Vital route for Russian grain and oil exports.
- 1913. 90% of grain exports used this route.

5 CENTRAL ASIA
- Newly acquired cotton fields developed from 1860s to supplement imports of raw cotton.
- 1880s. Production greatly boosted by improved railway links.

6 UKRAINE
- Major agricultural and industrial area.
- 1880s. Rapid expansion of new industries, especially because of railways.
- 1885. Railway linking Donets coal and Krivoi Rog iron ore.
- Ukraine replaced Urals as chief iron area; larger units, more advanced technology.
- Sugar beet developed as major agricultural industry from 1820s.
- By 1914, area produced 72% of Russia's iron ore, 70% coal, 57% steel.

7 DONETS COAL
- Major expansion.
- 1870   42,000tns
  1880   920,000tns
  1890   2,370,000tns

8 HUGHES AND EKATERINOSLAV
- 1871. Welsh industrialist Hughes set up New Russian Coal, Iron and Railway Company at Ekaterinoslav.
- Expanded by supplying rail orders for government.
- By 1884 biggest pig iron producer.
- New town named after him (Yuzhovska, now Donetsk). By 1904, 30,000 Welshmen employed in mines.
- Introduced new technology; had a demonstration effect.
- Shows role of foreign expertise.

9 BAKU
- Originally a fishing village, transformed into centre of oil industry, with 90% of output.
- Developed by Swedish Nobel brothers 1870s onwards, and then the French Rothschilds.
- Nobels built world's first oil tanker (in Stockholm) for Caspian Sea.

10 BAKU-BATUM RAILWAY 1883
- Allowed oil exports.

11 TRANS-SIBERIAN RAILWAY
- Chiefly constructed 1891 -1902: through route to Vladivostock only completed in 1917.
- 6400 km long. Journey took 13 days.
- Witte's prestige project, financed by government.
- Great hopes to:
  - boost heavy industry,
  - encourage French investors,
  - open up remote resources, especially coal, gold, timber,
  - encourage migration to Siberia (1903-1913, 1 million did so),
  - galvanise entire Siberian region,
  - channel China's commerce overland through Russia, not seawards.
- All except the last hope achieved to some extent, but,
- Construction standards poor, costs high,
- Not greatly used when first opened,
- Trebilcock calls it a 'monster devoid of purpose.'

16 OIL
- Developed from 1870s; in 1880s fastest growing industry.
- Taken by shiptanker, rail, river throughout European Russia.
- 1900. Russia the world's leading oil producer, (1897 - 1901, produced more than rest of world), but by 1913 only 1/3 of USA production.
- Oil (Kerosene) widely used, especially for lighting by peasants.

17 IRON
- By 1890s old Urals centre being overtaken by more modern Ukraine.

18 COAL
- Early on, most coal imported.
- Major expansion when 1880s railways helped open up Donets basin.

12 URALS
- Coal, iron, metallurgy.
- Old centre established by Peter the Great.
- Small scale units, largely serf labour till 1860s.
- Major exporter in 18th century, but during 19th century declined comparatively.
- Backward technology, ie. charcoal burning, and problems with timber supplies; no puddling till 1830s.
- Remote, costly transport.

13 MOSCOW
- Old area expanding.
- Textile, metal processing, chemicals.
- Knoop of Manchester presided over the modernisation of the textile industry.

14 ST. PETERSBURG
- Old area expanding
- Textiles, engineering (30,000 in Putilov works), metallurgy.
- Free trade policy of 1860s encouraged import of materials, machinery.
- The Jersey's of Manchester, and Mather and Platt of Oldham developed modern spinning methods.
- Siemans of Germany installed electric telegraph system, and built their own engineering works.

15 TEXTILES
- New industry, greatly expanded in 19th century.
- Initially relied on imported American raw cotton, and British thread.
- Assisted by Alexander II's free trade policies, and 1842, Britain's lifting of ban on the export of textile machinery.
- From 1860s, increasing use of raw cotton from Central Asia.
- 1890s. Production doubled; biggest industrial employer (1904 600,000 workers).

- Coal played key role in development of South, ie. metallurgy, railways, sugarbeet.

KEY

Ⓘ Four chief industrial areas, including 60% of all industrial workers, over half in factories over 1000 workers.

| COAL | Resource opened up by Trans-Siberian Railway.

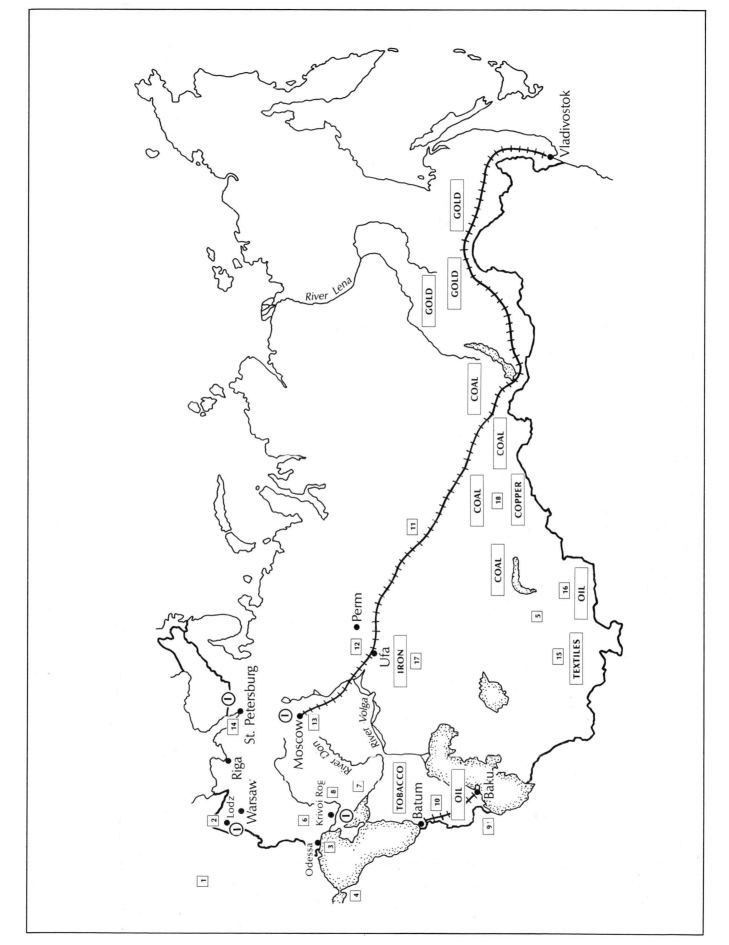

c) Extracts from the 1902 annual report to their Emperor from General Lobko, the state comptroller (minister responsible for surveying government expenditure):

'At present there is no more doubt that the crisis is caused by the artificial and excessive growth of industry in recent years. Industry, based on the protective tariff, extensive government orders, and the speculative increase of cheap foreign capital, grew out of proportion to the development of the consumer's market, which consists chiefly of the mass of the agricultural population, to which eighty per cent of our population belongs. An entirely sound existence for industry is guaranteed only by a corresponding development of the domestic market representing a sufficiently broad and constant demand for manufactured goods. That condition is particularly important for a young industry developing under the influence of protective tariffs, as it is in no position to count on the international market. Furthermore, the economic condition of our agriculture cannot be called satisfactory. The strenuous efforts of the government to plant industries has not been accompanied by equally intensive measures for the support and raising of the agricultural base of the welfare of the Russian people. In view of the inadequacy of the government measures the negative sides of the protective system show up all the more strongly in the agricultural population. The chief burden of that system lies undoubtedly upon the agricultural mass, seriously impairing its purchasing power. It has to bear almost the entire burden of direct and indirect taxes. As a result the demand of our domestic market cannot keep up with the excessive growth of our industry. The equilibrium between industry and the domestic market has been destroyed and with it the basis of successful economic development. This, according to my deepest conviction, constitutes the chief cause of the present difficulties.'

(Quoted by Kochan, L. (1967), *Russia in Revolution* pp.32-3)

Extract (a)

i) With what does Witte liken Russia in order to argue for industrialisation? Would this be a powerful argument in tsarist circles? (2 marks)

ii) Witte here is criticising Russia's dependence on European countries, yet that dependence increased as part of his policy. How can this be explained? (What was he using foreign expertise to do?) (2 marks)

Extract (b)

iii) What does this extract show about Witte's awareness of the effects of his policies? (2 marks)

iv) Why, despite the criticism, did he follow such policies? (2 marks)

v) Look at chart 7.3. Which other tsarist minister had called for sacrifices for the sake of building up Russia's economic strength? (1 mark)

vi) Were there any counterbalancing benefits for the Russian people

a) in the short term, b) in the long term? (2 marks)

vii) What were the dangers of such an approach? (2 marks)

Extract (c)

viii) Why does Lobko describe Russia's industrial growth as 'artificial'? (1 mark)

ix) For what reason does Lobko infer foreign capital is attracted to Russia? Were there other reasons? (3 marks)

x) Why does Lobko stress the need for a domestic market, and what is harming this? How does he imply the domestic market should be improved? (4 marks)

xi) Why might a general be interested in economic development? (1 mark)

xii) How powerful do you consider this criticism of Russian industrialisation? What did the government do after 1905 to try and improve the domestic basis of her economic growth? (see p.78) (3 marks)

C. Statistics on Russia's economic development

C.1. Interpretation of statistics on Russia's economic performance.

Study section A of chart 7.5 which contains two ways of presenting figures on Russia's economic growth. Then answer the questions which follow.

Industry

i) In which decades did industry expand fastest? (2 marks)

ii) Do any of the other figures help explain why iron production increased so rapidly? (2 marks)

iii) Compare the figures for population and industrial production. What might this suggest about the productivity of Russian industry? This is even better illustrated by comparing figures for urban population and industry; why? (3 marks)

Agriculture

iv) Over the period 1861-1913, as a whole, did agricultural production keep up with population growth? (2 marks)

v) What do the figures suggest about the economic effect of a) emancipation b) Stolypin's agrarian reforms? (See chart 7.8.) (4 marks)

vi) Do the figures prove that Stolypin's reforms were working? Explain (3 marks)

vii) What indication, if any, do they give of why Russia suffered from periodic famines in the nineteenth century, especially in 1891? (2 marks)

viii) Apart from figures for population and agricultural production, which other figures in the diagrams need to be considered when explaining:

a) the deaths from food shortages that occured, (2 marks)

b) the need for Russia to further improve her agriculture? (2 marks)

Continued on page 77.

Chart 7.5 Statistics on Russian Economic Development

A. Charts on rate of growth

a) Index number of economic growth 1861-1913

Year	Total ind A	Total agric B	Pop C	Urban pop D	Volume of grain exports E	Railways length F	Iron G	Govt revenue H
1861	1.00	1.00	1.00	1.00	1.00	1.00	1.00	1.00
1871	1.49	1.11	1.16	2.12	2.42	6.18	1.33	1.25
1881	2.52	1.12	1.36		3.59	10.50	1.67	1.60
1891	3.99	1.17*	1.62		5.04	13.95	3.33	2.19
1896	5.33	1.96	1.70	4.25	6.47	17.95	5.33	3.36
1901	7.50	1.81	1.83		7.40	25.64	9.67	4.41
1906	8.10	1.89	1.99		7.25	28.91	9.00	5.57
1913	11.65	3.09	2.32	6.96	7.83	31.91	14.00	8.38

b) Russian economic growth 1861-1913.

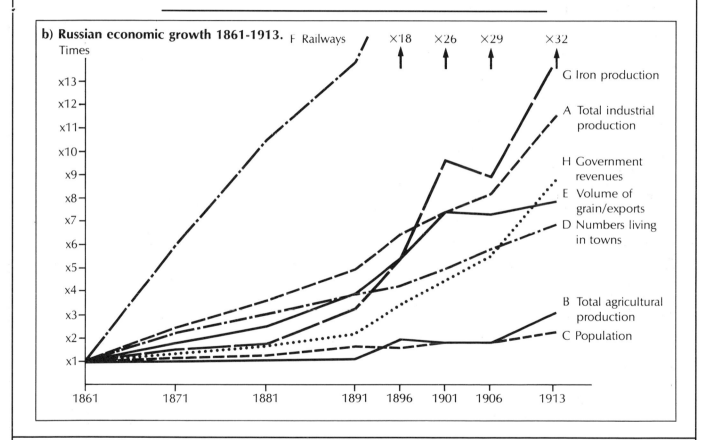

B. Foreign trade

a) Composition

Exports Percentage of total (1913) (by value)

Foodstuffs (mainly cereal, also sugar, meat, butter)	55%
Raw materials, animal products, and semi-manufactures (mainly timber, oil, flex, pelts)	39%
Manufactures chiefly to Asian, Baltic countries	6%

Imports

Industrial raw materials (eg cotton, wool, rubber, coal, iron)	50%
Finished goods, industrial machinery	30%

Russia was the world's largest importer of industrial machinery.)

b) Balance of trade (figures in millions of roubles)

Year	Exports	Imports	Balance
1861-70	222.7	225.9	-3.2
1871-80	454.8	488.2	-33.4
1881-90	622.2	471.8	+150.4
1891-1900	659.8	535.4	+124.4
1901-1910	1073.1	887.4	+185.7

C. International comparison

a) National Income (1913)

Per Capita National Income in gold roubles (about 10 to £).

USA	682	France	355	Italy	210	Russia	101
GB	505	Germany	300	Austria-Hungary	175	Bulgaria	97

b) Production

Comparative production of major industries in million tons (1914).

	Russia	France	Germany		USA	GB	Russ rank
coal	36	40	190	coal	517	292	5
pig iron	4.6	5.2	16.8	pig iron	31	10.4	5
steel	4.8	4.6	18.3	steel	31.8	7.8	4
*cotton	0.36	0.16	0.38	*cotton	1.04	0.74	3
oil	9.1	0	0	oil	33.1	0	2

*raw cotton consumed (1910)

Other industrial comparisons

Production of machines (1913) (as % of world production)		Electrical industry (1913) (as % of world production)		Alcohol production (1913) (In thousands of hectolitres)	
USA	50%	Germany	35%	Russia	5,196
Germany	35%	USA	29%	Germany	3,753
Britain	12%	Britain	16%	USA	3,659
Russia	3%	France	4%	France	2,954
Aus-Hung	3%	Aus-Hung	3%		
France	2%	Russia	2%		

c) Significance of industrial sector

Contribution of industry to GNP (gross national product) (1910)

Russia	30%
Austria-Hungary	47%
Germany	70%
Britain	73%

Proportion of National Product (1909-13) in Agriculture and Industry (Figures for 1880 in brackets).

	Agriculture	Industry
Britain	(11) 6	(40) 34
France	(41) 30	(30) 36
Germany	(36) 25	(32) 43
Italy	(57) 42	(15) 22
Russia	(66) 58 %	(14) 28 %

d) Output per head

Between 1860 and 1910 Russia failed to improve her ranking in terms of industrial output per head. She fell from 9th to 10th, below Italy.

e) Growth rate per annum (1880-1913)

Germany	3.75%
Russia	3.5%
USA	2.75%
UK	1.0%

f) Value of foreign trade (1913) (in million £)

Britain	1,223
Germany	1,030
France	424
Aus-Hung	199
Russia	190
Turkey	67

Chart 7.5 *continued*

g) Communications

i) Railways
Length of track (km) (1913)

USA	411,000
Russia	70,156
Germany	63,378
Aus-Hung	44,748
France	40,770
Britain	36,004

Comparative densities of networks (km of track per 100 square km of territory).

Russia	1
Germany	12
Aus-Hung	7
France	10
Britain	12

ii) Registered merchant ships (1910) (thousand tons)

Britain	1,556 (1)
Germany	2,890
France	1,452
Russia	723 (2)
Aus-Hung	414

(1) (only 10% sailing ships)
(2) (over half sailing ships)

h) Population

Population Size (1911) (in millions) (1860 in brackets)		Birth rate per 1000 (1913) (1860 in brackets)		Death rate per 1000 (1913) (1860 in brackets)	
Russia	160.7 (74)	Russia	43 (50)	Russia	27 (35)
Germany	64.9 (36.2)	Aus-Hung	32 (40)	Aus-Hung	20 (27)
Aus Hung	49.5 (35.5)	Italy	31 (38)	Italy	18 (31)
Britain	40.8 (23.1)	Germany	27 (36)	Germany	19 (23)
France	39.6 (37.4)	Britain	24 (36)	Britain	14 (21)
Italy	34.7 (25.0)	France	18 (26)	France	18 (21)

i) Agriculture (see chart 7.7)

D. Other indications of development

Education
a) Proportion of Population attending educational institutions (1910).

	Primary %	Secondary %	University %
Brit	14.9	0.46	0.07
Fra	14.5	0.33	0.11
Germ	15.9	1.56	0.11
Aus-H	14	0.46	0.10
Italy	9.7	0.47	0.08
Spain	7.7	0.24	0.10
Russia	5.2	0.39	0.07

b) Literacy (see also chart 6.4)
Statistics particularly unreliable, but Trebilcock gives the following figures for the proportion of literate bridegrooms/military recruits.

Prussia	90%	1855	Italy	50%	1886
England	80%	1870		70%	1907
France	80%	1873	Russia	30%	1892
				60%	1907

(Figures mainly taken from Trebilcock (1981) *The Industrialisation of the Continental Powers* 1780-1914, Falkus (1970) *The Industrialisation of Russia 1700-1914*, and Christian (1986) *Power and Privilege*.).

Government policy

ix) Compare the figures for government revenue and population rise. Given that most of this revenue came from indirect and direct taxation, what does this suggest about government tax policy, and its effects on the people? (2 marks)

x) What further evidence would the historian need to test this hypothesis? (2 marks)

General

xi) Which of the two diagrams (i or ii), presenting the same information in different ways, do you find most useful? Why? (2 marks)

xii) Study the following figures for coal production of two imaginary countries. Then answer the questions below.

Production	1890	1900	1910
Country A	10	50	100
Country B	100	170	250

a) Which country has the fastest growth rate over the period? (1 mark)

b) Which country has increased its production by the largest amount? (1 mark)

c) What has happened to the production gap between the two countries? (1 mark)

d) What is country A's growth rate for the period using 1890 as the base figure? (1 mark)

e) What is her growth rate (for the later period) if 1900 is used as the base figure? (1 mark)

xiii) Bearing the above exercise in mind, explain:
a) Why Russia had such great rates of growth 1860-1914. (2 marks)

b) Why the growth rate for railways was particularly high. (2 marks)

c) The significance of the choice of a particular base year for rates of growth. (2 marks)

d) Why, generally, historians must be cautious when dealing with growth rates. (2 marks)

xiv) Bearing in mind the above points about growth rates and base lines, was Russia's 6% p.a. growthrate of 1907-13 disappointing compared to her 8% growth p.a. of the 1890s? (3 marks)

Social effects

xv) Identify the various strains on Russian society that the figures in section A suggest. (3 marks)

xvi) What benefits, if any, might the Russian people gain from such economic growth? (3 marks) (Total 50 marks).

C.2. Study section B of chart 7.5, and read extract (a) from Witte's memo on page 71. Then answer the following questions.

i) Do the trade figures in section B support Witte's view of Russia as a semi-colony? If so, in what way? (4 marks)

ii) Why did Russia need to maintain a favourable balance of trade? (3 marks)

iii) Explain how successful she was in this respect. (3 marks) (Total 10 marks)

C.3. Consider section C of chart 7.5 on International Comparisons, then answer the following questions.

i) Would the Russian government be concerned about Russia's economic performance compared to that of other countries? Explain your answer. (3 marks)

ii) Why, despite her rapid industrial growth, do you think Russia failed to improve her ranking in ouput per head? (3 marks)

iii) Which of these statistics might a historian use if he/she were wishing to stress the economic backwardness of Tsarist Russia? Explain your answer. (3 marks)

iv) In which tables does Russia come out on top? Do these suggest the strength of the Russian economy? (3 marks)

v) Which are the more valuable railway statistics, those for length of track or density? What other railway statistics might be useful? (3 marks) (Total 15 marks).

D. Concluding Essay

Use of statistics.

Study chart 7.5 and 7.7 (on agriculture), and use the information in the charts, and the other material in this chapter, to write the following essay.

To what extent was Tsarist Russia a modern, industrialised power by 1914?

J   Agriculture

Examination of agriculture is vital for any study of Tsarist Russia. Well into the twentieth century over 80% of the population earned their living, wholly or in part, from the land. Two of the major reforms of the period, the Emancipation Edict and Stolypin's decrees were concerned with the position of Russia's agricultural masses. Yet despite this, most historians argue that the tsarist regime's agricultural policies were seriously flawed. Indeed, Trebilcock has argued that the government for much of the century developed no coherent policy for agriculture beyond that of 'to stagnate, to remain 'subservient, to render tribute.' (Trebilcock, C. (1981), *Industrialisation of the Continental Powers* p.250).

In truth, the agrarian question was very complex, involving far more than mere concern to assist farming. A vital consideration behind tsarist policy was the question of social control; the need to maintain order amongst Russia's peasant masses. This concern largely shaped the timing and nature of emancipation (see pages 18-20). Yet these social considerations served to hinder the improvement of agricultural efficiency. Similarly, the government's suspicion of mass education restricted a development which Japan showed could revolutionise peasant prosperity.

The agrarian question was further complicated when Russia embarked on her course of industrialisation, on the basis of inefficient agriculture, yet requiring the extraction of agricultural 'surplus' (see page 68). The vast peasant uprisings of 1902-6 showed that the regime had failed to maintain social cohesion. In addition, it was increasingly realised that the backwardness of Russian agriculture was preventing a securely based industrialisation (see page 74).

Whereas from the 1870s to 1905 agriculture suffered from neglect and comparative stagnation, after 1905 the agrarian question was at the centre of government policy. The Stolypin reforms were designed both to increase rural prosperity (thus stimulating industrial growth), and to restore order to the countryside by establishing a prosperous peasantry. Considerations of social control and economic advance seemed to point in the same direction. There is still, however, a vigorous debate over whether Stolypin's reforms did provide a sound base for a reinvigorated regime (see p. 52 and chart 7.8).

Eventually, under the pressures of war, tensions within Russia exploded. The peasantry exploited the collapse of the tsarist regime to impose their own long desired solution to the agrarian question, ie the seizure of gentry lands. Their satisfaction, however, was to be brief. In the 1930s the economic and political concerns of the Soviet regime led to a programme of forced collectivisation, probably the worst epoch in the sad history of the Russian peasantry. A solution to Russia's agrarian question remains to be found.

Chart 7.6 Agriculture in the late nineteenth century

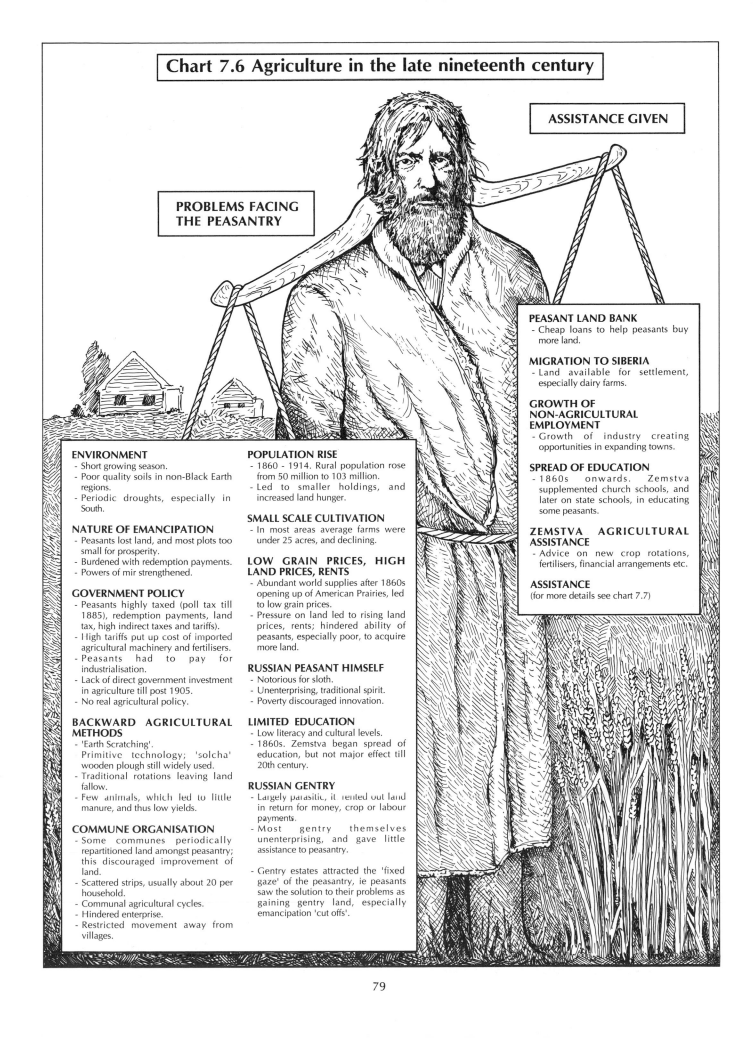

PROBLEMS FACING THE PEASANTRY

ENVIRONMENT
- Short growing season.
- Poor quality soils in non-Black Earth regions.
- Periodic droughts, especially in South.

NATURE OF EMANCIPATION
- Peasants lost land, and most plots too small for prosperity.
- Burdened with redemption payments.
- Powers of mir strengthened.

GOVERNMENT POLICY
- Peasants highly taxed (poll tax till 1885), redemption payments, land tax, high indirect taxes and tariffs).
- High tariffs put up cost of imported agricultural machinery and fertilisers.
- Peasants had to pay for industrialisation.
- Lack of direct government investment in agriculture till post 1905.
- No real agricultural policy.

BACKWARD AGRICULTURAL METHODS
- 'Earth Scratching'.
- Primitive technology; 'solcha' wooden plough still widely used.
- Traditional rotations leaving land fallow.
- Few animals, which led to little manure, and thus low yields.

COMMUNE ORGANISATION
- Some communes periodically repartitioned land amongst peasantry; this discouraged improvement of land.
- Scattered strips, usually about 20 per household.
- Communal agricultural cycles.
- Hindered enterprise.
- Restricted movement away from villages.

POPULATION RISE
- 1860 - 1914. Rural population rose from 50 million to 103 million.
- Led to smaller holdings, and increased land hunger.

SMALL SCALE CULTIVATION
- In most areas average farms were under 25 acres, and declining.

LOW GRAIN PRICES, HIGH LAND PRICES, RENTS
- Abundant world supplies after 1860s opening up of American Prairies, led to low grain prices.
- Pressure on land led to rising land prices, rents; hindered ability of peasants, especially poor, to acquire more land.

RUSSIAN PEASANT HIMSELF
- Notorious for sloth.
- Unenterprising, traditional spirit.
- Poverty discouraged innovation.

LIMITED EDUCATION
- Low literacy and cultural levels.
- 1860s. Zemstva began spread of education, but not major effect till 20th century.

RUSSIAN GENTRY
- Largely parasitic, it rented out land in return for money, crop or labour payments.
- Most gentry themselves unenterprising, and gave little assistance to peasantry.
- Gentry estates attracted the 'fixed gaze' of the peasantry, ie peasants saw the solution to their problems as gaining gentry land, especially emancipation 'cut offs'.

ASSISTANCE GIVEN

PEASANT LAND BANK
- Cheap loans to help peasants buy more land.

MIGRATION TO SIBERIA
- Land available for settlement, especially dairy farms.

GROWTH OF NON-AGRICULTURAL EMPLOYMENT
- Growth of industry creating opportunities in expanding towns.

SPREAD OF EDUCATION
- 1860s onwards. Zemstva supplemented church schools, and later on state schools, in educating some peasants.

ZEMSTVA AGRICULTURAL ASSISTANCE
- Advice on new crop rotations, fertilisers, financial arrangements etc.

ASSISTANCE
(for more details see chart 7.7)

A. Examining evidence on Russian agriculture

A.1. Statistical analysis.

Study the figures in chart 7.7, and answer the questions which follow. (Some useful precise references are given in brackets).

Production

Study the figures in section A.

i) What was happening during the late nineteenth century to:
  a) grain production,
  b) yields (output per area of land),
  c) productivity (output per head)?
  (3 marks)

ii) How was it possible for production to increase more than yields per acre? (2 marks)

iii) Look at (c) and (d). How did most Russian yields compare with those of other countries? (2 marks)

iv) Would you expect the most advanced agricultural country automatically to have the highest yields for every crop? Explain. (2 marks)

v) Are Russia's low yields necessarily a condemnation of the organisation of her agriculture? What other explanations could there be? (Refer to chart 1.3) (2 marks).

vi) Study (e) and (f). Why, despite her comparative inefficiency, was Russia still a major exporter of grain? (2 marks)

Agricultural methods

Study the figures in section B.

vii) Give at least three reasons why there was so little mechanisation in Russian agriculture. (Refer to information from sections B, C, D, E and F). (4 marks)

viii) Explain two ways industry could have helped agriculture. (2 marks)

Landholding

Study the figures in section D.

ix) What happened to the amount of land owned by the peasantry during the second half of the nineteenth century? (D.f) (1 mark)

x) What happened to the average size of a peasant's holding? (D.a) (1 mark)

xi) Which other set of figures in the chart explains this apparent paradox? (2 marks)

xii) Explain how peasant landholding could increase by more than the amount of land lost by the nobles. (D.f) (2 marks)

xiii) Did the average peasant have enough land to live off? (D.a,b) (2 marks)

xiv) How, then, did many peasants survive? (F.a) (2 marks)

xv) To what extent would giving peasants all the nobles' lands have ended their land hunger? (C.d. D.f,g) (3 marks)

Government policy

Study the figures in section E, and section D.d,e.

xvi) Use the information to assess the extent to which the government helped or hindered agriculture. (5 marks)

xvii) How important an advance does the evidence suggest the creation of the Peasant Land Bank was? (3 marks)
  (Total 40 marks)

A.2. Examining pictorial evidence.

Look at pictures A and B, below.

i) Explain the connection between them. (4 marks).

ii) 'Both are pieces of propaganda and so of no use to the historian.' To what extent do you agree with this comment? (6 marks)

A

'In this world there is a tsar. He is without pity. Hunger is his name.' Radical magazine, 1906.

B

Illustrated London News, 1891.

Continued on page 83.

Chart 7.7 Russian agricultural and rural society

Russian figures here have been converted into kilograms, tonnes and hectares. (For Russian measures see chart 1.2)

A. Production yields and exports

Production and yields

a) Grain harvest in million tonnes (3 year averages)

| 1861 | 28.2 | 1896 | 42.5 | 1881 | 33.9 | 1906 | 45.9 |
| 1871 | 32.9 | 1901 | 48.9 | 1891 | 34.4 | 1913 | 61.7 |

Between 1860-1913 overall output per head grew 1% per annum.

b) Trend of grain production related to rural population, European Russia, 1883-1914.

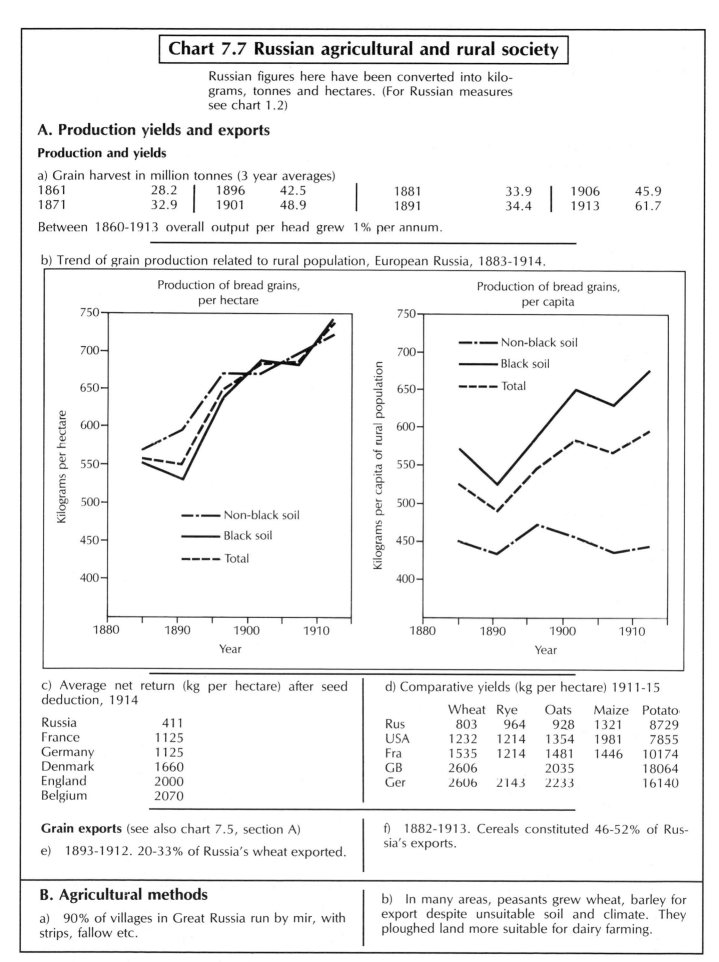

c) Average net return (kg per hectare) after seed deduction, 1914

Russia	411
France	1125
Germany	1125
Denmark	1660
England	2000
Belgium	2070

d) Comparative yields (kg per hectare) 1911-15

	Wheat	Rye	Oats	Maize	Potato
Rus	803	964	928	1321	8729
USA	1232	1214	1354	1981	7855
Fra	1535	1214	1481	1446	10174
GB	2606		2035		18064
Ger	2606	2143	2233		16140

Grain exports (see also chart 7.5, section A)

e) 1893-1912. 20-33% of Russia's wheat exported.

f) 1882-1913. Cereals constituted 46-52% of Russia's exports.

B. Agricultural methods

a) 90% of villages in Great Russia run by mir, with strips, fallow etc.

b) In many areas, peasants grew wheat, barley for export despite unsuitable soil and climate. They ploughed land more suitable for dairy farming.

Chart 7.7 *continued*

c) 1900   29%   no horse
             33%   only one horse
             25%   no cow
             50%   providing enough food for themselves
             16%   producing surplus

% (of 11 m European Russian peasant households)

d) 1892. A McCormick-reaper salesman covering about 10 provinces sold 1 binder, 21 mowers and 14 reapers.

e) 1911. European Russia had 66,000 reapers (West Siberia 36,000). European Russia 166 tractors (USA 14,000).

f) Production of artificial fertilisers, 1913.

Superphosphates	354,000 tons (less than Japan).
Basic slag	213,000 tons (less than Luxembourg).
Ammoniac fertilisers	26,000 tons (one third that of France).

C. Population

Numbers

a) 50 European provinces,   1860s 50m
                                1900   86m
                                1914 103m

b) 1860-1913. Proportion of population in agriculture fell from 90% to 85%.

c) 1860-97. Peasant population rose 50% from 50m to 79m.

Density

d) Estimates of surplus rural population by turn of century varied from 4 to 23 million, ie up to one quarter of total rural population.

e) Population density of main agricultural areas estimated at 3 to 8 times that of agricultural states of USA.

Migration to Siberia

f) 1861-1896   300,000
    1896-1905 1,300,000

g) In central, southern areas the natural population increase was 14 times greater than loss through migration.

D. Land holding

a) Average peasant holdings (in hectares)

	1860	1880	1890
Northern region	8.3	6.6	5.1
Central agric reg	3.9	2.7	2.2
Ukraine	3.6	2.7	1.9
South West	3.2	2.3	1.5

b) Estimated minimum land needed for survival:
6.5 hectares in Black Soil areas,
8.7 hectares in non-Black soil areas.

c) Average land prices rose 120% 1868-1897; in some fertile/congested areas far more.

d) Transfers via Peasant Land Bank (founded 1883, reorganised 1895)

1883-1895	sold	2.6m hectares to peasants
1896-1905		6.4m
1906-1913		9.2m

Stolypin transferred millions of acres of state lands to peasants via Land Bank.

e) With private banks' assistance, peasants bought 18.5 m hectares between 1877 and 1905.

f) Land held by Nobles, Peasantry (m hectares)

Date	Peasants	Nobles	State etc
1877	127 (31%)	102 (25%)	181 (44%)
1917 Jan	202 (47%)	69 (16%)	160 (37%)

g) Noble Land
1861 120m hectares
1905 79.3m
1914 35m (one tenth of arable land)

h) More extra land was being rented by peasants than bought. 1890s. Peasants rented 124m hectares, in return for increased money rents, share-cropping, and labour.

E. Government policy

a) A few financial concessions to peasantry, eg 1880s. Poll tax (paid by peasants alone) abolished; redemption dues lowered by 25%; 1883, 1894 some arrears written off, but no general reduction of debt.

b) Bunge introduced minor taxes on inheritance, commercial profits, investments; Vyshnegradsky considered income tax, (but not done until 1916).

c) Late 19th century. Proportion of taxes between direct and indirect was approximately 15: 85.

d) Sale of matches, vodka, tobacco, sugar, tea, kerosene (basic commodities for peasants) raised 5/6ths of revenue from indirect taxes.

e) High tariffs on imported fertilisers, agricultural implements, machines, livestock foodstuffs.

Chart 7.7 continued

f) 1860-1900
indirect taxes up 450%
direct taxes up 200%
population up 78%
(inflation very low)

g) 1883. Peasant Land Bank set up; advanced 25-50% cost of new land, at 5.5% interest, repayable over 24.5 or 34.5 years. Gentry Land Bank 1885 charged 4.5% interest; Lent twice as much as Peasant Bank.
1895. Peasant Land Bank reorganised; gave up to 100% loans, at lower interest, over extended pay back period.

h) Government initially favoured mir, but by 1900s policy being reassessed, and mir's powers reduced in 1903, just before major weakening of mir by Stolypin.

i) 1883. Government decree to establish system of lower agricultural schools; by 1888, 13 set up with total of 400 students; 1890, 43 agricultural schools with 2715 students; 3 agricultural colleges.

j) 1890s. Model farms set up in one third of zemstva districts to encourage improved methods and diversification.

k) 1889. Migration law; beginning of government help for migration, ie made easier to break from communal obligations, and financial help to those emigrating to Siberia.
1896. Resettlement Bureau in Ministry of Interior; helped spread literature about Siberia, especially opportunities for dairy farming.

l) Government expenditure on famine relief:
1891   444 million roubles
1901-1906   268 m.

F. Social Developments

Growth of wage labour

a)	1860	1913
In domestic Industry.	0.8m	3m
Agricultural wage labourers.	0.7m	4.5m
In Industry (factories, mines).	1.7m	6.9m
Other wage labour, eg transport, building.	0.9m	3.0m

Health

b) 1890. 64% peasant conscripts rejected as unfit.

c) Peasant consumption of wheat fell 20%, 1883-1896, to about three quarters below average for Western Europe. Many ate lower quality rye bread, not wheat.

d) Death rate rose from 24 per 1000 in early 19th century to 35 per 1000 by end of century, before falling. Higher in countryside than towns.

Literacy

e) 1897 census. 37% of males aged 25-59 illiterate. 1912. In rural population, 60% of males, 90% of women illiterate.

Indebtedness

f) 1876-1880. Direct tax arrears 22% of expected collections.
1896-1900. Direct tax arrears 119% of expected collections.
1903. Redemption arrears averaged 138%, ie in some areas the state was owed more in uncollected arrears from previous years than it proposed to raise in the current year.

(Figures mainly taken from Trebilcock (1981) *The Industrialisation of the Continental Powers* 1780-1914, Falkus (1970) *The Industrialisation of Russia 1700-1914,* and McCauley (1984) *From Octobrists to Bolsheviks).*

Worksection 7.2 continued.

A.3. Examining primary written evidence.

Read the following documents about Stolypin's reforms, then answer the questions which follow.

a) Nov 1906 Land Reform Decree.
'By Our Manifesto of 3 November 1905 redemption payments by peasants for allotment land were abolished as from 1 January 1907. From then on, those lands will be free from any restrictions imposed on them because of this payment and peasants will be granted the right to leave the commune freely, and individual households will be able to obtain part of the communal land stock as their own property . . .
We lay down the following regulations:
1. Each householder, holding allotment land from the commune, can at any time request that his share of this land be transferred to him as his private property . . .
12. Each householder who has had this land transfer-red to him as a result of the procedure in this law has the right to demand at any time that the commune should provide him with a single piece of land in exchange for his various separate pieces . . .
Whole communes, both those where land is held in communal tenure as well as those where it is held by individual tenure, may change to a system of consolidated holdings for each peasant, by a two-thirds majority of peasants eligible to vote at the village meeting.'
(Quoted by McCauley, M. (1984), *Octobrists to Bolsheviks* p.142-3)

b) Octobrist Golitsyn supports the reform Nov 1908.
'This edict of 9 November results from the eventual recognition of the need to discuss the question of our decrepit and obsolete forms of land ownership, to rescue our millions of peasants from the stagnant swamp of the commune, from general ignorance, lack of culture and inertia . . . which provides a

fertile ground for all kinds of propaganda . . . The defenders of the commune . . . support the belief that there is a great reserve of land available . . . which has been discussed in connection with the problems of land shortage and additional provision through compulsory expropriation (taking over of gentry land) . . . If we finally succeed in dispelling this belief in land being available, this will be recognised as one of the Third Duma's great services to history . . . Whilst the peasantry retain this belief, no educational or cultural measures will make them introduce improved methods of cultivation on their own lands. Whilst there is other land close by, there will always be an urge, impermissible in a cultured state, to appropriate it and this will make the peasant eye these lands greedily. There will not be sufficient stimulus for him to improve his own lands to produce benefits for himself.'
(Quoted by McCauley, M. (1984), *Octobrists to Bolsheviks* pp.144-5)

c) Representatives of the Moscow Zemstvo to the Committee on the Needs of Agriculture.

'The peasant is unable to understand why so little land was given to him at Emancipation. In many cases he believes that his allotment is small not because of the provisions of the Emancipation Act, but because he received less than he was entitled to.'
(Quoted by Florinsky, M. (1961), *End of the Russian Empire* p.187)

d) Peshekhonov, *'The Land Needs of the Village.'*

'"We need more land", this is the fundamental theme of the majority of statements made by peasants to the Committees of the Needs of Agriculture appointed in 1901-2. In the discussion of the committees the peasant members displayed remarkable unanimity in their approach to the problem of land shortage, and devoted to it most of their attention. Even stronger does this motive appear in the petitions and resolutions addressed to the committees by some of the village associations, and in the oral declarations of their representatives.'
(Quoted by Florinsky, M. (1961), *End of the Russian Empire* p.187)

e) Professor Kaufmann, an expert on Russian agriculture, describes peasant feelings in the early 20th century in 'The Agrarian Problem in Russia', 1919.
'Complaints of the shortage of land, demands for more land, a deep conviction that they are entitled to the land held by the nobility, all this found clear and unanimous expression in thousands of petitions sent by the peasants to Government departments, in the instructions given to the peasant deputies, in the speeches of the latter in the First and Second Dumas. The same complaints and the same demands were heard to the Old Believers' Congress which met in Moscow in 1906. Here, too, arose the clamour for more land. And it was particularly significant in this case, because it could not be treated as the result of party propaganda. On the contrary, the attitude of the Congress was that of strict loyalty to the sovereign. Its members vested all their hopes in the Tsar; they were openly hostile to what they called 'democracy', and they opposed the forcible solution of the agrarian problem. But in spite of all this they unanimously claimed more land, more land, more land.'
(Quoted by Florinsky, M. (1961), *End of the Russian Empire* pp.187-8)

Study document (a).
  i) Identify three major changes to the situation of a peasant outlined in the decree. (3 marks)
  ii) Under what circumstances might a peasant have the charge to consolidated holdings forced on him? (2 marks)

Study document (b).
  iii) What evidence is there here that the question of agriculture had been neglected? (1 mark)
  iv) How well does Golitsyn seem to understand the role of the commune? (3 marks)
  v) What evidence does Golitsyn provide of the political dimension of the Stolypin reforms? (Chart 7.8) (2 marks)
  vi) What does Golitsyn consider is preventing peasants from improving their lands? Does this seem a reasonable view? (3 marks)

Study documents (c), (d) and (e).
  vii) What peasant grievance is revealed in all these extracts? Why, according to document (c), has it arisen? (2 marks)

Study documents (b) and (e).
  viii) Does document (e) confirm Golitsyn's fears expressed in document (b) that political revolutionaries could easily exploit peasants? (3 marks)

Consult all the documents.
  ix) 'The documents show the gulf that existed between the ruling classes' view of the solution to the agrarian problem and the peasant view.' To what extent do you agree with this comment? (6 marks).
  (Total 25 marks)

A.4. Overall.

Discuss the comparative value of the three types of primary evidence studied above (ie statistical, pictorial and documentary). (10 marks)

A.5. General Assessment.

Study the primary evidence, chart 7.8, and page 52.

  i) Examine the diagrams of a notional Russian village. Is diagram 4 a 'typical' village? Why were there so many regional variations?
  ii) What changes caused by the Stolypin reforms does the diagram show?
  iii) To what extent were Stolypin's reforms similar to the English enclosure process?
  iv) Do you agree that Stolypin's reforms can be seen as the fulfilment of some of the hopes held of emancipation?
  v) Read the following three statements. Explain the extent to which you agree with each view.
  a) 'Stolypin should have redistributed land from the gentry to peasantry, rather than

have tried to redistribute it within the peasantry.'

b) 'Stolypin was correct in trying to encourage peasants to make more efficient use of their existing land because giving them gentry lands would not have solved the problem'.

c) 'The long term problem was not that the peasants had too little land but that, however the land was distributed, there were too many peasants.'

B. Problem Solving

The position of the Russian peasant in the late nineteenth century and government action.

Study the material above, especially chart 7.6. Below is a list of possible measures which might have been taken to improve the position of the Russian peasantry.

Possible measures
a) Reduce greatly the levels of indirect taxes, and establish an income tax.
b) Encourage consolidation of strips into compact farms.
c) Embark on a massive literacy campaign.
d) Improve communications.
e) Give government support to help raise grain prices.
f) Encourage birth control.
g) Expropriate (take over) gentry's lands, and give them to peasants.
h) Give state lands to peasants.
i) Sell or rent state lands to peasants on favourable terms.
j) Force the gentry to improve the terms for peasants renting lands.
k) Expand industry.
l) Control land prices.
m) Establish cheap loans to help peasants buy gentry land.
n) End redemption payments.
o) Give financial assistance to those migrating to Siberia.
p) Establish agricultural colleges.
q) Encourage emigration to U.S.A.
r) Reduce the powers of the mir to allow peasants to break free from its controls.
s) Provide cheap fertilisers/ agricultural implements/ improved seeds.
t) Encourage greater agricultural diversification.
u) Allow zemstva to assist agricultural innovation.
v) Give famine grants.

i) Either
a) Decide the best ten measures that you think ought to have been taken to help Russian agriculture, and rank them in order of importance. Explain your choice.
Or
b) Do the above exercise but consider the problem realistically from the viewpoint of a tsarist minister and select and rank ten points.

(Some members of the group could do (a), some (b) and then responses could be compared.)
ii) Try to sort out the various proposals into the following broad approaches:-
a) improving agricultural efficiency,
b) tackling the land problem,
c) tackling the population problem,
d) improving the financial position of the peasantry,
e) other.
Which of these broad approaches would you consider most important?
iii) Study charts 7.6 and 7.7. Then divide the list of possible measures into four columns:-
a) measures taken in the 19th century,
b) measures taken after 1905,
c) measures taken by peasants themselves in 1917,
d) measures not taken.

C. The Russian village 1860-1910. Change and continuity

Study the four diagrams of a typical Russian village between 1860 and 1910 (charts 3.1. and 7.8).

i) In which period does there appear to have been most change?
ii) Which diagrams show most continuity?
iii) 'The broad structure of the Russian village remained remarkably stable between 1860 and 1914.' Using the diagrams and other information, explain how far you agree with this statement.

D. Debate

'The tsarist regime stands condemned for its treatment of the Russian peasantry'. Considering all the above evidence, debate whether you consider this comment justified.

E. Concluding essay. An overview of economic development

Discuss the nature and effects of economic change in Russia between 1870 and 1914.

Advice. The chapter should have provided you with the material needed for this essay which can be approached in a very structured way, as follows.
Introduction. Briefly explain why the Russian government was concerned to modernise her economy.
Core.
i) Industry.
Identify nature of Russian industrialisation (see pp. 66-68 and chart 7.3).
Discuss whether, as optimists argue, development after 1906 was less artificial than before (see pp. 52-53).
Effects; consider points in chart 7.3. Consider economic effects as well as social and political ones. Here various types of figures would be useful, eg production figures, rates of growth

(very significant in terms of social effects), and comparisons with other countries.

ii) Agriculture.

Contrast the major developments in industry with the neglect of agriculture until 1905. Although the question begins in 1870, the effects of emancipation need discussing as this greatly influenced agriculture throughout this period. Do not neglect the massive population rise, nor the gradual transfer of land to the peasantry. Discuss thoroughly the Stolypin reforms, and the debate over them.

Conclusion. Debate continues as to whether economic changes of this period provided potential base for continued development under tsarism, or whether they raised tensions which the tsarist government was unable to contain.

Chart 7.8 Stolypin's agrarian reforms.

A. Chief features

Redemption payments ended (as promised in 1905). Power of mir reduced to allow:

  a) individual peasants, not mir, to own farms,
  b) peasants to leave restrictions of mir, and consolidate strips into one farm,
  c) peasants free to totally leave their village.

Encouragement of individual enterprise. As well as weakening the mir, the power of land captains was reduced, and the internal passport system weakened.

Greater financial assistance to buy land, via State Bank, from gentry and state.

Help given to those wishing to migrate to Siberia.

ie to encourage development of prosperous peasantry ('wager on the strong') by freeing them from mir, and encouraging them to buy up land from less enterprising.

B. Process

  a) A few minor reforms (over collective responsibility for redemption payments) in early 1900s.
  b) Nov 1905. Promise to end redemption payments by 1907.
  c) 1906. Edict issued under Article 87.
  d) Third Duma eventually passed a range of elaborating laws.
  e) 1911. Terms for leaving commune made easier, and elements of compulsion increased.
  f) Changes delayed by lack of officials to supervise the reorganisation of agriculture.
  g) From 1913, Ministry of Agriculture relaxed the pressure for implementation as problems were realised.
  h) Reforms largely suspended on outbreak of war, 1914.

Chart 7.8 *continued.*

C. Impact

Aim	Achievements
Economic To establish independent household ownership.	– By 1914, 2.5 million households (ie 25%) had newly gained full legal title to their own land. – 4 million others (from non-repartitional communes) were declared owners. No real change, but brought total of private ownership to nearly two thirds.
To consolidate scattered strips into one holding, ideally around a new farmstead away from the village (ie 'khutor' farm), rather than with home still in village (ie 'otrub' farm).	– By 1916 1.2 million (ie 10%) households had set up consolidated farms, enclosing 10% of allotment land. Most other land remained in strips. – Only 320,000 of these consolidated holdings were 'khutor' farms.
To reduce power of mir, and eventually disband it.	– Commune proved resilient; peasants preferred guarantee of collective welfare to uncertainties of individual farming. – In the most populated central areas, few left the commune. – In 1917 Revolution 95% returned to the mir.
To improve the efficiency of agriculture.	– Limited impact. 'Separators'/consolidators sometimes ruined the soil by exhaustive methods. – Run of favourable weather concealed lack of major improvements. – Population in Central Russia rose more than production. – Productivity only increased 1% p.a. – Legal changes by themselves inadequate to greatly improve efficiency.
To encourage land transfers, especially from poor, less enterprising to sturdy and strong.	– 1908-16. 1.1 million households sold farms. – 1906-14. 4 million desyatins purchased via State Bank from nobles.
To encourage migration to Siberia.	– 5 million migrated to Siberia, mainly to set up dairy farms. – One sixth returned.
Political To reorientate tsarism from a declining gentry to a new, prosperous peasantry. To divert peasants' gaze from gentry lands to commune.	b) – Freely elected First and Second Dumas dominated by radical peasant deputies wanting gentry land confiscation; electoral law had to be changed to give dominant influence to gentry. – After 1902-6, disturbances declined, but during 1917 Revolution there was a new peasant upsurge to seize gentry land in 'Second Emancipation'. – Tension in countryside continued, now directed at resented separators.

D. Assessment

– Misjudged character of Russian peasantry, who preferred collective security to individual enterprise.
– Made least impact in areas with worst problems, especially central region.

– Assumed that individual ownership would improve farming, and the mir could not; neither was automatically true.
– Initial rush to leave the commune died out.
– But might have helped regime survive if given more time.

E. Notional* Russian village before and after Stolypin Reforms.

(compare to map of same village in 1860 and 1870 in chart 3.1

Map 3. 1900

KEY

▬ Strips worked by one peasant household.
Have been reallocated by mir since 1870, and number of strips reduced due to increased population in village.

M Meadow. Lord's section has been sold off to mir, and part turned over to arable to ease pressure on arable land.

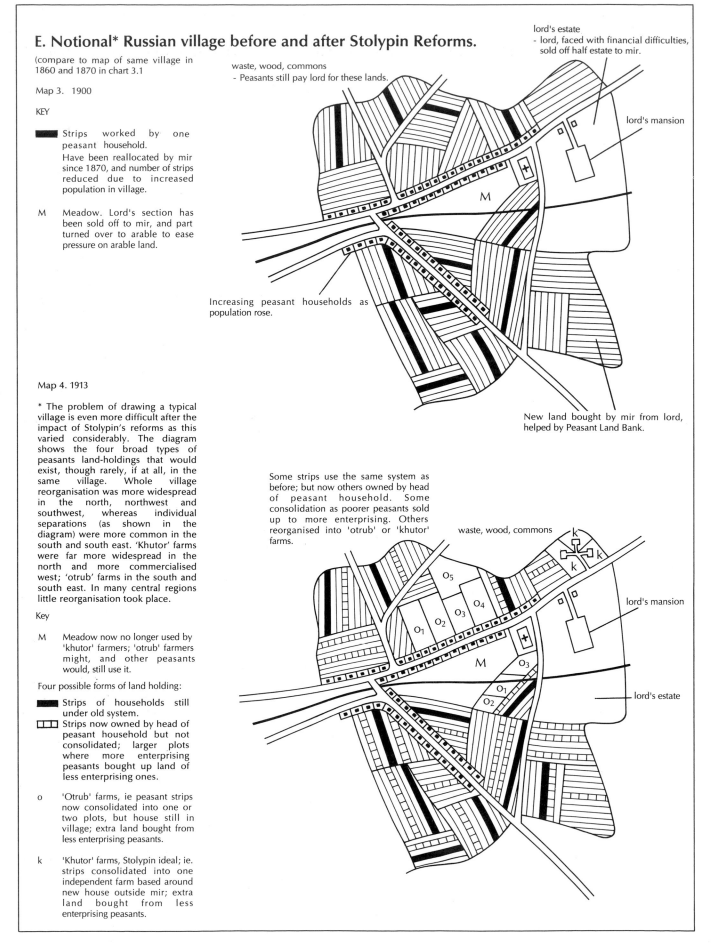

lord's estate
- lord, faced with financial difficulties, sold off half estate to mir.

lord's mansion

waste, wood, commons
- Peasants still pay lord for these lands.

M

Increasing peasant households as population rose.

New land bought by mir from lord, helped by Peasant Land Bank.

Some strips use the same system as before; but now others owned by head of peasant household. Some consolidation as poorer peasants sold up to more enterprising. Others reorganised into 'otrub' or 'khutor' farms.

waste, wood, commons

k k

k

k

lord's mansion

O₅
O₄
O₃
O₂
O₁

M   O₃
O₁
O₂

lord's estate

Map 4. 1913

* The problem of drawing a typical village is even more difficult after the impact of Stolypin's reforms as this varied considerably. The diagram shows the four broad types of peasants land-holdings that would exist, though rarely, if at all, in the same village. Whole village reorganisation was more widespread in the north, northwest and southwest, whereas individual separations (as shown in the diagram) were more common in the south and south east. 'Khutor' farms were far more widespread in the north and more commercialised west; 'otrub' farms in the south and south east. In many central regions little reorganisation took place.

Key

M Meadow now no longer used by 'khutor' farmers; 'otrub' farmers might, and other peasants would, still use it.

Four possible forms of land holding:

▬ Strips of households still under old system.
▭ Strips now owned by head of peasant household but not consolidated; larger plots where more enterprising peasants bought up land of less enterprising ones.

o 'Otrub' farms, ie peasant strips now consolidated into one or two plots, but house still in village; extra land bought from less enterprising peasants.

k 'Khutor' farms, Stolypin ideal; ie. strips consolidated into one independent farm based around new house outside mir; extra land bought from less enterprising peasants.

88

8 Opposition

A Introduction

During the nineteenth century the tsarist government had to confront increasing pressure from opposition movements. These sought to change, through peaceful pressure or violence, the political and in many cases the social system. Although tsarism was eventually overthrown, it is easy to exaggerate the importance of these movements. They were symptomatic of the tension in Tsarist Russia, but the organised groupings were not primarily responsible for either of the revolutions of 1905 and February 1917. The second revolution of October 1917 was, however, organised by the Marxist Bolsheviks.

Though discontent amongst the ordinary people was widespread, the chief critics of tsarism came from the educated elite. These were themselves, however, as distant from the masses, as they were from the government, and they often bemoaned their impotence. It was only when, in the early twentieth century, the intelligentsia and the people briefly joined forces that the regime was forced to make concessions, and in 1917 was eventually swept away.

B Broad trend of events

The first major outbreak of organised political opposition, in contrast to the peasant unrest and aristocratic intrigue which had always existed, was the Decembrist Revolt of 1825. This had attempted to exploit the confusion following the death of Alexander I to establish a liberal form of government. The attempt had been badly organised, geographically and ideologically split, and had failed to gain much support beyond a group of army officers. It achieved nothing except to reinforce the new tsar's repressive inclinations, though the rebels' martyrdom also served as an inspiration to others.

Unlike in the more advanced countries of Europe, in Russia there was no attempted revolution during the European economic slump of 1847-8. There was, however, a growing tide of peasant unrest, and some contemporaries feared Russia was near revolution following her Crimean defeat. This was one reason for Alexander II's great reforms, though by arousing expectations that were not fulfilled, and by introducing an aura of political debate, his reign actually served to increase tensions in Russia. The creation of zemstva and the spread of education also increased the number of people desiring liberal reforms.

The mid century also saw the development of an intelligentsia at odds with the regime. Many sons and daughters of the aristocracy were moved by the position of the peasantry. They expressed their feeling either in novels (thus seeking to avoid censorship), or by forming revolutionary groups dedicated to liberate the people from their oppression. Such groups were characterised by idealistic impatience to remedy the great ills they saw. Attempts at gaining mass support from the peasantry, or to spark off revolution by assassinating the tsar,

both failed. The 1880s saw a decline in opposition activity, as Alexander III's repression worked, and many politically disillusioned idealists redirected their activities into social work. At the same time, however, a new Western revolutionary ideology, Marxism, began to make an impact. At first confined to a tiny minority of intellectuals, Marxism took deeper root as Russia began to industrialise rapidly, and activists became involved in industrial unrest.

By the 1890s the refusal of the government to accommodate even moderate requests for wider participation in government, the impact of rapid industrialisation, and such horrors as the 1891 famine served to revitalise opposition movements. Once again intellectuals took the lead. Nicholas I's earlier fear of Moscow University as the 'wolves' den' was now partially justified, as student unrest grew, and graduates were prominent in opposition movements. The teacher whom the traveller Pares found buying Marxist library books, encouraging attacks on the gentry and referring to 'Nicholas the Last' may not have been unique as at the First All Russian Congress of Teachers in 1913 nearly half the delegates belonged to revolutionary socialist parties. This illustrates again how Russia's modernisation encouraged the growth of social groups potentially hostile to the regime.

C The various groups (See chart 8.1)

By the late nineteenth century, the opposition groups can be broadly divided into three main strands, although there were considerable differences within each group.

i) Populism and the Socialist Revolutionaries

The tendency that made the greatest impact during the nineteenth century was probably the Populists. The members of this group were mainly young intellectuals, often from fairly favoured backgrounds. They were inspired by the misery of the ordinary people, especially the peasantry, to work for both social and political change. They tended to look to the mir, the traditional communal organisation in the countryside, as the basis for a socialist rural society in which the landowners would lose their land, which would be divided amongst the peasantry. The tsarist government would be overthrown, and replaced with a democratic republic.

The Populists (or Narodniks) were divided over tactics. As their name suggests ('narod' is Russian for people), they looked to the ordinary Russian peasants to rise up against their oppressors. One might have expected them to have been able to exploit the discontent caused by the inadequacies of emancipation. However, this was not the case. The thousands of students who organised the 'To the People' movement in the 1870s, (some hoping to stir up revolution, others to serve the people through education), were met with apathy or actual hostility by the uncomprehending peasantry. Most of these still revered their 'father' tsar. They blamed their misfortunes on the nobles and

Chart 8.1 Opposition

Populists	Liberals	Marxists
Groups 1876. Land and Liberty, and Black Partition. 1879. 'People's Will'. 1900. Socialist revolutionaries to bring all groups together.	No real organised parties until the 20th century. Zemstva associations. 1902. League of Liberation. 1904. Union of Liberation. 1905. Moderate Octobrists, radical Constitutional Democrats (Kadets). 1908. Progressists.	1883. Emancipation of Labour. 1895. Russian Social Democratic Labour Party (RSDLP). 1903. Split into majority radical Bolsheviks and minority moderate Mensheviks.
Key figures Lavrov Chernov	Shipov, Zemstva leader. Milyukov, Kadet leader. Guchkov, Rodzianko, Octobrist leaders.	Plekhanov, founder of Russian Marxism. Lenin, leader of Bolsheviks. Martov, Menshevik leader. Trotsky, President of St Petersburg Soviet 1905.
Bases of support Mainly concentrated on peasantry (85% of population), though claimed to speak for all toilers. In the 20th century SR's gained some support amongst proletariat who, with artisans, formed 50% of their membership.	Strong in zemstva assemblies, especially amongst gentry, and in expert professionals employed by zemstva, the 'Third Element'. Intellectuals, especially in Universities. Some commercial and industrial support, eg Progressists.	Looked to industrial proletariat as creators of socialist revolution. Lenin also identified revolutionary role of peasantry. Actual leaders predominantly middle and upper class.
Aims Constituent Assembly to establish democratic socialist republic of self governing associations. Agarian socialism ie land redistributed to peasantry.	Constituent Assembly to establish democracy and basic civil liberties.	Firstly, establish bourgeois, democratic state with basic civil liberties. Ultimately, create a socialist republic.
Tactics Propaganda amongst masses to stir up mass revolt. Individual acts of heroism, and assassinations.	Joint meetings of zemstva leaders, eg 1896, lst Congress of Zemstva Presidents. Various legal professional bodies, eg Law societies, as vehicles to discuss liberal ideas. Moderate pressure on government to pass reforms. Some illegal propaganda for a constitution.	Secret cells, and study groups. Propaganda amongst workers. Organised demonstrations, strikes.
Key acts Assassinations. eg Alexander II 1881, Plehve 1904, Grand Duke Sergei 1905, Stolypin 1911. In 1907, assassinated some 2000 government officials. Helped arouse peasantry 1905; influential at Peasant Union Congress. Also helped to organise some strikes.	Banquetting campaign and initial support for strikes, 1905. Moderate liberals rallying to the government, Oct. 1905, helped its recovery. Failure of Vyborg protest in 1906.	Helped organise wave of industrial strikes 1890s, especially in 1896-7 in St Petersburg. Dec 1905. Bolsheviks behind failed Moscow rising. Involved in St Petersburg July 1914 strike, though unable to control it.
Strength Early Populist groups had little support, ('People's Will' about 400 members), but the 20th century SRs were developing a wide base, seen in 1917 elections. SRs only held their first national con-	Limited numerically, but Kadets largest party in lst Duma Divorced from masses. Even legal organisations after 1905 largely based in just a few major cities.	1870s. Small discussion groups, but 1890s Marxist ideas more influential as Russia embarked on industrialisation. 1904. 40,000 members 1906. 150,000 members

Chart 8.1 *continued*

Populists	Liberals	Marxists
gress in Dec 1905, and drew up programme. In 1906, claimed 50,000 members, with further 350,000 'under party influence', but declined rapidly thereafter. 30 members in second Duma despite officially boycotting election; their sympathisers, the Trudoviki, had about 100. Weakened by penetration by police double-agents, eg Azev.		1906. SDs elected to 2nd Duma 1910. 10,000 members 1912. Legal Bolshevik daily paper 'Pravda' print run of 40,000 Weakened by police informers, double-agents, eg 1914, 3 of 7 Central Committee were police agents. RSDLP weakened by internal feuds; after the set-back of 1905, Menshevik support grew, especially among new, legal trade unions working for reforms; but increasingly from 1912 support switched to Bolsheviks.
Importance Assassination tactic, and attempts at stirring unrest, strengthened position of reactionaries, especially 1870s-80s. Arguably delayed reforms. Rural unrest largely spontaneous, although SR agitation may have contributed to the spread of 1902-7 risings. Populists attracted intelligentsia, thus depriving government of able servants.	Limited, as government unresponsive to liberal requests until crisis of 1905. Backwardness of Russia, and tradition of lack of initiative from below, made Russian liberalism weak. Caught in dilemma: how to force autocracy to yield without destroying whole basis of society, and being swept away by socialists. Liberals' failure to secure parliamentary regime after collapse of tsarism February 1917 indicative of their weakness.	Only given chance because of late 19th century industrialisation. Easy to exaggerate importance, over-influenced by their success in October 1917. Industrial unrest would have occurred anyway, but also fomented by Marxists.

officials, and distrusted upper class intellectuals.

This failure forced some to change tactics. They resorted to acts of terror as a means to dislocate the government, and thus pave the way for mass revolt. Although thousands of tsarist officals, and several government ministers and members of the royal family were to become victims of this policy, it did not lead to the hoped for revolution. Their greatest apparent success, the assassination of Alexander II by the so called 'People's Will', clearly illustrates this. It merely led to a general revulsion against radicals, a rallying to the government, and intensified repression which produced a decade of political calm. However, it could be argued that the assassination of Interior Minister Plehve, and Grand Duke Sergei, given the general context of mass discontent and pressure on the government, did have an effect in forcing Nicholas, belatedly, to make concessions in the 1905 Revolution.

In the early 20th century, the Populist tradition was reformed in the Socialist Revolutionary Party (SRs). This was an attempt at a broad umbrella grouping, with a loose, doctrinally flexible organisation. It continued to engage both in mass propaganda, chiefly amongst the peasantry, by now becoming more restless, and in acts of assassination carried out by their Battle Organisation. Whereas the Populists had seen capitalism as an alien process irrelevant to Russian traditions, their SR heirs now accepted it. They looked for support to 'all toilers', the industrial working class as well as the peasantry. Although the Socialist Revolutionaries were formed in 1900, it was not until 1906 that they held their first congress and drew up a clear programme.

After the failure of the 1905 Revolution, their influence seemed to decline, a trend increased by the exposure of one of their leaders Azev as a police spy. Support, however, may have increased again in the 1910s. They were certainly the most popular group in Russia's only genuinely democratic elections held after the overthrow of tsarism in 1917.

Worksection 8 part 1 Populism

A. Primary evidence about revolutionaries in the late nineteenth century

A.1. Study the following five pieces of evidence, then answer the questions below.

a) Revolutionary Manifesto September 1861:
'The sovereign has betrayed the hopes of the people; the freedom he has given them is not real and is not what the people dreamed of and need.'
(Quoted by Christian D. (1986), *Power and Privilege* p.73)

b) 'Young Russia' 1862:
'The group that is oppressed by all and humiliated by all . . . is the common people. Over it stands a small group of contented and happy men. They are the landowners . . . the merchants . . . the govern-

ment officials, in short all those who possess property, either inherited or acquired. At their head stands the tsar. They cannot exist without him, nor he without them. If either falls the other will be destroyed . . .

There is only one way out of this oppressive and terrible situation which is destroying contemporary man, and that is revolution, bloody and merciless revolution, a revolution that must radically change all the foundations of contemporary society without exception and destroy the supporters of the present regime.'
(Quoted by Christian, D. (1986), *Power and Privilege* p.74).

c) An extract from the memoirs of Catherine Breshkovskaya, a noble's daughter who, disguised as a peasant, took part in the 'To the People' Movement. Here she explains the lack of response:

'To the request that he help me in my revolutionary propaganda . . . the old man answered, "I have no strength left. I have been cruelly punished." (Other peasants) made no protest against my proposal to prepare the soil for a general revolt: but it was evident that the recent punishments (after the 1861-3 uprising) had made a terrible impression on them. They said as one man: "if everyone agreed to rise at the same time, if you went around and talked to all the people, then it could be done. We tried several times to rise. We demanded the rights to the land. It was useless. Soliders were sent down and the people were punished and ruined." '
(Quoted by Christian, D. (1986), *Power and Privilege,* pp.75-6)

d) *'Educating the People in the Ideals of Liberty'*, painting produced during 1905.

e) Extract from the Programme of the People's Will 1879:

'The organisation and consummation of the revolution. In view of the oppressed and cowed condition of the people, and of the fact that the Government, by means of partial concessions and pacifications, may retard for a long time a general revolutionary movement, the party should take the initiative, and not wait until the people are able to work without its aid.'
(Quoted in ed.Dmytryshyn B. (1974), *Imperial Russia. A Sourcebook'* p.312)

i) What common attitude of the revolutionaries towards the people is suggested by evidence (a), (b) and (d)? (3 marks)

ii) What evidence do sources (b) and (c) give of the use of violence, by revolutionaries, peasants, and the government? (3 marks)

iii) Did the peasantry tend to share the views towards the tsar held by the revolutionaries in sources (a) and (b)? Whom did they tend to blame for the disappointments of emancipation? (3 marks)

iv) Was 'Young Russia's' view of the relationship between the tsar and the whole governing system proved right by the events of 1881? (3 marks)

v) What major problems does source (c) reveal about the peasantry as a potential revolutionary force? (2 marks)

vi) Why, according to Breshkovskaya in source (c), did the peasantry not respond to the revolutionaries? (2 marks)

vii) To what extent does source (e) support this view? Can you think of other reasons? (3 marks)

viii) Can the views expressed in source (e) be partly explained by the failure of the 'To the People' Movement? How did the 'People's Will' consider they could take the initiative? (3 marks)

ix) To what extent does painting (d) support the evidence in extract (c) as to how the peasantry greeted revolutionaries? (3 marks)

x) How reliable do you consider sources (c) and (d) as historical evidence? (5 marks)
(Total 30 marks)

A.2. General analysis of historical documents.

Read the following extracts from the literature of the 'People's Will' movement.

a) Extract from the Programme of the 'People's Will', 1879:

'Destructive and terroristic activity. Terroristic activity consists in the destruction of the most harmful persons in the Government, the protection of the party from spies, and the punishment of official lawlessness and violence . . . The aim of such activity is to break down the prestige of Governmental power, to furnish continuous proof of the possibility of carrying on a contest with the Government, to raise in that way the revolutionary spirit of the people and inspire belief in the practicality of revolution, and, finally, to form a body suited and accustomed to warfare.'
(Quoted in ed.Dmytryshyn, B. (1974), *Imperial Russia. A Sourcebook* p.312)

b) Extract from an 'Open Letter of the Revolutionary Executive Committee' of the 'People's Will' sent to Alexander III on 23 March 1881 after the assassination of his father:

'Majesty, although the executive committee understands very well the mood which now possesses you, it does not regard itself justified . . . to postpone the following declaration. There are higher duties than even the most justified human feelings; these are the duties towards our country, duties which command every citizen to sacrifice himself, his own sentiments, and even those of others . . . .

The tragedy was no accident and should not have surprised anyone. After the events of the last ten years it appears rather as an unavoidable necessity. During a whole decade the revolutionary movement has grown in spite of all the measures taken to suppress it. The best elements of the country . . . those most willing to sacrifice themselves, step forth to enter the ranks of the revolution. For three years the revolution and the government were linked in desperate combat.

Guilty and innocent were hanged; the jails and far off places of exile were crowded. The so-called leaders of the revolution were . . . executed . . . but their death did not stop the revolution . . . A revolutionary movement, Your Majesty, does not depend upon individuals. It is a process carried on by the people, and therefore gallows, erected for the most energetic representatives of this process, are . . . powerless to save the obsolete order . . . The government may continue with its arrests, and executions as long as it wishes; it may perhaps succeed in destroying some revolutionary organisations . . . Yet the government will not be able to prevent the further course of events. It is this course of events which creates revolutionaries, the general dissatisfaction among the masses and the development of new social forms in Russia.

A whole nation cannot be suppressed and the dissatisfaction of a nation can even less be extinguished by mere severity. On the contrary severity will increase not only dissatisfaction but also its energy and its forces . . . The revolutionary organisations must in the course of time gain in number and strength. Finally, a terrible explosion, a blood-drenched revolution will convulse the whole nation and destroy the old order of things.

Yes, Your Majesty, this is a sad and terrible perspective. Please do not think it an empty phrase . . .

Whatever good intentions the emperor may have, the actions of the government have nothing in common with the aspirations and the welfare of the people. The Russian government has brought the masses to such a state of poverty and misery that they haven't even the freedom to act for their common welfare and that even in their own homes they are not safe against secret police.

There are only two ways out of such a situation; a revolution which cannot be prevented by executions, or the voluntary transfer of the supreme power to the people and their participation in the government. In the interests of the country and in order to preclude such a terrible misfortune as a revolution always is, the executive committee appeals to Your Majesty to follow the second alternative . . .

These conditions must be fulfilled so that the revolutionary movement gives way to a peaceful development . . . first, a general amnesty for all political criminals, for they have committed no crimes but have simply done their civic duty. Second, a convocation of an assembly of representatives of the whole people to discuss the new foundations of the forms of social and political life, in accordance with the desires and wishes of the people . . .

And now Your Majesty, you must decide for yourself. Two roads are open before you. The choice is yours. We can only hope that your reason and your conscience will dictate to you the only decision which is compatible with Russia's welfare, with your own dignity, and with your duties toward the fatherland.'
(Quoted by Kohn, H. (1957), *Basic History of Modern Russia* pp.148-50)

Comment on the approach of the Populists as revealed by these documents. Refer in particular to; the reasons for their action; their tactics; their attitude to the government, and to the tsar; their attitude to violence; their analysis of the balance of forces in Russia.

B. Group debate. Violence and terror

Consider how the 'People's Will' justify their use of terror, any evidence to suggest they could be considered idealists, and the effects of their actions. In particular, try to resolve the following questions.

i) Do you agree with the Liberal leader Struve who considered their actions 'historically inevitable and morally justified'?
ii) Can assassination, and the use of terror, ever be justified?

ii) Liberalism

Liberalism (the belief in the importance of individual rights such as free speech, the rule of law, and representative government) was classically a Western European doctrine. As such it never gained a strong foothold in Russia which lacked the advanced middle classes which elsewhere provided the social foundation for liberal parties. Ever since the impact of the French Revolution and Napoleon, there had been small groups from the educated elite who wanted Russia to follow the path of Western Europe. After the failure of the Decembrist Revolt, their only hope of success was if liberal reform was initiated from on top, by the government. Liberal hopes rose during the new era after the Crimean defeat. However, although Alexander II was prepared to support liberal reforms in some areas (see chart 3.2), he was a firm believer in autocracy. His social and administrative reforms did, though, lead to an increase in the professions, such as lawyers and teachers, which increased the numbers of people attracted to liberal ideas. The creation of zemstva and open law courts allowed a more liberal atmosphere to develop in Russia, and the zemstva have been called the 'seedbeds of liberalism'. Russian liberalism, due to its weak class base and the peculiar conditions in Russia, tended to be more concerned with social issues than their Western counterparts, accepting the need to satisfy peasant land hunger and worker grievances.

The more cautious liberals, such as Shipov, anticipated a gradual development of reforms through the actions of an enlightened tsar. This would allow a greater role for the zemstva, with forces outside the bureaucracy helping to shape government policy, and perhaps eventually lead to a national assembly based on the zemstva. But Russian tsars and their bureaucrats were jealous of any encroachment on their powers, and they tried to prevent wider zemstva organisation. By the 1890s, however, congresses of zemstva leaders were meeting, providing a national forum for moderate liberalism.

Another strand of liberalism was more radical. This looked directly to the parliamentary regimes in the West, and demanded a similar system in Russia, arguing that a gradualist approach was too slow. This view, led by Miliukov, even gained majority support at a zemstva representatives meeting in 1904, showing the leftward trend of liberalism, given the absence of reform from above. In 1902 an illegal radical liberal newspaper, 'Liberation', was founded. Two years later a secret Union of Liberation was established in St Petersburg, demanding a national assembly elected by direct universal suffrage. With an illegal organisation and paper, the tactics of these liberals resembled those of revolutionary groups.

Neither of these liberal tendencies had much political influence. However, they did contribute to the pressure for change in 1904-5, when they became organised in the Union of Unions, holding a series of banquets to spread their views. It was, however, the unrest of the masses that forced the granting of a parliament. This was sufficient to satisfy the more cautious liberals who formed the Octobrists, accepting the government's reforms; the radical Kadets (Constitutional Democrats) rejected them. The weakness of this group was seen in 1906 in the Vyborg Manifesto, when in protest against the dissolution of the first Duma, the Kadet leaders went to nearby Vyborg in Finland and called upon the Russian people to adopt civil disobedience and to refuse to pay taxes. They got little response, but just made themselves liable to arrest and disqualification from the second Duma, in which their influence declined (see chart 6.4).

After the reforms of 1906, political parties were legal in Russia, though no parties further left than the Octobrists were in fact allowed to register. The liberal element formed a variety of parties from the moderate conservative Octobrists, to the Progressists and Kadets. However, torn between trying to co-operate with the government and keeping their principles, and with many afraid of a repetition of what they saw as the mass anarchy of 1905, they had little effect on developments. When briefly propelled into power with the collapse of tsarism in 1917, they were unable to secure a moderate democratic government, being overthrown by the Bolsheviks.

Worksection 8 part 2 Liberalism

A. Primary evidence on Liberalism

A.1. Read the following extract.

Liberal reply in an Open Letter to Nicholas after he rejected hopes for allowing participation in government as 'senseless dreams', 1895:

'We do not know whether you clearly understand the situation created by your 'firm' utterance. But people who do not stand so above and so far off from actuality can easily comprehend what is their own and your position concerning what is now the state of things in Russia . . . No zemstvoist has put the question as you put it, and no voice was raised in any Zemstvo assembly against autocracy . . . The question was only to remove the wall of bureaucracy and court influences which separate the tsar from Russia; and these were the tendencies which you in your inexperience and lack of knowledge ventured to stamp as 'senseless dreams' . . . Russian society realised very well that not an ideal autocrat has spoken to them on January 29, but a bureaucracy jealous of its omnipotence (exercising full power) . . . If autocracy in word and deed proclaims itself identical with the omnipotence of bureaucracy, if it can exist only so long as society is voiceless, it is lost. It digs its own grave, and soon or late, at any rate, in a future not very remote it will fall beneath the pressure of living social forces.

You challenged the Zemstva and with them Russian society, and nothing remains for them now but to choose between progress and faithfulness to autocracy. Your speech has provoked a feeling of offence and depression; but the living social forces will soon recover from that feeling. Some of them will pass to a peaceful but systematic struggle for such scope of action as is necessary for them. Some others will be made more determined to fight the detestable regime by any means. You first began the struggle; and the struggle will come.'
(Quoted by Mazour, A. (1960), *Rise and Fall of the Romanovs* p.170)

i) What initial attitude towards the autocracy did the zemstva representatives hold? What indications are there that this was changing? (3 marks)
ii) How do they view Nicholas II? (2 marks).
iii) To what extent do they agree with the attitude of the petitioners in 1905 (see pp. 39-40) about the greatest problem with the government? (3 marks)
iv) What do they claim is their own relationship with society? Was this view justified? (3 marks)
v) Compare this letter with that received by Alexander III on acceding to the throne. Although the first document was from avowed revolutionaries and the second was from representatives of the moderate wing of liberalism, is there any similarity? Explain your answer. (4 marks).
vi) 'A far more cautious statement than that of the 'People's Will', but in its own way more ominous for the tsarist regime.' Do you agree with this statement about the zemstva letter? Give reasons for your answer. (5 marks).
(Total 20 marks)

A.2. Read the following extract from the speech by the liberal Petrunkevich, July 1905, to the Congress of Zemstvo delegates:

'Until now we have hoped for reform from above, but now the people are our only hope . . . The ineptitude and impotence of the regime has brought on the revolution . . . Our duty is to devote all our efforts to avoiding bloodshed. We cannot stop the storm, but we must in any case take care that a strong shock is avoided.'
(Quoted by Christian, D. (1986), *Power and Privilege* p.103)

   i) To what extent does this speech contain further evidence of the changing approach of some liberal elements, as suggested in the first source?

   ii) What attitude to 'the people' is shown in this speech?

   iii) Does it give support to the view of those Marxists who argued that the Russian middle class would be unable to carry through a genuinely democratic revolution? (Reference to chart 8.2 on Marxism mights be useful here.) Explain your answer.

B. Assessing Russian Liberalism

Read the following analysis by Deutscher, a Marxist historian:

'The economic preponderance of the state, the numerical weakness of the middle classes, the predominance of foreign capital in industry, the absence of a middle class tradition, all combined to make Russian bourgeois liberalism still born.'
(Deutscher, I. (1970), *Prophet Armed* p.152)

   i) Some historians might consider this a rather harsh judgement. Can you think of a Russian liberal force which Deutscher does not refer to?

   ii) Might Deutscher be prone to underestimate the strength of Russian liberalism in the early 20th century? Give reasons for your answer.

iii) Marxists

Though it was the Marxists who eventually became the rulers of Russia, one must be careful not to exaggerate their importance before 1917. Like liberalism, Marxism was essentially a Western European political theory, being largely based on Marx's studies of the British economy, German philosophy and French political thought. Marxists stressed the role of classes and class struggle in history, which progressed through a series of revolutions from feudalism, to capitalism, to socialism-communism (see chart 8.2). They called themselves Social Democrats as they believed liberal democracy meant freedom only for the prosperous elite, not for the exploited masses who needed social revolution to establish genuine democracy in a socialist society.

Marx himself had considered backward Tsarist Russia as one of the least likely countries to have a socialist revolution. However, the growth of industry, and hence of an industrial proletariat, made Marx's scientific analysis of capitalism seem more appropriate. It also attracted young critics of the tsarist system, especially after the failure of Populism. Neither appeal to the peasant masses, nor action as a vanguard without support had worked. Now many Russian dissidents followed Marx in looking to the proletariat as the source of their revolution; these would first overthrow the autocracy, and then pressurise the new bourgeois government to grant reforms like mass education and political freedom. The advance of industry would eventually create the conditions for a socialist revolution. In the meantime, Marxists helped organise a series of strikes in the 1890s seeking to turn basic economic grievances into hostility to the whole social and political system. The various groups, such as the 1880s Emancipation of Labour, were small numerically, hindered by the conditions of secrecy and repression in which they had to operate, and torn by factional disputes. However, they gradually attracted more adherents than the SRs, probably being the largest group by 1904, but falling back afterwards.

In 1903, five years after its founding, the Russian Social Democratic Labour Party split, primarily over organisational issues, into the Bolsheviks, followers of Lenin, and the Mensheviks. The latter favoured a broader party compared to Lenin's tightly knit, disciplined structure. Most of the leaders of both factions were in exile. So when both the 1905 and February 1917 revolutions occurred largely spontaneously, the Marxist leaders had to rush back to try and channel discontent into what they saw as the proper lines, with limited success. Though Marxists did play a role in fomenting the increasing industrial unrest that marked the last years of Tsarist Russia, most historians would argue that it was only after the collapse of tsarism in February 1917 that the Marxists played a major role.

Worksection 8 part 3 Marxism

A. The Marxist view of history

A.1. Study chart 8.2.

   i) In which stage of history would Marxists consider nineteenth century Tsarist Russia was?

   ii) What though, according to this scheme, was unusual about Russia by the end of the century?

   iii) How did Lenin argue the 'bourgeois revolution' would have to be achieved in Russia?

A.2. Read the following extract, and study chart 8.2. Then answer the questions below.

Extract from the Manifesto of the Russian Social Democratic Labour Party, 1898:

'Fifty years ago the invigorating storm of the revolution of 1848 burst over Europe. For the first time the modern working class appeared on the scene as a major historical force . . .

Chart 8.2 Marx's view of history. A simplified view

Marx argued that all societies broadly developed along the following lines.

Stage 1. PRIMITIVE COMMUNISM

Political: No government.
Society: No classes.
           Very few commodities.

As the later nostalgic radical song claimed: 'When Adam delved and Eve span, who was then the gentleman?'

Stage 2. FEUDALISM

Political: Some form of monarchy, usually absolute.
Society: Dominant social group: Aristocracy.
           Mass of population: Peasantry.
           Revolutionary class: middle class (merchants etc)
(though occasional peasant revolts).

(Growth of trade, commerce enlarges middle class who eventually seek power to reshape society and government to give them freedom to develop their talents further.)

Stage 4. SOCIALISM

Political: Workers control the state to resist counter-revolution.
           'Dictator ship of the proletariat'. As the threat diminished, so state becomes less powerful.
Society: Becoming more equal, and class system breaking down. Wealth, goods created under capitalism now fairly distributed.

Lenin

Stage 3. CAPITALISM

Political: Parliamentary democracy, defending 'bourgeois' liberal principles.
Society: Dominant social group: Middle class (especially industrialists).
Mass of population: Working class (proletariat, ie industrial workers).
Revolutionary class: Proletariat.
(According to Marx, these would automatically develop socialist consciousness).

(Industry expands dramatically, thus enlarging the proletariat, the eventual 'grave-diggers' of capitalism. Capitalism produces great wealth and material goods but they are unfairly allocated, and the workers are exploited.)

Stage 5. COMMUNISM

Political: No state, just the 'administration of things'.
Society: No classes; all equal. Plentiful goods fairly shared.

'From each according to his ability, to each according to his needs.'

Problems of Applying Marxism to Early Twentieth Century Russia

- Russia an example of 'uneven and combined development' (Trotsky), ie. a mixture of traditional feudal, and imported advanced elements, ie. politically still autocratic with powerful aristocracy and impoverished peasant masses, but rapid industrialisation created a growing proletariat. This did not fit into orthodox Marxist schema.
- Mass of population still peasants, a group which Marx did not consider important (as irrelevant to the socialist revolution).
- Russian bourgeoisie had not developed strongly enough to carry through the bourgeois revolution. They might also be frightened by the presence of a socialist-inclined proletariat, and thus be prepared to compromise with the autocracy (as the Octobrists did during the 1905 Revolution).

Lenin's Adaptation of Marxism to Russian Conditions

- Need small, disciplined party of professional revolutionaries to develop socialist consciousness in proletariat. (key issue causing split with Mensheviks 1903)
- 'Bourgeois revolution' had to be carried out by the proletariat, assisted by poor peasantry, rather than by the bourgeoisie itself. (Idea developed by Lenin as a result of the experience of 1905. Trotsky developed a similar idea.)
- Workers take control after they have carried out the 'bourgeois revolution', and gradually move towards socialism (with the help of foreign socialist countries).
- ie, workers should attempt to seize power, and not just wait for the bourgeoisie to accomplish the 'bourgeois revolution', (the orthodox Marxist line, retained by Mensheviks).

These ideas were gradually developed by Lenin. The Bolsheviks only fully adopted them in the months before the October 1917 Revolution, which was inspired by them.

96

All this time Russia apparently remained aside from the main road of historical movement. The class struggle was not apparent there, but it was there . . . The Russian government, with laudable zeal, itself planted the seeds of class struggle by cheating the peasants, patronizing the landlords, fattening up the big capitalists at the expense of the toiling population. But the bourgeois-capitalist order is unthinkable without a proletariat or working class. The latter is born together with capitalism, grows together with it, gets stronger, and in proportion to its growth is thrown more and more into conflict with the bourgeoisie.

The Russian factory worker, serf or free, has always carried on a hidden struggle with his exploiters. In proportion to the development of capitalism, the proportions of this struggle have grown, they have embraced more and more layers of the working class population.

And what does the Russian working class not need? It is completely deprived of what its foreign comrades freely and quietly enjoy: participation in the administration of the state, freedom of speech and of the press, freedom of organisation and assembly . . . Political freedom is necessary for the Russian proletariat like fresh air is necessary for healthy breathing. It is the basic condition for its free development and the successful struggle for partial improvements and final liberation.

But the Russian proletariat can only win the political freedom which it needs by itself.

The farther east one goes in Europe, the more the bourgeoisie becomes in the political respect weaker, more cowardly . . . and the larger are the cultural and political tasks which fall to the share of the proletariat. On its broad shoulders the Russian working class must bear and will bear the cause of the fight for political freedom. This is essential, but it is only the first step towards the realisation of the great historical mission of the proletariat, towards the creation of that social order in which the exploitation of man by man will have no place. The Russian proletariat will throw off its burden of autocracy so that with all the more energy it will continue the struggle against capitalism and the bourgeoisie until the complete victory of socialism.

The Russian Social Democratic party continues the cause and the traditions of all the preceding revolutionary movements in Russia; taking as the principal immediate task of the party the goal of conquering political freedom, Social Democracy moves towards the goal which has already been marked out by the glorious activists of the old 'People's Will'. But the means and the path which Social Democracy chooses are different. The choice of them is determined by its conscious desire to be and remain a class movement of the organised working masses. It is firmly convinced that 'the liberation of the working class can only be its own business,' and it will undeviatingly make all its action conform to this fundamental basis of international Social Democracy.'

(Quoted by Daniels, R. (1960), *A Documentary History of Communism* pp.5-8)

i) Explain the reference to 'cheating the peasant', and 'fattening up the big capitalists at the expense of the toiling population.' (2 marks)
ii) How many references are there to 'the people'? What words are used instead? Why is this the case? (3 marks).
iii) How do the Social Democrats consider tsarism is, as Marx would have said, creating its own gravediggers? (2 marks)
iv) How, according to the Social Democrats, does Russia compare to Western Europe, with regard to:
   a) its historical development,
   b) conditions for its working class,
   c) the nature of its middle class?
   (3 marks)
v) What is the first task of the proletariat? What is its final task? (2 marks)
vi) Who would have to lead the struggle for political freedom (contrary to classical Marxism as shown in chart 8.2)? Who might initially co-operate with it? Would such co-operation be firm or likely to last? (4 marks)
vii) Did the events of 1905 bear out this analysis? Does the view of the bourgeoisie described here also help explain what happened after the overthrow of tsarism in 1917? (4 marks)
viii) How does the Social Democratic Party view the Populists? (Discuss their agreements and disagreements.) (2 marks)
ix) Like the extracts from Liberal and Populist opposition movements, this Marxist document suggests an air of optimism. Is that surprising? What reasons does the Manifesto give which suggest why Social Democrats should be optimistic about their prospects? (3 marks)
(Total 25 marks)

Power and privilege — a social democratic cartoon of 1900. From the top, captions read: 'We reign over you'; 'We govern you'; 'We mystify you'; 'We shoot you'; 'We eat for you'. *The banner reads: 'To live in freedom, to die in struggle'*

A.3. Marxist propaganda.

Look at the Marxist propaganda poster of 1901 on the previous page.

i) What groups does it identify as exploiters of working people?
ii) Explain the reference. 'We mystify you'. How does this support Marx's view of religion as 'the opium of the masses'?
iii) Many of its potential audience might be illiterate. Explain whether you think the poster might still be effective on someone who could not read the writing.
iv) Does the poster just describe the existing situation, or does it also suggest that change could happen?

Worksection 8 part 4 overall

A. Interpretations

A.1. Comparing the groups.

Having studied the above material, and closely examined charts 8.1, 8.2, complete the following exercise (preferably without referring back to the information so you can see how much you have learnt.)

Below are a series of statements about the three main opposition tendencies in Tsarist Russia. Draw up three column headings for the three groups, (Populism, Liberalism, Marxism) and divide the statements between them. (A word of warning. You may consider some of the statements do not apply to any group, and a few to more than one. Discuss this afterwards.)

a) Organisations

Battle Organisation
Bolsheviks
Union of Liberation
'People's Will'
Mensheviks

Octobrists
Emancipation of Labour
RSDLP
Kadets
SRs

b) Ideas

Looked to Western traditions. Stressed need for a Constituent Assembly. Stressed importance of the mir. Believed in a socialist society. Saw capitalism as a necessary progressive stage.

c) Tactics and action

Wave of assassination. Concentrated on proletariat. Assassinated Alexander II. Looked largely to peasants for support. 'To the People' movement. Looked to the tsar for reforms. Considered zemstva should develop into national system of representation. Stressed role of propaganda bringing socialist consciousness to the working class.

d) Strength and significance

Strong base in zemstva.
Considerable role in 1890s strikes.
Infiltrated by police spies.
Considerable role in causing 1905 Revolution.
Their violent action provoked government into repression.
Greatly benefited from growing industrialisation.
Largely product of reforms of Alexander II.
Influential in top circles of central government.
Probably most popular group by 1917.

Played major role in overthrow of tsarist government. Group that eventually controlled Russia.

A.2. Contemporary comments.

Analyse the following statements:

a) Decembrist motto: 'From the spark shall grow the flame.'
(Quoted by Rogger, H. (1983), *Russia in the Age of Modernisation and Revolution* p.134).

b Zhelyabov, member of the 'People's Will':
'History is terribly slow, it must be pushed forward.'
(Quoted by Kochan, L. and Abraham, R. (1983), *Making of Modern Russia* p.218)

c) Lenin 1902 'Give us an organisation of revolutionaries and we shall overturn Russia'.
(Quoted by Rogger, H. (1983), *Russia in the Age of Modernisation and Revolution,* p.148)

d) Plekhanov, whilst boating with fellow Marxists on Lake Geneva:
'If this boat sinks, it's the end of Russian Marxism.'
(Quoted by Kochan, L and Abraham R, (1983), *Making of Modern Russia* p.234)

e) Interior Minister Durnovo, February 1914: 'The Russian opposition is intellectual throughout, and this is its weakness, because between the intelligentsia and the people there is a profound gulf of misunderstanding and distrust.
(Quoted by Dmytryshyn, B. (1974) *Imperial Russia, A Sourcebook* p.463)

A.3. Historians' views.

i) Westwood, discussing the Populists, argues: 'Violence was a reflection of weakness as was, essentially, the violence practised by the government. ((1973) *Endurance and Endeavour* p.120).
Do you agree with these two judgements, a) for the 1870s, b) for any other period?
ii) 'There was far more agreement amongst Russia's opposition political groups about aims than about methods of achieving them.'
To what extent do you agree with this view? (It might be useful to distinguish between short term and final aims).

B. Concluding essay

Analyse the nature and importance of opposition to tsarism between 1870 and 1914.

Advice. Nature. Under nature you should consider ideas / aims, organisation, sources of support, methods / strategy and strength. Discuss the three main strands of opposition identified above. Try to avoid too many references to numerous groups and people, but concentrate on broader points to identify nature.

Also refer to other areas of opposition, such as minority groups. Peasant discontent might also be worth considering, though the question is about opposition to tsarism. You would need to identify how, although rural discontent was growing for most of this period, it was not really directed against tsarism, but more against the local lords. Reference to the failure of the 'To the People' movement might be useful here.

The difficulties facing the various groups, particularly repression and infiltration by police spies, could be identified, and the extent to which the groups were torn by factional struggles. The necessity for most of their leaders to live mainly in exile, and the variety of tactics used, especially the role of propaganda, are other areas worth considering.

Importance. This is a difficult area to assess, partly due to the lack of reliable evidence. Stone ((1983) *Europe Transformed* p.214) ingeniously refers to the SRs distributing three hundredweight of propaganda in 1904 as a way of indicating popularity. Some reference to the number of people in the various groups might be useful, (though how reliable is the evidence?). In addition, consider that groups can be far more important than their size might suggest. A further problem is that both the parties themselves, and, for example the secret police, might, for their own different reasons, claim the groups were more influential than they really were.

One way to assess importance is to look at what the groups achieved. Here the 1905 Revolution needs to be considered although be careful about exaggerating the role of parties within this. The parties' role in rural and industrial unrest generally during the period needs consideration, and the extent to which the political parties were successful in a) provoking unrest, and b) channeling it into political directions. It has also been argued, both by contemporaries such as Milyutin (see pages 26, 29), and historians, that revolutionary groups actually strengthened reactionary forces, and so prevented reforms. This, might, however, as some revolutionaries argued, in the long term assist the build up of revolutionary pressures.

The impact of assassinations needs discussion, with perhaps contrast made between that of Alexander II in 1881, and Grand Duke Sergei in 1905. Reference could be made to Kennan's point of how the opposition groups served to attract talented youth away from government service which contributed to the eventual disintegration of the tsarist system. A look ahead to 1917 might serve to reinforce a cautious assessment of the importance of the organised groups themselves, for most historians argue that the February Revolution was more of a collapse by tsarism than an overthrow by political parties; it was only in October 1917 when the Bolsheviks were able to exploit anarchy to seize power that a particular party took control of events. Finally, you might like to consider Pearson's view ((1974), *Russia in Revolution* p.7) 'Tsardom was not only its own worst enemy, but its only effective enemy.'

9 Key Individuals

A Introduction

This chapter examines the work of five individuals who played a major role in the final years of tsarism. Three of them, Nicholas II, Rasputin and Pobedonostsev have been blamed for tsarism's collapse, and the others, Witte and Stolypin, have usually been seen as potential saviours.

B Witte, Stolypin, Pobedonostsev and Rasputin

Their work and influence are conveyed in a series of analytical charts, combined with exercises based on a range of primary and secondary material.

Worksection 9 part 1

A. Identification of the individuals

A.1. Study charts 9.1 to 9.4 on Witte, Stolypin, Pobedonostsev and Rasputin. Below are a series of statements made by them. Decide who said what, and explain your choice. (There are two statements by each individual, plus statement (a) where one of the ministers is addressing another; here identify the two people.)

a) 'The working class? I know of no such class in Russia . . . I do not understand what you are talking about. We have peasants. They form 90 percent of the population. They include a relatively small number who go to work in mills and factories, but who still remain peasants. You are trying to create artificially a new class, a sort of social relationship completely alien to Russia. In this respect . . . you are a dangerous socialist.'
(Quoted by Crankshaw, E. (1978), *Shadow of the Winter Palace* p.343)

b) 'To the present epoch has fallen the difficult task of making up for what has been neglected in an economic slumber lasting two centuries.'
(Quoted by Kochan, L. (1970), *Russia in Revolution* p.27)

c) 'The Government has placed its wager, not on the needy and the drunk, but on the sturdy and the strong; on the sturdy individual proprietor who is called to play a part in the reconstruction of our Tsardom on strong monarchical foundations.'
(Quoted by Kemp, T. (1969), *Industrialisation in Nineteenth Century Europe* p.144)

d) Parliamentary government 'is the greatest false-hood of our time.'
(Quoted by Floyd, D. (1969), *Russia in Revolt* p.6)

e) 'Sexual indulgence is the true path to humility and, through humility, to eternal salvation.'
(Quoted by Dymtryshyn, B. (1974), Imperial Russia. A Sourcebook p.439)

f) 'The power of the state is based solely on the unity of consciousness between the people and the state, in the national faith . . . The church is identical and inseparable from the history of the Russian Narod . . .

and is the life, truth, and full foundation of our existence . . . The Church and the Church alone has allowed us to remain Russians and to unite our scattered strength.'
(Quoted by Byrnes, in ed. Stavrou, T. (1969), *Russia under the Last Tsar* pp.55-7)

g) Letter written to the Tsar, December 1916.
'I feel I shall leave life before January 1 . . . If I am killed by common assassins . . . you, Tsar of Russia, have nothing to fear . . . But if I am murdered by nobles, and if they shed my blood . . . then no one of your family, that is to say none of your children or relations will remain alive for more than two years. They will be killed by the Russian people.'
(Quoted by Elliott, J. (1974), *Fall of Eagles* p.175)

h) 'At present the political strength of the Great Powers which are called to fulfil great historical tasks in the world is created not only by the spiritual valour of their peoples but also by their economic organisation. Even the military preparedness of a country is determined . . . by the degree of its industrial development. Russia with her vast multinational population, her complex historical tasks in international relations and her many sided interests needs perhaps more than any other country a proper economic foundation for her national policy and her culture.'
(Quoted by von Laue, in ed.Stavrou, T. (1969), *Russia under the Last Tsar* p.128)

i) 'As the revolution is so strong, I must carry through effective measures of reform, and at the same time I must face revolution, resist it, stop it.'
(Quoted by Floyd, D. (1969), *Russia in Revolt* p.121)

A.2. Below are a series of statements by historians about the same four individuals. (There are two about each person.) Decide whom is being referred to, and explain your choice.

a) His 'economic significance (was) approached by probably no other single individual in nineteenth century Europe.'
(Trebilcock, C. (1981), *Industrialisation of the Continental Powers* p.231)

Continued on page 106.

Chart 9.1 Witte. A potential saviour of tsarism?

A. Basic details

1849 Born Sergi Yulevich to noble mother; father of Dutch ancestry. Married Jewish divorcee. Joined government railway department where he showed great efficiency.

1891 Transport Minister.

1892 Finance Minister.

1903 Dismissed in reaction to unrest and disruption caused by European economic slump.

1905 Negotiated peace with Japan.
Advised granting of Duma.
President of Council of Ministers.
Organised repression of unrest.

1906 Negotiated crucial massive French loan.
Then dismissed in April.
Jealous of successor Stolypin; helped weaken his position.

1914 Opposed Russian entry into war.

1915 Died embittered, predicting revolution.

B. Character

- Self-confident, dynamic, boastful, ambitious.
- Practical, business-like.
- Outstanding statesman.

C. Ideas and aims

- To modernise Russia and maintain her position as a great power, and prevent her becoming a 'European China'.
- To use state power not just for repression and preserving the status quo, but to enact radical changes in the economy.
- To combine Western technology with Russian autocracy, thus sustaining autocracy by economic advance.

D. Work

i) Economic

- Assisted massive economic expansion of 1890s.
- Built on work of predecessors, but now greater urgency, coherence, ie the 'Witte System' (see next page).
- Great propagandist as well as manager of industrialisation, ie used press, organised competitions, exhibitions.
- Great advocate of railways; grew from 30,000 km in 1890 to 60,000 by 1904.
- As Transport Minister, helped initiate Trans-Siberian railway.
- 1894. Established state liquor monopoly, eventually producing 30% of state revenue.
- 1897. Put rouble on Gold Standard.
- Budget doubled in the 1890s; money poured into investment.
- Reformed company law.
- Developed Russian steamship companies.
- Challenged educational philosophy of conservative Russia as inadequate for modern, industrial state. Favoured spread of technical education. 1894-1904, technical schools grew from 8 to 100.
- 1902. Chaired Conference on the Needs of the Agricultural Industry, which detailed faults of the mir.

ii) Political

- Originally believed in autocracy, but in 1905 advised the creation of a Duma as he realised Nicholas was unable to uphold the autocracy.
- Appointed President of Council of Ministers October 1905; in effect, first constitutional Prime Minister of Russia.
- Helped restore foreign confidence in Russia, and negotiated vital French loan.
- April 1906. Dismissed (technically he resigned) just when Duma met, as he was no longer required by the tsar.
- Had weak political base; disliked by many for selling out Russia to foreign capitalists.
- Despised by Nicholas as an upstart, too dynamic.
- Was attacked as both a revolutionary and reactionary.
- Twice dismissed from key jobs (1903,6) and given nominal posts.
- Worked in an unsympathetic environment, and was defeated by it.

iii) Diplomatic

- 1890s. Favoured expansion of Russian influence in East to open up resources, especially via railways, but he criticised Russia's aggressive approach.
- This helped cause his dismissal in 1903. Out of office when Russia got involved in disastrous Russo-Japanese War.

Chart 9.1 *continued*

– Aug 1905. Successfully negotiated lenient peace with Japan.
– 1910s. Criticised those advocating an assertive foreign policy. Urged need to maintain peace. Saw war in 1914 as a catastrophe.

E. Criticism of Witte

i) Industry

– Chiefly concerned with heavy industry (railways, metallurgy, engineering). Neglected light industry, eg textiles. Neglected need to build up smaller, sophisticated machine and electrical industries to reduce reliance on imports.
– Concern for prestige projects like Trans-Siberian Railway which were in advance of Russia's immediate requirements.
– Dependence on foreign capital, especially in key areas like iron, made Russia vulnerable to fluctuations in international confidence, eg 1901-2 collapse, when 2400 firms closed.
– Ruthless pursuit of good of state at expense of the individual.

ii) Finance

– High taxes, especially indirect, put great burden on masses, and harmed the domestic market.
– High tariffs put up costs of imported agricultural machinery, fertilisers etc.
– Budget only balanced by having two accounts, an 'ordinary' (balanced), and an 'extraordinary' (in deficit) to pay for military, railways and debt servicing.

iii) Agriculture

– Neglected needs of agriculture. Criticised for having no agricultural policy.
– Increased extraction of grain from peasants by over 20%. Peasant consumption levels fell 25%.

iv) Political

– Aimed to reinvigorate autocracy, but created social unrest. Helped cause 1905 Revolution through growth of volatile proletariat, financial pressure on peasantry, contact with West, and raised expectations.
– Had no real sympathy for Duma system he had helped set up.
– High-handed. Failed to co-ordinate his policy with that of other branches of the government.

F. Defence of Witte

– Worked in unfavourable climate; bitterly critical of quality of Russian entrepreneurs, and lack of trained, efficient, uncorrupt bureaucracy.
– Failed to receive sustained commitment to his policies from Nicholas and whole sections of ruling elite.
– His economic policy was diverted by non-economic factors, eg the military requirements of railways, and the social stability need to maintain the mir.
– Was aware of agriculture's problems and hoped industrial advance would eventually help it. He followed List's view, 'What is good for industry, is good for agriculture.' By 1900s had come to see problem of mir, but unprepared to tackle this sensitive issue.

G. Overall assessment

– Name synonymous with Russian industrialisation, but chief features preceded him.
– Sacrificed present for future gains; gambled that industry would produce benefits before the masses revolted.
– Although he intended his industrialisation programme to reinvigorate tsarism, it has been argued it helped undermine it.
– However, his mixed role as diplomat, reformer, repressor and financial negotiator played major role in saving tsarism during the 1905 Revolution.
– His political reforms might have allowed tsarism to develop, but his tenure of office was too insecure and brief.

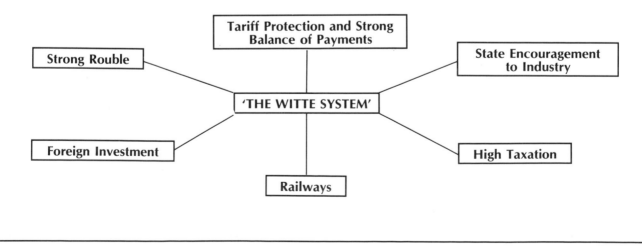

Chart 9.2 Stolypin. A potential saviour of tsarism?

A. Basic details

1862 Born Pyotr Arkadyevich to gentry family. Became civil servant, then Governor of Saratov Province.

1906 May, Minister of Interior. July, President of Council of Ministers.

1906-7 Organised post 1905 repression.

1907 June, Electoral law.

1906-11 Agrarian reforms.

1911 Assassinated.

B. Character

— Cold, tough, abrasive.
— Resolute, convinced right, ambitious.
— Superb organiser.

C. Ideas and aims

— Technocrat. Determined to improve efficiency of tsarism through conservative reforms.
— Great nationalist, with deep love of Russia.
— Initially saw a powerful Duma as obstacle to effective government, but after 1905 accepted it had a role to play.

D. Work

i) Economic

— Agriculture. (see chart 7.8)
Reforms 1906-11 to encourage private ownership, consolidation of strips, improved efficiency, so as to create prosperous, stable, loyal peasantry.

ii) Political

a) Repression after 1905 Revolution.
— 'First pacification, and then only then, reform.'
Courtmartials and 'necktie' (hangings). Repression of Kadet signatories of Vyborg proclamation.

b) Approach to Duma.
— July 1906. Reluctantly agreed to dismiss lst Duma, and issue agrarian reforms by decree.
— 2nd Duma also too hostile to co-operate, so dismissed
— June 1907 electoral law, 'Stolypin's coup'. Restricted franchise to reduce influence of radicals and national minorities.
— At first worked with Third Duma. Effective public speaker, able to sway Duma. Good relations with Octobrist Guchkov, but increasingly came to rely on Right Nationalists.
— 1911. Upset Duma over his use of emergency decrees over extension of zemstva.
— By 1911 had alienated both Right and Liberals.

c) Cabinet government.
— Enforced overhaul of government, and move towards proper cabinet.
— Greater coherence of government; break with tradition of weak ministers.

d) Nicholas.
— Nicholas increasingly disliked Stolypin (as he defended Duma, and criticised Rasputin); but retained him as he managed the Duma.
— Court intrigue against Stolypin, and 1911 zemstva quarrel meant Stolypin near dismissal before his assassination.

e) Other points.
— Strong nationalist; imposed Russification on Finland. Anti-semitic.
— Stressed religion as a conservative political force.

E. Assessment

— Has been seen as Russian Bismarck; conservative reformer who might have preserved tsarism.
— In this view, his assassination seen as tragedy, harming consolidation of Duma system.
— Also agrarian reforms could have brought prosperity and contentment to countryside but for outbreak of World War.

But:-
— Can be argued, his political base weak, and his dismissal likely.
— Agrarian reforms ill-conceived, and made limited impact.
— Also, Stolypin's own role not crucial. Agrarian reforms were likely in any case: Idea of weakening mir had long been advocated, and Nicholas's 1905 decision to end redemption payments removed one role from mir.
— Reform schemes originated from Danish official within bureaucracy, rather than Stolypin himself, though he showed determination in enacting them.
— Stolypin's death in 1911 had no effect on continuance of agrarian reforms.

Chart 9.3 Pobedonostsev. An unintentional destroyer of tsarism?

A. Basic details

1827 Born, son of priest professor. Studied law. Became university law lecturer and civil servant. Assisted legal reforms.
1861 Appointed tutor to future Tsar Alexander III.
1880 Director General of Holy Synod.
1881 Chief adviser to Alexander III. Tutor to heir Nicholas.
1894 Chief advisor to Nicholas II.
1905 Dismissed as Director General in October
1907 Died.

B. Character

– Dry, reserved.
– Pessimist.

C. Ideas and aims

– Great philosopher of absolutism; saw it as historically justified and basis for unity of state.
– Admired reign of Nicholas I which he saw as an honest, paternalist administration.
– Saw man as weak, vicious, so God gave power to autocrat to overcome this.
– Considered parliamentary government encouraged greedy, ambitious, manipulating politicians, and would lead to disintegration of Russia.
– Government must maintain stability, and rally nation based on land, family and national church.
– Anti-semitic; once suggested Jewish problem could be solved by killing one third, expelling another third, and assimilating the remaining Jews.

D. Work

i) As tutor

– Considerable influence as tutor to last two tsars.

ii) As government adviser.

– Helped persuade Alexander III to reject 1881 Loris-Melikov proposals and dismiss him.
– Had JPs replaced by new land captains to restore landed nobility to rightful place as guardian of peasant.
– Greatest influence in 1880s as arch exponent of repression, reinforcing natural tendencies of Alexander III.
– Responsible for Nicholas's 'senseless dreams' speech in 1895.

iii) As Head of Orthodox Church

– Great influence on education.
– Favoured spread of Church-run primary education as vehicle for consolidating religion, respect and Russian culture.
– Saw education as a moral not intellectual process. Favoured a restricted curriculum based on faith, not reason.
– Saw non-Orthodox subjects as disloyal. Consequent repression of them made this a self-fulfilling allegation.

E. Assessment

– Served to determine character and policies of last two tsars; reinforced their opposition to change just when Russia needed it.
– Not notable for any particular major policy (unlike Witte, Stolypin) but great influence in resisting change in declining years of tsarism.
– Earned nickname 'Grand Inquisitor'. His beliefs, and even appearance, seen by opponents as symbolising worst features of hated regime.
– Seen as great philosopher behind the throne who actually did more than anyone else to destroy it.

But:-

– Possible to exaggerate his influence, particularly after 1890 when he increasingly withdrew from court.
– Most famous advocate of unbending autocracy, but there were numerous others.
– Just reinforced a policy likely to occur anyway.

Chart 9.4 Rasputin. An unintentional destroyer of tsarism?

A. Basic details

(Early life as obscure as his death is legendary.)

1862 or after — Born Grigory Yefimovich to Siberian peasant family. Developed reputation as seer and profligate. Given nickname Rasputin (degenerate).

1904 — At last a son (Alexis) born to Alexandra, but soon discovered to be a haemophiliac.

1905 — Well received in polite St Petersburg society. In Nov. Nicholas recorded in his diary meeting 'a man of God named Grigori'.
Helped to stop Alexis's bleeding. Influence on Alexandra grew; Nicholas ignored police reports about his behaviour.

1911 — His behaviour a scandal. After death of hostile Stolypin, Rasputin's influence increased.

1914 — Stabbed in assassination attempt, June 28. Seriously ill, but pleaded with Nicholas to avoid war.

1915 — Nicholas made himself Commander in Chief near front; left Alexandra in virtual charge of government, and Rasputin had great influence over government appointments.

1916 — Dec. Poisoned, shot and eventually drowned by disgruntled aristocrats. Buried at royal residence at Tsarskoe Selo.

1917 — Body disinterred and burnt.

B. Character

- Very powerful personality. Hypnotic eyes.
- Drunkard womaniser.
- Some sympathy for ordinary poor people.

C. Ideas and aims

- Little evidence about his ideas.
- Believed sin was one way to gain salvation.
- Firm believer in monarchy, and hostile to Duma where both his behaviour and influence were criticised.
- Opposed to war in 1914; predicted disaster.
- Claimed to speak for the ordinary people from whom he came.

D. Work

- Probably through hypnosis, he had calming influence on Alexis, and may have saved his life in 1907.
- Seen by Alexandra and Nicholas as the only person able to prolong the life of Tsarevich Alexis.
- Held no formal position, and little evidence of influence on actual policy decisions except government vodka policy and pacific line in 1913 Balkan crisis.
- Received thousands of petitions, but on minor issues.
- Influence on appointments, eg Protopov as Interior Minister, Sturmer as Prime Minister in 1916.

E. Assessment

- Rasputin's career not unique as other humble mystics had gained patronage from Russian upper classes, especially women.
- Has been seen as major cause of the revolution as he discredited Nicholas, especially with aristocrats, tsarism's natural supporters.
- Partly responsible for poor appointments, especially 'ministerial leapfrog' after 1915 when his influence strongest, and tsarism under greatest pressure.
- Boasted of great influence, which served to discredit tsarism. Even if this influence was exaggerated, it was believed by contemporaries to be great.
- Considerable influence on Alexandra, and through her on Nicholas, though his advice was not always taken.
- Has been suggested his murder was the first step to revolution as it showed respect for the tsar's wishes had disappeared. Possible prelude to 'right wing revolution' to save dynasty by replacing Nicholas.
- Easy to confuse notoriety with historical importance.
- More a symptom of decay of tsarist system than a cause of it.

b) 'He was a superb organiser, and he was tireless; he was also swift, decisive, and harsh . . . He was a burning patriot, and this meant he had no choice but to believe in the peasants, who were the country.'
(Crankshaw, E. (1978), *Shadow of the Winter Palace* p.431).

c) 'For all his steel spectacles and his desiccated appearance, (he) was a reactionary in the high romantic manner. He believed in the total incapacity of mankind to govern itself intelligently, or even to behave in a reasonable and decently intelligent manner over any length of time . . . More than any single man he was to be the evil genius of the dynasty, all through the reign of Alexander III and well into that of Nicholas II, working with a single-minded dedication for the upholding of suicidal policies.'
(Crankshaw, E. (1978), *Shadow of the Winter Palace* p.312)

d) 'outstanding in his brazenness and boldness, and the mesmeric quality of his gaze. He appealed strongly to the debatable idea that the bigger the sinner the nearer he is to God.'
(Crankshaw, E. (1978),*Shadow of the Winter Palace* p.438)

e) He 'believed with passion that he was leading his country to a glorious future beneath a reinvigorated autocracy. And indeed he performed miracles. But it may also be argued that with his crashcourse of industrialisation he had a great deal to do with the creation of the conditions which made the country's stability hopelessly vulnerable to the imbecilities of Nicholas II.'
(Crankshaw, E.(1978), *Shadow of the Winter Palace* p.338)

f) He ' . . . accepted the new state of affairs in which basic civil liberties and political rights had been proclaimed . . . He wished to part with 'the old police order of things' and to collaborate with the Duma. Yet he was in an older tradition, that of the masterful enlightened bureaucrat who preferred to promote and control reforms from above, and had little taste or talent for politics . . .
He was an oldfashioned, almost chauvinistic patriot and deeply devoted to monarchy. He suffered . . . from the hostility of reactionary opponents of change, from the suspicions of liberals and, naturally, from the hatred of revolutionaries whom he repressed with fierce effectiveness. Above all, he suffered from the limitations and weakness of the monarch, which restricted his freedom of action . . . (He) may not have been the Russian Bismarck his admirers saw, but he loomed very large on the Russian scene.'
(Rogger, H. (1983), *Russia in the Age of Modernisation and Revolution* p.37)

g) 'In this new world of flux, when all manner of alien political and philosophic doctrines threatened Russia's precarious stability the autocracy was more necessary than ever as an agent of the status quo. Autocracy denoted a practice and a theory that initiated and justified the enforcement of uniformity of belief and conduct in every sphere of life. The church and the schools must inculcate the virtues of conformity to the whole prevailing order . . . On this basis, (he) defended the censor and denounced freedom of the press as an avenue to the dissemination of falsehood; parliamentarianism as a facade for intrigue; Jews, Poles and Catholics as aliens within the Russian body politic; and an independent and irremoveable judiciary as a shackle on the freedom of the state.'
(Kochan, L. (1970), *Russia in Revolution* p.64)

h) 'a pernicious pervert whose activity accelerated the downfall of imperial Russia.'
(Quoted by Dymtryshyn, B.(1974), Imperial Russia. A Sourcebook p.439)

B. Assessment of individuals

B.1. Comparative chart exercise.

Use charts 9.1 to 9.4 and the quotations above to fill in the comparative chart below. You might not be able to complete all the sections, but this itself might be informative.

	Witte	Stolypin	Pobedonostsev	Rasputin
Character				
Key positions				
Aims				
Attitude to autocracy				
Economic ideas				
Other important aspects				
Major achievements				
Importance				

B.2. Role of the individual. Debate about Pobedonostsev, Witte, Stolypin and Rasputin.

One of the key tasks of a historian is to assess the significance of the work of individual people. Some historians still support the old tradition which sees history largely as the story of the heroic (or villainous) lives of great individuals. Others tend to stress more the context within which individuals acted. They consider broader factors, such as economic and social developments, and political structures, as more significant. In this view, individuals may influence particular events but do not determine the whole course of a country's development.

Late nineteenth century Russia provides fertile ground for this debate. Some historians have suggested that but for Nicholas II, or Rasputin, or even Pobedonostsev, tsarism might have survived. It has also been argued that if only Witte had not been dismissed or Stolypin assassinated, they might have saved the regime.

The contrasting view sees the work of such individuals as largely the product of the situation, such as the need to industrialise and make changes after the 1905 Revolution. Even the apparently unique Rasputin can be set within the context of the Russian aristocracy's tendency to believe in 'holy men'; in addition, his actual influence has been disputed.

Such points should emerge during a debate about which of the above ministers and advisers had the most important influence on Tsarist Russia. It could be organised as follows:

i) One student, or a small group, chooses one of the above four, and makes a brief speech stressing his importance.
ii) Each 'individual' is then assessed by the class, with marks given both for 'Presentation' (ie the way the case has been argued), and for 'Historical Importance'.
iii) The two 'individuals' gaining the highest marks, then enter the 'second round', where they argue between themselves why one was more important than the other.
iv) A new set of marks is then taken to decide the 'winner', ie the most important.
v) The exercise is then reviewed.

The idea of marks and a 'winner' is obviously false, but the exercise should be an enjoyable way to explore the issue of historical importance.

When trying to assess the importance of an individual it might be useful to consider these and other questions:

a) **What did he achieve?** ie what did he do? What effect did his actions have, short term, long term? Did his work last? Were his ideas and policies wise? How difficult was the situation facing him? Did he tackle the problems? Did his work fulfil its purpose? Were there unintended effects?
b) **What did he not do?** ie was there a need neglected? An alternative path rejected?
c) **How responsible was he for the measures attributed to him?** Might they have happened anyway? Consider the hypothetical question, what might have happened if he had not lived?

B.3. Contemporary satirical prints on tsarist ministers and advisers.

Study the prints in chart 9.5

i) Identify individuals 1,2 and 3. (3 marks)
ii) Why was person 1 called the 'Evil Genius of Russia', and portrayed the way he was? (3 marks)
iii) What feature of Tsarist Russia in 1905-1906 do prints (b), (c) and (e) all identify? (Examine the border of print (b), and the cellars in print (e), and consider what 'Moscow Red' represents in print (c). (3 marks)
iv) What reason for person 3 being so resented is illustrated in prints (d) and (f)? Which of them do you consider makes the point more effectively? Why? (3 marks)
v) What additional reason for his being criticised is evident in cartoon (e)? (2 marks)
vi) Most historians would consider his portrayal in cartoons (d) and (f) (if not (e)) is exaggerated. Does this, however, greatly reduce the value of the cartoons as evidence? (Consider: What do they suggest about people's attitudes? How important were these? (6 marks)

C. Concluding essay

'Witte and Stolypin came too late to save the tsarist' regime.'
Discuss.

C. Nicholas II. The views of historians

Although the preceding individuals helped shape the development of tsarism, one could argue that the one person most responsible for the eventual collapse of tsarism was Nicholas II. He held the power to appoint and dismiss such ministers, and ultimately claimed, and took, responsibility for the actions of the Russian government. The following section looks at a range of primary and secondary evidence about Nicholas.

Chart 9.5 Cartoons on Russian ministers and advisors

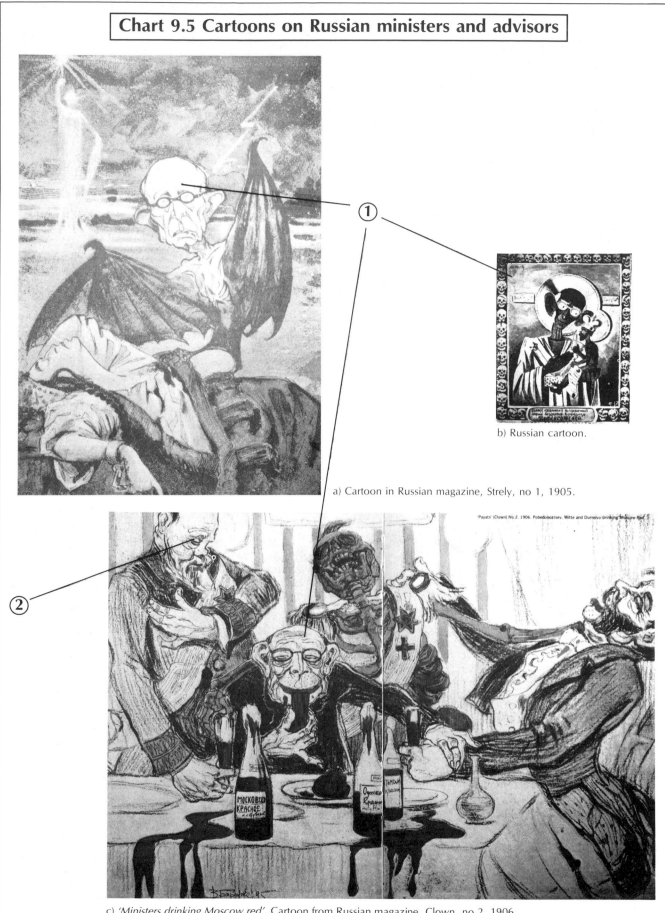

a) Cartoon in Russian magazine, Strely, no 1, 1905.

b) Russian cartoon.

c) 'Ministers drinking Moscow red'. Cartoon from Russian magazine, Clown, no 2, 1906.

Chart 9.5 *continued*

d) Russian cartoon.

e) Russian cartoon.

f) *A satirists impression of the Imperial household in 1916.* Russian cartoon.

Worksection 9 part 2

A. Evidence on Nicholas II

A.1. Organising material. Secondary evidence.

The following exercise shows one way of organising a range of evidence so as to develop a clearer picture of a topic.

i) Draw up a chart as follows to organise the following evidence from historians about aspects of Nicholas II.

> The seven aspects are as follows:
> 1) his upbringing 2) his character 3) his attitude towards autocracy 4) his intentions 5) his attitude to and treatment of his ministers 6) his attitude towards his people, and his understanding of them 7) his understanding of Russia's needs, and his general fitness to rule.

Historian	Aspect:	1	2	3	4	5	6	7
a) Charques								
b) Stephenson								
c) Kennan								
d) Seton-Watson								
e) Rogger								
f) De Jonge								
g) Keep								

ii) Read the following secondary sources about Nicholas II, and select evidence from them to fill in the chart.

iii) Which historian do you consider most sympathetic to Nicholas? Explain your decision.

iv) Which do you consider most harsh? Why?

Historians' views.

a) Charques:
   'No Russian Emperor was more completely posses-

sed by his prerogative as autocrat. In that strange region of the mind where men believe they are anointed by God, Nicholas staked faith, duty and all else upon the dogma of autocracy . . . He looked upon the absolute power he had inherited as an inviolable trust, to be transmitted whole and unimpaired to his successor. Through every mischance and portent of crisis in his reign, his first rule of conduct was to seek to preserve it . . .

It was his indifference to those who served him which

blunted the edge of Nicholas's good intentions. Charles I and Louis XVI, both monarchs by similarly divine right, meant equally well. In his pathetic ineffectualness Nicholas recalls Louis; in his duplicity and obstinacy, as in the ingratitude with which he cast off those who might have saved him and set himself to digging his own grave, the likeness with Charles I is unmistakable.'
(Charques, R. (1965), *Twilight of Imperial Russia* pp.49-51)

b) Stephenson:

'As a deeply religious man he took literally the words which he had spoken at his coronation. He believed that even were he to agree to a constitution he would still, in the eyes of God, be responsible for what happened to his subjects. By surrendering to the politicians he would have deprived himself of the power to fulfil his responsibilities . . .
This simple, honourable, industrious, pious, obstinate and bigoted family man did not possess the intellectual equipment necessary for the analysis of the choices facing him.'
(Stephenson, G. (1969), *History of Russia* p.189-190)

c) Kennan:

'Poorly educated, narrow in intellectual horizon, a wretchedly bad judge of people, isolated from Russian society at large, in contact only with the most narrow military and bureaucratic circles, intimidated by the ghost of his imposing father and the glowering proximity of his numerous gigantic uncles, helpless under the destructive influence of his endlessly unfortunate wife, Nicholas was obviously inadequate to the demands of his exalted position; and this was an inadequacy for which no degree of charm, of courtesy, of delicacy of manner, could compensate . . . Time and again, in the record of his reign, one finds the evidences of his short-sightedness and his lack of grasp of the realities of the country.'
(Kennan, G. (1979),*The Breakdown of the Tsarist Autocracy,* in Ed.Emsley, C. *Conflict and Stability in Europe* p220-1)

d) Seton-Watson:

'If one tries to see the reign of Nicholas in perspective, one can hardly maintain that he had made so conspicuous a success of affairs for the last twenty years as clearly to justify the belief that he and his immediate circle could best rule Russia alone, without the help, and in direct conflict with the wishes of the great majority of the politically conscious Russians, and indeed of the whole educated part of the nation . . .
The truth is that the insuperable obstacle was his dogmatic devotion to autocracy, which had been deeply implanted in him.'
(Seton-Watson, H. (1967), *The Russian Empire* p.717-8)

e) Rogger:

'If Nicholas was weak-willed and devious, if he had so little confidence in his own judgement that he distrusted his ministers and failed to back them up, was this not as much an indictment of autocracy as of the autocrat? . . . Nicholas was not lacking in firmness or, depending on one's view, obstinacy . . . when it came to the integrity of his power or the defence of cherished prejudices . . . The problem was rather an excess than a want of firmness; more precisely, an inability to distinguish between flexibility and weakness, strength and mulishness.
Even more poorly prepared than his father for the burdens of kingship, Nicholas had no knowledge of the world of men, of politics or government to help him make the difficult and weighty decisions that in the Russian system the tsar alone must make. His training was adequate only for the one role he would not play, the ceremonial one of the constitutional monarch. The only lodestars he recognised were an inherited belief in the moral rightness and historical necessity of autocracy, and a religious faith, bordering on fatalism, that he was in God's hands and his actions divinely inspired . . .
A simple man himself, he was convinced until the very end that the simple people were on his side and that this made him the best judge of the country's mood. Protest and dissent were temporary aberrations traceable to agitators, Jews or selfish politicians.'
(Rogger, H. (1983), *Russia in the Age of Modernisation and Revolution* p.16-19)

f) de Jonge:

'It is hard to imagine anyone less well equipped to steer Imperial Russia into the twentieth century than Nicholas II. A family man first and foremost . . . as an autocrat he was hopeless. He had not even had the benefit of proper preparation for his task. His education had essentially been that of a cavalry officer . . .
Nicholas's personality did not help him overcome the limitations of his education. A short, neat figure of a man, five feet seven inches tall, he was timid, introverted and weak, in the sense that he was incapable of making up his mind and sticking to his decisions. However, it must be said that he always commanded great love and loyalty in his immediate entourage, together with a considerable amount of respect. He had great charm . . .
Yet despite his considerable majesty of manner, as an emperor he lacked stature and that taste for power which is . . . vital for an autocrat . . .
Yet weak though he may have been as a ruler, he possessed that peculiar dogged obstinacy that sometimes accompanies weak men in power. On the rare occasions on which he made up his mind definitely he was impossible to move; no argument, however convincing, could reach him . . .
Nicholas sincerely believed that he had received Russia from God, and was personally responsible for her well-being. This meant he did not have the right to delegate or dilute his power in any way. It also meant that when he heard the voice of conscience advise a certain course nothing could dissuade him from taking it. Obstinacy, mysticism, and weakness combined to shape perhaps the most disastrous of all his characteristics: a deadly fatalism'
(De Jonge, A. (1983), *Life and Times of Rasputin* p.118-121)

g) Keep:

'The acute tensions which had (by the 1890s) developed in Russian society posed a formidable threat to the absolutist regime. It could overcome them only by showing extreme foresight and flexibility. But the throne was next occupied by a monarch deficient in such qualities. Nicholas II . . . inherited his father's faults without his modest virtues. Though a stubborn advocate of firm government, he was weak in character and intellect. He mistrusted ministers whose abilities surpassed his own, preferring to rely on backstairs advisers, often of unsavoury reputation . . . By his own actions he helped isolate the monarchy from the whole of Russian society, not excluding even the most moderate elements who were its natural allies against revolution.'
(*Cambridge Modern History Vol XI,* (1962), p.372)

A.2. Primary Evidence. Contemporaries' comments on Nicholas.

Read the following primary sources on Nicholas II.

i) What further evidence do they provide about the seven aspects identified in exercise A.1.?
ii) Are there any conflicts of evidence? Give examples.
iii) Choose any four of the contemporary sources, and comment on each one's reliability.
iv) How does the last extract suggest why Croce has argued that 'all history is contemporary history'?

a) Witte:

'His character is the source of all our misfortunes. He is incapable of steering the ship of State into a quiet harbour. His outstanding failure is a lack of willpower. Though benevolent and not unintelligent, this shortcoming disqualifies him totally as the unlimited autocratic ruler of the Russian people.
The Emperor's character may be said to be esentially feminine . . . His Majesty would not tolerate about his person anyone he considered more intelligent than himself or anybody with opinions differing from those of his advisors.'
(Witte describes Nicholas' view of ruling?)
'I do what I please, and what I please to do is good. If people do not understand it, that is because they are ordinary mortals, while I am God's annointed.'
(Quoted in Elliot, J. (1974), *Fall of Eagles* p.124, and Floyd, D. (1969), *Russia in Revolt* p.6)

b) Kaiser Wilhelm II:

'The way to deal with him is to be the last to leave the room.'
(Quoted in Elliot, J. (1974), *Fall of Eagles* p.149)

c) Grand Duke Alexander Mikhailovich:

'He was always timid, almost painfully so, and when by a strong effort of will he conquered that timidity, he came out with what he wanted to say in an almost brutal manner . . . He never had an opinion of his own . . . his want of mind making him always endorse the judgement of the last person he speaks to.'
(Quoted by de Jonge, A. (1983), *Life and Times of Rasputin* p.121)

d) Former Interior Minister Prince Sviatopolk Mirsky:

'One could never trust him. What he approved today will be cancelled by him tomorrow.'
(Quoted by Halpern, in ed. Kochan M. and L. (1967), *Russian Themes* p.118)

e) Rasputin:

'The tsar can change his mind from one minute to the next; he's a sad man; he lacks guts.'
'Papa understands nothing and cannot cope.'
(Quoted in de Jonge, A. (1983), *Life and Times of Rasputin* pp.318,337)

f) Empress Alexandra:

'My poor Nicky's cross is heavy, all the more so as he has nobody on whom he can thoroughly rely and who can be a real help to him. He has had so many bitter disappointments, but through it all he remains brave and full of faith in God's mercy. He tries so hard, works with such perseverance, but the lack of what I call 'real' men is great . . . On my knees I pray to God to give me wisdom to help him in this heavy task.'
(Quoted by de Jonge, A. (1983), *Life and Times of Rasputin* p.126)

g) Courtier Count Paul Benckendorff:

'His real affection was for his family, with which he was identified, and which was always the object of his unique adoration. Intelligent, good, well-meaning, his character did not allow him to respond to the gigantic events of the closing years of his reign. Weary and overburdened as he was, these events crushed him.'
(Quoted by Lyons, (1974), *Nicholas II, the Last Tsar* p.216)

h) Kerensky, socialist member of the 3rd and 4th Dumas, and Prime Minister August to October 1917.

He describes Nicholas in his memoirs *Crucifixion of Liberty.* (1934):

'He merely believed what his father and Pobedonostsev has instilled into him; there would be no Russia without autocracy; Russia and the autocracy were one; he himself was the impersonation of the autocracy. So the magic circle closed. There was no way out, unless it was into disaster and void . . . Living in the twentieth century, he had the mentality of the Muscovite Kings.
The daily work of a monarch he found intolerably boring. He could not stand listening long or seriously to ministers' reports, or reading them. He liked such ministers' reports, or reading them. He liked such ministers as could tell an amusing story and did not weary the monarch's attention with too much business . . .
When it came to defending his dvine right his usual indifference left him; he became cunning, obstinate, and cruel, merciless at times.'
Kerensky (in his 1929 book, *The Catastrophe),* describes a visit to Nicholas after his abdication:

'I think the Red terror has already made some people, and will make many others, reconsider the personal responsibility of Nicholas II for the horrors of his reign. I for one do not think he was the outcast, the inhuman monster, the deliberate murderer I used to imagine. I began to realise there was a human side to him. It became clear to me he had acquiesced in the whole ruthless sytem without being moved by any personal ill-will and without even realising that it was bad. His mentality and his circumstances kept him wholly out of touch with his people. He heard of the blood and tears of thousands upon thousands only through official documents, in which they were represented as 'measures' taken by the authorities 'in the interest of the peace and security of the state' . . . From his youth he had been trained to believe that his welfare and the welfare of Russia were one and the same thing, so that 'disloyal' workmen, peasants and students who were shot down, executed or exiled seemed to him mere monsters who must be destroyed for the sake of the country and the 'faithful subjects' themselves.'
(Quoted by Mazour, A. (1960), *Rise and Fall of the Romanovs* p. 171-2, and Stacey, A. (1968), *Lenin and the Ussian Revolutions* pp. 31-32)

A.3. Comments by Nicholas II

Read the following comments by Nicholas II.

  i) Which aspects identified in exercises A.1 and A.2 are reinforced by Nicholas' statements?
  ii) What evidence do they provide of how Nicholas viewed the Duma?
  iii) Discuss the three extracts which you consider most powerfully help explain the tragedy of Nicholas II.

a) 'I have a firm, and absolute conviction that the fate of Russia — that my own fate and that of my family — is in the hands of God who has placed me where I am. Whatever may happen to me, I shall bow down to His will with the consciousness of never having had any thought other than that of serving the country which He has entrusted to me.'
(Quoted in Massie, R. (1968), *Nicholas and Alexandra* p.vi)

b) Nicholas on becoming tsar after the surprise death of his father aged 49, 1894:
'What is going to happen to me . . . to all Russia?. I am not prepared to be the Tsar. I never wanted to become one. I know nothing of the business of ruling. I have no idea of even how to talk to ministers.'
(Quoted by Massie, R. (1969), *Nicholas and Alexandra* p.329)

c) Addressing Zemstva representatives Jan 1895:
'Let it be known to all that I, while devoting all my energies to the good of the people, shall maintain the principles of autocracy just as firmly and unflinchingly as did my unforgettable father.'
(Quoted by Seton-Watson, H. (1967), *The Russian Empire* p.549)

d) Nicholas's address to first Duma, April 1906:
'With ardent faith in the radiant future of Russia I greet in you those best men whom I ordered my beloved subjects to choose from their midst . . . May this day be henceforth remembered as the day of the rebirth of the moral fibre of the Russian land, the day of the rebirth of her best forces.'
(Quoted by Riha,T. *Constitutional Developments in Russia,* in ed. Stavrou T. (1969) *Russia under the Last Tsar* p.87)

e) Nicholas to his mother March 1907:
'I have been constantly receiving messages from True Russian Men all over Russia expressing their indignation at such disrespectful behaviour in the Duma . . .
I am getting telegrams from everywhere petitioning me to order a dissolution; but it is too early for that. One must let them do something manifestly stupid or mean, and then, slap! And they are gone!'
(Quoted in ed. Bing, E. (1937), *Letters of Tsar Nicholas and Empress Marie*, p.229)

f) Nicholas in November 1905:
'Nine tenths of the trouble-makers are Jews; the people's whole anger has turned against them.'
(Quoted by Kochan, L. (1970), *Russia in Revolution* p.63)

g) Nicholas to Stolypin rejecting a proposal to relax restrictions on Jews:
'I pondered on the matter night and day.
Despite the most convincing arguments in favour of my approving the matter, my inner voice tells me more and more insistently that I should not take the decision myself. Up to now my conscience has never deceived me. Therefore, in this case I intend to follow its guidance.
I know that you believe that the 'Tsars's heart is in God's hands.'
Let it be so.
I bear a fearful responsibility to God for all the powers granted to me and I am ready at any time to give account of them to Him.'
(Quoted by McCauley, M. (1984), From *Octobrists to Bolsheviks* p.53)

h) Nicholas' reply to Alexandra in 1916 who had urged him to 'be the emperor, be Peter the Great, Ivan the Terrible':
'Tender thanks for the severe written scolding. Your poor little weak-willed hubby'.
(Quoted by de Jonge, A. (1983), *Life and Times of Rasputin* p.333)

i) Nicholas to Grand Duke Paul's request for political reform, December 1916:
'The day of my coronation I took my oath to absolute power. I must leave this oath intact to my son.'
(Quoted by Kochan, L. (1970), *Russia in Revolution p.191)

j) Nicholas to Buchanan, the British Ambassador in January 1917:
'Do you mean that I am to regain the confidence

of my people or that they are to regain my confidence?'
(Quoted by Kochan, L.(1970) *Russia in Revolution* p.18)

k) Nicholas just before his abdication, January 1917:
   'Is it possible that for 22 years I have tried to act for the best, and that for 22 years it was all a mistake?'
(Quoted by Grey, I. (1970), *The Romanovs* p.348)

l) Nicholas's comment on the Duma president's request for a government possessing the confidence of the country, February 1917:
   'That fatty Rodzianko has sent me some nonsense, which I shan't even answer'
(Quoted by Seton-Watson, H. (1967), *The Russian Empire* p.725)

m) His letter of abdication, March 1917:
   'In these decisive days in the life of Russia we have considered it our duty to make it easier for our people to unite and organise all their forces for the swift attainment of victory, and in agreement with the Imperial Duma we have decided for the good of the country to abdicate the throne of Russia and lay down the supreme power.'
(Quoted by Mazour, A.(1960), *Rise and fall of the Romanovs* p.179)

B. Nicholas II. An overall assessment

B.1. Make a list, in descending order of importance, of Nicholas's six greatest faults. Briefly explain your choice. What can be said in his defence?

B.2. Write a speech that you think Nicholas might have written after the February Revolution of 1917 defending his previous policies.

B.3. Construct an analytical chart (similar to those on Alexander I, Nicholas I, Alexander II and III) on the reign of Nicholas II.

C. Concluding essay

Re-read chapters five and six, and pages 107, 109-113. Then write one of the following essays:
   i) 'Nicholas II was totally unfitted to deal with the problems facing his country and dynasty.' To what extent do you agree with this judgement?
   ii) 'Nicholas II wished the best for his country, but made a series of stupid mistakes, and failed to understand the grave problems Russia faced.' Discuss this comment.

Advice. Both these essays cover similar material, but each essay needs to be structured around the precise title set. They both concentrate on Nicholas's fitness to rule, the latter giving some assistance as to how this might be assessed. Both also involve consideration of the problems facing Russia. This might serve as an introduction.

In the first essay the phrase 'totally unfitted' is a very strong one, and might be modified. The 'problems facing the dynasty' need distinct treatment as they are highlighted in the title; these might be largely covered in general problems, but particular reference could be made to maintaining the three hundred year old Romanov dynasty, and the problem of Alexis (for when Nicholas finally produced a son, he was a haemophiliac).

This essay might be best approached by developing an argument demonstrating Nicholas's unfitness, then modifying it. The former might be easier, but counter points, perhaps stressing the greatness of the problems rather than Nicholas's inadequacies, could be made.

The second essay might be most effectively approached by discussing in turn the three particular aspects about Nicholas in the title. This is more likely to ensure a direct response. The issue of motivation is a difficult but interesting one. How does the historian assess what inspired Nicholas's policies? One would need to consider his statements about his beliefs, but such evidence needs to be treated cautiously. One could look at comments by contemporaries who had access to the inner discussions of the government, such as Witte, but he in particular illustrates the need to be critical of evidence. One could also look at Nicholas's actions, which ought to suggest whether high sounding statements of intent actually meant much. However, it is still possible genuinely to wish something, but be unable to achieve it.

One must also be careful not to assume that Nicholas's determination to uphold the autocracy is necessarily evidence against his good intentions. He may well have been misguided in his belief that the autocracy was vital for Russia's well-being, but that does not disprove good intent. Reference back to Alexander II (p29) might be illustrative of this point.

10 Foreign Policy and Conclusion

A Foreign policy

Russia's foreign policy was partly determined by domestic developments. Concern to maintain her position as a great power also inspired both emancipation and industrialisation. In addition the main wars in which she became involved had significant domestic effects.

Worksection 10 part 1

A. Russian foreign policy. Key features

A.1. Study charts 10.1 and 10.2 where the chief features of tsarist foreign policy are identified.

i) Explain some of the general problems Russia faced in foreign affairs due to her geographical position.

ii) What were the chief areas of interest for Russian foreign policy?

iii) Can any trends be seen in her diplomacy?

iv) To what extent was foreign policy influenced by domestic considerations, and vice versa? Refer in particular to the following wars: Napoleonic, Crimean, Japanese and First World War.

v) What evidence is there for the view that the Balkans were the 'graveyard of Russian diplomacy'?

vi) Discuss Westwood's view that 'Like a good chess-player, Russia moved in to fill accessible power vacuums while showing no interest in attacking strong positions.'

A.2. Analytical chart assessing foreign policy.

Draw up a chart with two columns, one headed 'Foreign Policy Successes', the other 'Foreign Policy Failures'. Select material from charts 10.1 and 10.2 to fill in the columns.

A.3. Primary evidence on foreign policy.

Read the following extracts. Describe the aspects of Russia's foreign policy revealed by each one.

a) The historian Pogodin in the 1830s:
He urged Russia to unite with 'the thirty million of our brothers and cousins who are scattered across the face of Europe from Constantinople to Venice . . . who are bound to us in a spiritual unity by origin and language despite geographical and political separation.'
(Quoted by Catchpole, B. (1976), *Map History of Russia* p.28)

b) Navy Minister Grigorovich 1913:
'The Straits in the hands of another state would mean the complete control of the economic development of southern Russia by a foreign power, and the transfer to that state of the hegemony (mastery) of the Balkans and the key for an aggressive advance into Asia Minor.'
(Quoted by McGrew, in ed. Stavrou T. (1969), *Russia under the Last Tsar* p.208)

c) Dostoevsky in his 'Diary of a Writer':
In Europe Russians 'were hangers-on and slaves, whereas we shall go to Asia as masters . . .
When we turn to Asia . . . in Russia there may occur something akin to what happened in Europe when America was discovered . . . With an inspiration for Asia, our spirit and our forces will be regenerated . . . Our civilising mission in Asia will bribe our spirit and drive us thither . . . Build only two railroads; begin with one to Siberia, and then to central Asia . . . Do you know that in Asia there are lands which are less explored than the interior of Africa? And do we know what riches are concealed in the bosom of these boundless lands?'
Quoted by McGrew, in ed. Stavrou, T. (1969), *Russia under the Last Tsar T* pp.220-1)

d) Grand Dukes Nikolai Nickolayevitch and Michailovitch arguing in favour of mobilisation during July 1914 crisis:
'A peace bought with cowardice would unleash revolution at home.'
(Quoted by Kochan, L. (1970), *Russia in Revolution* p.175)

e) Kadet Shingarev Sept 1915:
'After the thunder of Sevastopol Russian slavery ceased. The war with Japan sowed the seeds of a Russian constitution. Out of the torment of this war will come freedom for the nation and our liberation from old forces and instruments of power.'
(Quoted by Charques, R. (1965), *Twilight of Imperial Russia* p.225)

Chart 10.1 Russian foreign policy. 1

A. Influencing factors

Personalities
Officials on ground far from St Petersburg followed own policies, eg Chernayev in Tashkent, Muravyov in Manchuria.
Nicholas II prone to pressure for expansion in East.
Particular officials (eg Witte with 1905 Peace Terms, Izvolsky 1908 Bosnia-Herzegovina muddle, Hartwig in Balkans 1912-1914, Kokovtsov over mobilisation debates 1912-4), could influence course of events.

Military Factors
Military might main determinant of foreign policy.
Military strength (real or perceived) encouraged more assertion eg 1904 against Japan, and weakness encouraged caution, eg 1908-13 Balkans.
Concern to protect vital strategic areas, eg Straits.
Need to gain secure borders, eg in Asia.

Economic Factors
Great power status was increasingly dependent on economic strength.
Desire for economic resources encouraged expansion, eg in East.
Development of railways allowed influence to be extended, eg Siberia, Central Asia, China. Also military use.
Need for foreign loans influenced diplomacy, eg French alliance.
Concern to secure trade routes, especially the Straits.

Historical Factors
Early Kiev and Muscovy states conquered by Tatars from East. Imposed harsh rule and terror. Also attacked from West by Teutonic Knights.
By 16th century, Muscovy freed itself from Tatars, and itself expanding East.
In 18th century Russia defeated Sweden and Poland in struggle for supremacy in North. Russia then looked more to the West. State, surrounded by hostile forces, had maintained itself through strong government, tightly organising its scarce resources, and through military might.

FACTORS

Domestic Political Factors
Domestic problems could curb foreign policy aspirations, eg post Crimean War, post 1905 revolution.
Expansion abroad could also be seen as way to divert discontent, eg 1904 War against Japan; some also argue the First World War.
Domestic weakness might make government reluctant to risk further criticism with weak foreign policy, eg 1914 crisis.
Domestic pressures, eg from 1870s increasing Panslav agitation and after 1907 nationalist Duma pressure to defend Russia's prestige.

Geographical Position
Vast land mass required massive commitment to military.
Few natural defensive boundaries, particularly in West, her richest area; very vulnerable to attack.
Need to gain access to trade routes, ie Russia's 'urge to the sea'; seen with concern to secure head of the Baltic, to settle on the Black Sea and gain control of the Straits, and to establish base on the Pacific.

Ideological Factors
Concern to defend established authority, eg Holy Alliance, 1849 Hungary.
Panslav desire to lead federation of Slav people; (but easy to exaggerate degree of influence on government policy).
Religious desire to re-establish Christian control of Constantinople, and 'Holy Russia' mission to protect Orthodox Christians, eg Crimea.
'Civilising' mission in Asia.

International Context
19th century Russia greatly affected by rise of Germany in Europe, an increasingly powerful neighbour.
Internal problems of Austrian Empire, and her concern for Balkans.
Decline of neighbouring Ottoman Empire.
Growth of Slav nationalism.
Expansion of Japan, Britain and other European states in Asia, and the weakness of China.

B. General aspects

i) Areas of concern
Europe, especially Poland, Balkans,
Asia, ie Caucasus
Central Asia
Far East

ii) Pattern of interest
Interest fluctuated: generally if she received a set back in one area, eg Europe in Crimea 1856, Berlin Congress 1878, then Russia switched to concentrate elsewhere, eg Asia, where resistance less strong.

The 1905 defeat in Asia encouraged reconcentration on Balkans, leading to the First World War.

Chart 10.2 Russian foreign policy

POLAND

- Eastern parts acquired during 18th century partitions.
- After defeat of Napoleon, Alexander I claimed all Poland 1815, and gained most of it at Congress of Vienna. This 'Congress Poland' had its own constitution; considerable autonomy.
- 1830-31. Revolt met by repression; incorporated into Empire.
- 1863. **Revolt led to increased Russian control.**
- 1905. Revolt forced concessions on key issue of language, education, religion, but later retracted by Stolypin.
- Occupied by Germany during First World War.
- 1917. Provisional Government promised Poland independence.
- Formally gained independence 1919 after German defeat.

FINLAND

- Great strategic concern for Russia, as area considered vital for defending St Petersburg.
- Conquered from Sweden 1809; special rights, constitution of Grand Duchy confirmed.
- Well treated till 1890s Russification; infringements of Finnish rights created anti-Russian feeling.
- Evident in unrest 1905; forced concessions, but later retracted by Stolypin.
- 1917. Bolsheviks granted Finland independence.

BRITAIN

General
- Usually poor relations, as suspicious of each other's expansion, and competed for influence in Near and Far East, especially Persia, Afghanistan and route to India. Relations improved in 20th century.

Events
- Fought Russia in Crimean War, 1854-6.
- 1902. Allied with potential Russian enemy, Japan.
- 1905. Dogger Bank incident nearly led to war.
- 1906 onwards. Relations improved, as Russia was seen as weaker; also after 1882 Britain had control of Suez Canal, (alternative route to India) so she was less concerned about the Straits. Britain increasingly worried by Germany.
- 1907. Colonial disputes (Persia, Afghanistan, Tibet) settled by agreement, leading to so called 'Triple Entente' of First World War.

FRANCE

General
- Tsarist Russia initially hostile to France, seen as home of revolutions, but by 1890s mutual economic and military interests led to alliance.

Events
- 1854-6. France fought Russia in Crimean War.
- 1880s. Growing financial ties with France, and political differences played down. 1894, Russia reluctantly made formal military alliance directed at mutual enemy Germany.
- 1906. French loan crucial in helping tsarism recover from 1905 Revolution.
- 1914. Massive loan to finance Russian railways to help Russian mobilisation.
- 1914. The 1894 alliance, and German Schlieffen Plan, determined that France and Russia fought on same side in First World War.

GERMANY

General
- Crucial area as on Western border; agreement with Germany would secure this key frontier. Lasted till 1890, then antagonism grew.
- Pro-German elements in Russian government, especially among Right; favoured fellow semi-autocratic country. Many Russians had close industrial and banking connections with Germany. Also close royal family ties, eg. Nicholas II and William II cousins; most tsars' wives were German, eg. Alexandra. Large German communities, especially around the Baltic.
- Common concern to control Poles, seen in 1863.

Events
- First half of 19th century, Russia co-operated with Prussia in Holy Alliance to maintain status quo; reaffirmed at Munchengratz 1833.
- After Russia's Crimean defeat, conservative policy less prominent, and Russia agreed not to intervene against Prussia in her 1860 wars with Denmark, Austria and France, in return for Germany's support for revising Black Sea clauses of Treaty of Paris.
- From 1871, Russia was faced with growing power of Germany on her border.
- Whilst Bismarck was German Chancellor, relations generally good, and 1873-7, 1881-7 formed Dreikaiserbund with Germany and Austria-Hungary, but broke down over quarrels in Balkans.
- Also economic tension with Germany, eg. 1879, German tariffs hit Russian grain exports, and in 1888 Germany refused to renew loans to Russia; French filled the gap.
- 1887. Bismarck negotiated Reinsurance Treaty with Russia, but his successors did not renew it in 1890. Russia moved closer to France. She now had to rely more on military might for security in West.
- 1900s. Growing tension between powerful neighbours, each fearing the other would attack.
- 1905. William II and Nicholas II negotiated Bjorko Treaty, but rejected by both governments.
- German penetration into Ottoman Empire, and support for Austria-Hungary in Balkans worsened Russo-German relations, 1908-13.
- 1913. Tension over German General Liman von Sanders in Constantinople.
- Mutual fears eventually led to Russian mobilisation, July 1914, and German declaration of war.

AUSTRIA-HUNGARY

General
- First half of nineteenth century co-operated in conservative Holy Alliance, but territorial clash of interests in Balkans drove them apart.

Events
- 1849. Russia sent troops to crush Hungarian rebels, and persuaded Prussia to climb down to Austria at Olmutz 1850.
- Austria's failure to back up Russia in Crimea, and threat of hostile intervention, ruined Austro-Russian relations. Russia refused to intervene to prevent changes in Italy and Germany at Austria's expense.
- This non-interventionist stance by Russia crucial in allowing Italian and German unification to succeed.
- 1870s, 1880s. Improved Austro-Russian relations in Dreikaiserbunds, but broke down over conflicts in Balkans.
- Later rapprochements, eg. 1897-1908, also ruined by Balkan issues, as increasing suspicion of each others' actions in this crucial area.
- Austrian hostility to Russia's ally Serbia led to series of Balkan crises, and eventual war in 1914.

BALKANS

General
- Vital area of interest for Russia.
- Racial ties with fellow Slavs; desire to develop client states, or unite Slavs (panslavism).
- Religious sympathies for fellow Orthodox Christians, mainly ruled by Muslim Turks.
- **Strategically important for control of Straits.**
- Russia really needed an ally to support forward moves here as Britain and Austria would oppose her, but Bismarck would not support change to the status quo, and Russia's later ally France was cautious.

Events
- 1827-8. Nicholas I eventually intervened to help Greek rebels against Turkey.
- 1877. Intervened to help Bulgarian and Serb rebels. Gained creation of 'Big Bulgaria' at San Stefano, but upset other powers, and forced to lose most gains at Congress of Berlin. Seen as diplomatic humiliation.
- 1885-7. Tried to create client state in Bulgaria, but eventually lost influence.
- After 1905 Far Eastern defeat, renewed interest in Balkans, especially as the economic importance of Straits grew, and because of Nationalist pressure in the Duma.
- 1908-9. Tried to resist Austrian annexation of Slav Bosnia-Herzegovina, but too weak after war and revolution so forced to back down.
- 1912. Russia helped form Balkan League, primarily intended as defensive against Austria, but it turned on Turkey.
- 1912-13. During Balkan wars Russia again backed down to Austro-German threats.
- 1914. Determined to back Serbia in post-Sarajevo crisis; mobilisation led to First World War.

STRAITS AND BLACK SEA

- Vital concern for Russia, as only outlet from the Black Sea.
- Military concern. Ideally wanted to possess Straits to allow free passage of her warships. If full control not possible, wanted agreement to prevent passage of foreign warships through Straits.
- Also increasingly important as trade route for Russian grain exports and importation of Western machinery.
- Also religious desire to re-establish Christian control of Constantinople, former centre of Orthodox church.
- Various conventions over Straits during 19th century, some favourable to Russia, eg, Unkiar Skelessi 1833, some not, eg Peace of Paris 1856 neutralisation of Black Sea, ie. forbidding Russian fleet there.
- Renunciation of these clauses chief Russian foreign policy concern till 1870, with German support, renounced them: confirmed in London 1871.
- Closure of Straits for two weeks during Turkish-Italian War 1912 greatly harmed Russia's trade.
- 1913. Crisis with Germany over General Liman von Sanders.
- Various plans to seize Straits considered; Black Sea fleet vastly enlarged.
- 1915. Secret treaty with Allies awarded Russia Constantinople:

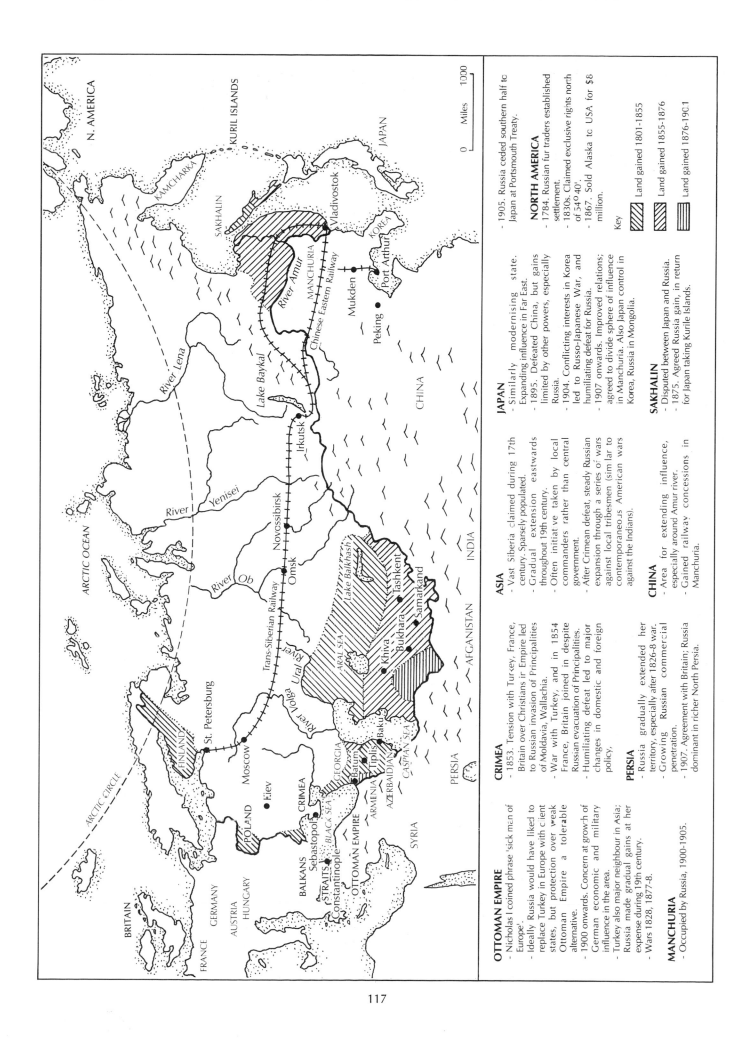

OTTOMAN EMPIRE
- Nicholas I coined phrase 'sick men of Europe'.
- Ideally Russia would have liked to replace Turkey in Europe with client states, but protection over weak Ottoman Empire a tolerable alternative.
- 1900 onwards. Concern at growth of German economic and military influence in the area.
- Turkey also major neighbour in Asia; Russia made gradual gains at her expense during 19th century.
- Wars 1828, 1877-8.

MANCHURIA
- Occupied by Russia, 1900-1905.

CRIMEA
- 1853. Tension with Turkey, France, Britain over Christians in Empire led to Russian invasion of Principalities of Moldavia, Wallachia.
- War with Turkey, and in 1854 France, Britain joined in despite Russian evacuation of Principalities.
- Humiliating defeat led to major changes in domestic and foreign policy.

PERSIA
- Russia gradually extended her territory, especially after 1826-8 war.
- Growing Russian commercial penetration.
- 1907. Agreement with Britain; Russia dominant in richer North Persia.

ASIA
- Vast Siberia claimed during 17th century. Sparsely populated.
- Gradual extension eastwards throughout 19th century.
- Often initiative taken by local commanders rather than central government.
- After Crimean defeat, steady Russian expansion through a series of wars against local tribesmen (similar to contemporaneous American wars against the Indians).

CHINA
- Area for extending influence, especially around Amur river.
- Gained railway concessions in Manchuria.

SAKHALIN
- Disputed between Japan and Russia.
- 1875. Agreed Russia gain, in return for Japan taking Kurile Islands.

JAPAN
- Similarly modernising state. Expanding influence in Far East.
- 1895. Defeated China, but gains limited by other powers, especially Russia.
- 1904. Conflicting interests in Korea led to Russo-Japanese War, and humiliating defeat for Russia.
- 1907 onwards. Improved relations; agreed to divide sphere of influence in Manchuria. Also Japan control in Korea, Russia in Mongolia.

- 1905. Russia ceded southern half to Japan at Portsmouth Treaty.

NORTH AMERICA
- 1784. Russian fur traders established settlement.
- 1830s. Claimed exclusive rights north of 54° 40'.
- 1867. Sold Alaska to USA for $8 million.

Key
- Land gained 1801-1855
- Land gained 1855-1876
- Land gained 1876-1901

0 Miles 1000

B Conclusion. Continuity and change

Russian history illustrates well the complexity of the concept of continuity and change in history. In broad terms one could argue that tsarist governments of the later nineteenth century embarked on considerable economic changes, yet tried to maintain the traditional autocracy. This approach has been seen as essentially contradictory, leading to the tensions that finally erupted in 1917. However, such a neat contrast between economic change and political continuity might be considered too simple. For just as many aspects of the old economic and social system were preserved, thus restricting Russia's economic development, so also tsars faced increasing pressures for political changes, and were forced to make concessions.

Furthermore, one might expect the history of Soviet Russia to show little continuity with that of its predecessor, for the Soviet Union was the product of a revolution whose principles were in stark contrast to those of tsarism. Yet the study of Soviet Russia might soon reveal considerable continuities.

Worksection 10 part 2

A. Continuity and change

A.1. Consider one of the following aspects of Tsarist Russia, and identify evidence of continuity and change within the area.

i) Agriculture. (Diagrams 1 and 2 p. 23, and 3 and 4 p. 88 will help here).

ii) Industry. (Apparently an area of great change, but consider closely the nature of the Russian workforce and structure of industry, as well as the source of inspiration for economic advance.)

iii) Administrative and political development (particularly the administrative changes of Alexander II, and forced political reforms of Nicholas II).

iv) Opposition groups. (Consider their aims, organisation and methods.)

v) Foreign policy.

A.2. Tsarist and Communist Russia.

i) Are there any broad reasons why one might expect considerable continuity in Russia's history even after the Communist revolution? (Chart 1.3. might help here.)

ii) Can you think of any elements of continuity between Tsarist and Communist Russia? (Consider the above areas, and others such as the police, civil rights, the idea of an empire.)

iii) Why do you think Stalin has been called a 'Red Tsar'?

iv) Refer back to worksection one exercise A.2 p.5. Discuss which of the adjectives applicable to Tsarist Russia would also apply to Soviet Russia.

B. Pictorial evidence on themes in Tsarist Russia

Look at the contemporary paintings and photographs of Tsarist Russia in charts 10.3 and 10.4.

i) What do the pictures in Aspects I have in common? Explain the activities portrayed, and comment on their implications for the autocracy.

ii) What do you consider the 'Two Themes' illustrated in Aspects 2 could be? Sort out the pictures into the two themes, and explain the significance of each event.

C. Concluding assessment. The strengths and weaknesses of tsarism

Most historians stress the growing problems facing tsarism in the nineteenth century. Aware that the regime collapsed in 1917, they tend to suggest this was inevitable. This popular view, held by many contemporaries as well, is represented by the cartoon on the front cover, and the postcard on the back cover. However, this approach has been criticised as too deterministic, and one leading to the neglect of the strengths of the tsarist regime. Certainly considerable advances were made in the nineteenth century. The 1905 Revolution, often seen as a 'dress rehearsal' for 1917, can also be seen as illustrating tsarism's resilience, in that it survived an unfortunate combination of circumstances. It took an even more exceptional situation to cause the February Revolution of 1917, and even then events might have taken a different course, perhaps leading to a reshaped monarchy under a new tsar.

Refer back to material already covered, in particular the debate on 1906-1914 in chapter six, and the assessment of the role of individuals in chapter nine. Then discuss one of the following issues, either as an essay or in a class debate.

i) What were the strengths of the tsarist system in the nineteenth century?

ii) Pearson has summarised the Soviet view of tsarism thus:
'A political dinosaur, large of bulk but small of brain, tsardom was doomed to extinction.' ((1974), *Russia in Revolution* p.31)
Do you agree with this judgement?

Chart 10.3 Aspects of Tsarist Russia 1

a) *Members of the Ivanovo-Voznesensk Soviet of Deputies in 1905.*

b) *Meeting of a village commune.*

c *A Zemstva Council session.*

d) *The State Duma meets in the Taurida Palace, St Petersburg, 1906.*

Chart 10.4 Aspects of Tsarist Russia 2

a) *Assassination of Alexander II, 1881.*

b) *Shooting of strikers, 1906.*

c) *Victims of Pogrom.*

d) *Moscow strike, 1905.*

e) *March to Tsar, January 1905.*

f) *Arrest of Populists, 1870s.*